The making of a bourgeois state

The Dutch Republic about 1650

Marjolein C. 't Hart

The making of a bourgeois state

War, politics and finance during the Dutch revolt

Manchester University Press
Manchester and New York
Distributed exclusively in the USA and Canada by St. Martin's Press

Published by Manchester University Press
Oxford Road, Manchester M13 9PL, UK
and Room 400, 175 Fifth Avenue, New York, NY 10010, USA

Distributed exclusively in the USA and Canada
by St. Martin's Press, Inc., 175 Fifth Avenue, New York, NY 10010, USA

British Library Cataloguing-in-Publication Data
A catalogue record for this book is available from the British Library

Library of Congress Cataloging-in-Publication Data applied for

ISBN 0 7190 3807 3 *hardback*

Photoset in Linotron Sabon
by Northern Phototypesetting Co. Ltd, Bolton

Printed in Great Britain
by Bookcraft (Bath) Limited

Contents

List of tables

List of figures

Acknowledgements

I have incurred many intellectual debts in writing this work. Comments of friends and colleagues, who read considerable parts of the manuscript, helped to pursue my study. I would like to thank Julia Adams, Gerbert Beekenkamp, Karel Davids, Wantje Fritschy, Karin Iest, Clé Lesger, Henk van Nierop, Maarten Prak, Wayne Te Brake, Frits Wegenwijs, Harry de Wit, and Jan Luiten van Zanden. Above all, I am grateful for the understanding and encouragement of Wim Blockmans and Charles Tilly. They shared the task of supervising my PhD thesis, which was presented at Leiden University in 1989. Critical remarks from members of the PhD reading committee, in particular from J.R. Bruin, A.Th. van Deursen and J.J. Woltjer, spared this work from several errors.

Institutions have provided space and intellectual discourse: the Department of Sociology in Groningen, the Historical Departments of Leiden, the Vrije Universiteit in Amsterdam, the Erasmus University in Rotterdam, and the University of Amsterdam. Especially, I have enjoyed my stay at the Center for Studies of Social Change, which is affiliated to the New School for Social Research in New York. The logistics of my enterprise were developed with the help of Raul Zambrano and Peter Doorn. Financial support was kindly provided by the Vera List Fellowship of the New School for Social Research in New York, the Dr Hendrik Muller's Vaderlandsch Fonds, and Sigma Xi. Finally, I would like to express my gratitute for the services of the Algemeen Rijksarchief in The Hague, the Rijksarchieven in Groningen and Utrecht, and the Gemeente Archieven of Amsterdam, Rotterdam and The Hague.

Chronology of major events

1515–55	The Low Countries become part of the Habsburg empire under Charles V
1566	Iconoclastic revolts in the Netherlands
1568	Spanish governor Alva crushes revolt. Stadhouder William I of Orange commences military campaigns, 'start' of Eighty Years' War against Spanish Habsburgs
1579	Signing of the Union of Utrecht, eventually constituting the Republic of the Seven United Provinces (Holland, Zeeland, Utrecht, Gelderland, Overijssel, Groningen and Friesland)
1590–1600	Consolidation of republican territory through conquests of Stadhouder Maurice of Orange
1609–1621	Twelve Years' Truce with Spain
1618	Outbreak of Thirty Years' War; increased involvement of the Dutch in anti-Habsburg leagues in central Europe
1621	Expiration of Twelve Years' Truce and resumption of Eighty Years' War
1625	Death of Stadhouder Maurice of Orange. He is succeeded by Frederick Henry of Orange
1644–1645	Dutch naval expeditions against Denmark force the merchant passage of the Sound
1647	Death of Stadhouder Frederick Henry. He is succeeded by William II of Orange
1648	Treaty of Munster. End of both Eighty Years' War and Thirty Years' War

1650	Premature death of Stadhouder William II; no new Stadhouder appointed until 1672
1652–1654	First Anglo-Dutch War
1665–1667	Second Anglo-Dutch War
1672–1674	Third Anglo-Dutch War and invasion of the Republic by the French; re-establishment of the Stadhoudership in favour of William III of Orange
1794–1795	French invasion of the Dutch Republic. Stadhouder William V of Orange flees to England. Old régime collapses
1813–1814	Re-establishment of Dutch independence. William of Orange becomes King of Holland

Introduction

> 'But when', asked Pantagruel, 'will you get rid of your debts?'
>
> 'When hell freezes over', answered Panurge, 'when the whole world is happy, and when you are your own inheritor. Pray God I never reach that stage. I would not find anyone who would lend me a penny any more. . . . Always be in debt to someone. That person will constantly pray God to give you a long and happy life. Fearing that he might lose his loan, he will always speak well of you and get you new creditors.'
>
> [François Rabelais, *Le Tiers Livre*, 1552, 25]

The humanist François Rabelais, who wrote the stories of *Gargantua* and *Pantagruel* in the sixteenth century, tackled a fundamental problem of many early modern states in Europe: debts. Pantagruel – his name might be translated as something like Lord of the Thirsty – had given the lordship of Salgimondis in Dipsodia to his friend Panurge. It was a rich gift, with an annual revenue of 6,789,106,789 royaux, not including the yield from maybugs and roman snails, which varied – averaging good years and bad years – between 2,435,768 and 2,435,769 *moutons à la grande laine*. Bearing in mind that a *royal* was equivalent to thirteen or fourteen golden francs and a *mouton à la grande laine* about sixteen golden francs, the king of France disposed of far inferior revenues!

Be that as it may, according to Rabelais's story Panurge managed to run through three years' revenue in two weeks. His debts soon accumulated. The situation caused Pantagruel anxiety, but Panurge pointed to the rich possibilities of filling one gap with another, or, in other words, of robbing Peter to pay Paul. As long as he had debts, his creditors would pray for his health and well-being. They would even search out new creditors for him. Thus, in his opinion, by being indebted he was actually serving a good cause in preserving peace and order in the realm.

Panurge's argument seemed watertight. Indeed, he was partly right, as debt did give lenders an interest in the ruler's survival. However, when debt charges rose disproportionately they were often destructive, maybe not in the fictional Dipsodia of Panurge, but at least in the real European principalities of the sixteenth and seventeenth centuries. Regular funds were indispensable to meet interest payments and to maintain the solvency of the state. The moment public credit collapsed, any state faced catastrophe. And, indeed, debts recurrently brought about state bankruptcies, destroying alliances with domestic elites that had been built up through the institutions of the state.

Despite the destructive side-effects of debt, most rulers could not do without borrowing. Loans gave a state great advantages, as in rapid mobilization for war, especially since warfare had evolved from feudal service to paid (infantry) troops, to expensive fortifications and garrisons, and to guns and powder which were available in international arms markets. In early modern Europe, wars were increasingly monetized.[1]

Given this paradoxical challenge for all early modern states, the Dutch Republic (1579–1795) set an eccentric example to neighbouring principalities. In the early seventeenth century, the costs of war pressed extremely hard, due above all to the lengthy Eighty Years' War against Spain. The public debt, indeed, rose out of all proportion and reached sky-high levels. Yet throughout, Dutch credit was strong, and it even promoted enduring alliances between the state and influential urban elites. It was a wonder to all visiting statesmen and scholars that the integrity of the state was never endangered. In the meantime, this tiny nation, numbering a mere 1.5 million inhabitants, managed to achieve a world hegemony for a century or so. Obviously, the Dutch had found a peculiar solution to the ever increasing demands of war.

How did the Dutch manage to wage the long and expensive wars of the seventeenth century without endangering the state's credit? How was it that they did not need a large, permanent administrative apparatus as compared with rival states? How could they fund their warrior republic upon credit, where others failed? These three fascinating questions stand at the centre of this book.

Present theories of the state fail to provide a satisfactory answer. Customarily, leading scholars have followed such analysts as Max Weber and Otto Hintze, who established the paradigm that the capacity of a state to wage war was dependent on the creation of a massive bureaucracy. Apparently, the heavy external pressures of war generated centralized institutional responses from within. How states reacted to that pressure was crucial for their survival. As Paul Kennedy states:

> The post-1540 waging of war was intimately connected with 'the birth of the nation-state'. Between the late fifteenth and the late seventeenth centuries, most European countries witnessed a centralization of political and military authority, usually under the monarch (but in some places under the local prince or a mercantile oligarchy), accompanied by increased powers and methods of state taxation, and carried out by a much more elaborate bureaucratic machinery than had existed when [. . .] national armies were provided by a feudal levy.[2]

Kennedy argues that the monopolization and bureaucratization of military power by the state was a process with a reciprocal outcome: the state gained enhanced authority because of the military establishment, while the collection of funds created for the armed forces a degree of permanence which had not existed a century earlier.[3] A new dynamic of power emerged, involving a struggle for prestige and authority, as 'every political structure naturally prefers to have weak rather than strong neighbors'.[4] The processes of bureaucratization and centralization were regarded as the most self-evident means of increasing control, the more so, as an interlocking European state system with a *kriegerischen Staatsräson* forced rival monarchies to extend their powers within and beyond their boundaries. Rulers and bureaucrats observed more succesful examples elsewhere and tried to copy the military, fiscal, and political institutions of their more fortunate rivals. Obviously, war was a recurrent imperative enforcing state formation.[5]

In most of Europe, state formation had an internal drive as well, as, once appointed, bureaucrats tended to expand their powers. In the terminology of Norbert Elias in his *Civilizing Process*, their success was determined by two monopolization processes: one of violence and one of taxation. The first implied that no one, except officers in the service of the state, came to be entitled to bear arms and use force; the second entailed the sole right to impose levies and duties upon the area and population in question.[6] Officialdom continued to increase in numbers, a process that was believed to be 'representative of general European trends'.[7] Moreover, the bureaucrats changed the character of domination by the state:

> The rise of centralized domination under the leadership of autocrats, whether kings, princes, prime ministers, or political cardinals, wrought profound changes in the functions of central government; in the methods of political and administrative management; in the recruitment and behavior of men in authority; and in the conception of the rights and duties of officeholding. [. . . The new state rulers] built up a new bureaucratic empire. They raised sizeable permanent armies, imposed ever larger taxes, multiplied fiscal exactions. They extended and intensified the regulative and administrative intervention of the dynastic government into the sphere of private rights and local home rule.[8]

In the legitimation and extension of their powers rulers used the language of reciprocity:

> Kings call their subjects 'my' people, or 'our' people. What ruler has ever denied that he had the obligation to serve and protect his or her people? [. . .] In general, rulers and dominant groups talk in terms of reciprocity (though they may not use that expression) to stress *their* contribution to the social units they head, and to praise the virtues and necessities of harmonious social relationships therein. In this fashion the notion of reciprocity readily becomes a form of mystification, an ideological cover for exploitation.[9]

True, the new state was never a mere negative imposition upon society. Even the most absolutist state had to bargain, as the cooperation of domestic elites was crucial to reduce the costs of domination. In return for obedience or compliance, local rulers obtained state posts, state prestige, and privileged positions in the revenue-raising machine. Armies, navies, and bureaucracies also provided new opportunities, new sources of revenue for those who were able to obtain some access to the state-making process. Indeed, for some elites the acceptance of new formats of public domination could imply a significant advance in status.[10]

Yet as bureaucratization and centralization hardly advanced in the Dutch Republic, the example of this tiny but powerful nation seemed to defy those causal notions between war and state formation. The country followed a deviant path from the general solutions within early modern Europe.[11] Partly, the puzzle originated because most leading scholars had been preoccupied with the absolutist and bureaucratized models of France and Prussia while overlooking the Low Countries. Yet even when significant attention was paid to the Dutch achievements, confusion remained. Indeed, the Republic was ahead of others with respect to the effective organization of its military and finances, as was shown by Geoffrey Parker and James Tracy in their studies of the military and financial revolutions in early modern Europe.[12] But why, then, did France became a model state for Europe, and not the Netherlands? Were modern methods of military and financial administration not inevitably leading towards more bureaucracy, as Max Weber, Otto Hintze and Hans Rosenberg have stressed?

Clarity of vision was impeded when Immanuel Wallerstein called the Republic the first core state of the capitalist world system. Despite the fact that a central state hardly existed, he denied any weakness in the Dutch political system. On the contrary, he stressed that the Dutch state was strong, 'strong' in the sense of being 'a partially autonomous entity' with 'state managers and a bureaucracy'. After all, in his theory, core states were the 'most centralized' of all, prone to stimulate nationalism, 'a mass sentiment resulting from homogenization of the population', which even implied collective solidarity.[13]

Simon Schama's study *The embarrassment of riches*, however fertile in depicting essential Dutch cultural traits in the seventeenth century, increased the confusion about the character of the Dutch state. Explicitly, Schama believed that a unique national identity was constructed, mentioning 'a belief in themselves as a common tribe', 'patriotic steadfastness' and a 'community of the nation'.[14] Yet these concepts are quite problematic for the history of the Low Countries, as the Dutch Republic was only weakly integrated. The revolt of the 1570s and 1580s against Spain had reinforced centrifugal identities, reviving the power and privileges of former communities, thus intensifying borders and boundaries that made it extremely difficult to 'think' of the Dutch as a nation. On the contrary, one should rather stress the cultural fragmentation, as Johan Huizinga did:

> The Hollander and Zeelander knew little of their eastern and northern cousins. The Frisians were probably closest to them, for in Friesland lay the Stadholder's Court as a visible token of the glory of the House of Orange. Groningen with its lush and boggy surroundings seemed a more remote and backward region, despite its university. To the south of Groningen lay the vast moors of Drenthe, barely touched by the centuries, then lonely and humble Overijssel, the Veluwe and finally Het Gooi, a long strip dividing the rest from the heart of the country.[15]

However, the image of the overall strength of the Dutch state was reiterated by Jonathan Israel in his *Dutch primacy in world trade.* The hegemony of the Netherlands, in his words, was supported by 'a powerful state' to 'protect and promote the vital interests of the first world-trade entrepôt'.[16] Yet it seems misplaced to speak of a strong state or to point to shared national feelings. Israel, Schama, and Wallerstein overlooked the contradictions among the multiple mercantile and entrepreneurial factions within the Netherlands. No powerful central institution existed which acted as an arbiter deciding what those 'vital interests' should look like, and Dutch policies – although they may have had the appearance of quick-wittedness for outsiders – were determined by continuously changing coalitions of provinces, cities, and factions.

Thus, despite long and expensive wars, despite a hegemonic position in the world of the seventeenth century, and despite advanced methods in military organization and finance, no powerful structures were imposed by 'The Hague', the meeting place of the representatives of the seven provinces in the Estates General. This theoretical imbroglio calls for a re-evaluation of the causal regularities that underlie the histories of states.[17] In particular, the regularity cited above – how war influenced state formation – needs closer scrutiny.

Perhaps the concept of the state should be clarified here. The state can best be defined as three elements. First, it is a set of institutions, staffed by the state's own personnel. Second, these institutions are at the centre of a geographically bounded territory, usually referred to as a society. Third, the state monopolizes law-making within its territory. This tends towards the creation of a common political culture shared by all citizens.[18] State formation, then, is understood as the growth of public institutions and the extension of their power from above. From below, it is the acceptance of those institutions by the population. State formation may coincide with nation-building, but it is a separate development.[19]

From above, no well designed outline for the formation of a state existed. Kings, princes, urban magnates, or top civil servants could act as 'state makers', yet none of them envisaged the omnipresent bureaucratic and public domination of the national states of our times. State formation was always an unintended outcome of several processes of interaction. Society imposed its logic, wars enforced theirs, elite groupings demanded influence, and the rulers had to take decisions amidst manifold political traditions, stubborn convictions, and material limitations.

From below, acceptance could be bought through bargaining with relevant elites, through cherishing an appropriate ideology or religion, or even through outright deterrence.[20] From above, the discourse about the pursuit of military goals predominated. By 1600, European states were still marginal to their domestic social environment, but they were central in wars. Their international, geopolitical position together with the aims of competitive rulers determined the start of wars in the first place.[21] Through wars, then, frontiers were extended. Through wars other states were absorbed. And internally, states had to extend their functions, their legitimation, and their penetration into society.

Above all, wars forced states to look for financial solutions. This constituted the direct cause of a renewed confrontation between state and society. Always, the successes and failures of a state formation process had their reverberations in the realm of state finances. According to Shmuel Eisenstadt's *Political system of empires*, the struggle of rulers to create, and to hold, resources not committed to primary groups or traditional elites lay at the heart of the formation of bureaucratic empires.[22] By the same token, acceptance of tax demands by the population was an indicator of penetration of the state into society. The extent of taxation, then, became a measure of the cohesion between individuals and the state.[23] In the words of Joseph Schumpeter:

> We have seen that without financial need the immediate cause for the creation of the modern state would have been absent [. . .]. The tax is not merely a surface phenomenon, it is an expression of this development which it summarizes in a particular direction [. . .]. The tax system was the organ the development of which entailed other organs. Tax bill in hand, the state penetrated the private economies and won increasing domination over them. The tax brings money and calculating spirits into corners in which they do not dwell as yet, and thus becomes a formative factor in the very organism which has developed it.[24]

Recently, Charles Tilly has set out the contrast between 'coercion-intensive' and 'capital-intensive' routes in state formation. Several states were heavily bureaucratized and centralized, others became only weakly integrated. The extractive capacity of state institutions provided an explanation for distinct paths in state making.[25] This study aims to follow the Dutch example within this perspective by analysing the complex relations between wars, taxes, debt, the socio-economic structure and state making. Although it concentrates on the early seventeenth-century Netherlands, during the unravelling of mechanisms at work in state formation this work may serve to increase understanding of the development of other nation-states as well.

Part I sets the context of the Dutch Republic and its wars. Of major impact for the development of the state was the Eighty Years' War against Spain (1568–1648). Most data are derived from the last phase of this war, the decades in which the Dutch republican state machinery was consolidated, collected from evidence in the central state archives in The Hague (Algemeen Rijksarchief). Chapter One delineates the relevant historical facts. Chapter Two asks how the military revolution could be held responsible for monetizing the burden of war.

Any shift of the war burden always resulted in a political crisis of some sort.[26] Such a crisis is labelled 'relative' in case a solution can be found within existing institutions and domination. The outcome of the shifting process was crucial. Part II is the core of the book, describing how that financial burden was shifted onto society. Chapters Three to Six deal respectively with the shift of the war costs, the central means of the Republic, the tax revenues from the provinces, and the public loans.

Part III, finally, analyses the effects of the transfer process upon bureaucratization and state formation in the Republic. Matters such as (the absence of) centralization, increased control, regimentation of the bureaucracy, and local bureaucratization are discussed. A final chapter relates the Dutch experience to existing social theories of the state.

In short, the argument follows the path as designated in Fig. 1.1. Much of the evidence stretches over the first half of the seventeenth century. It was an era that determined the fate of many European states. All were challenged by increased military and financial demands. Internal control, by the same token, became crucial, yet several greater powers were in turmoil in the 1640s (the English Civil War, the Fronde in France, the revolts of Portugal and Catalonia in Spain). Highly indicative was the fact that many frontiers were set after the end of the Thirty Years' War (1648). Externally, the Republic emerged stronger than ever. Internally, though, it witnessed a renewed emphasis on rule by the provinces and the cities at the expense of the centre. This case study makes it possible to reconstruct the working of the state finances during a period of prolonged warfare. A specific bourgeois state structure emerged that

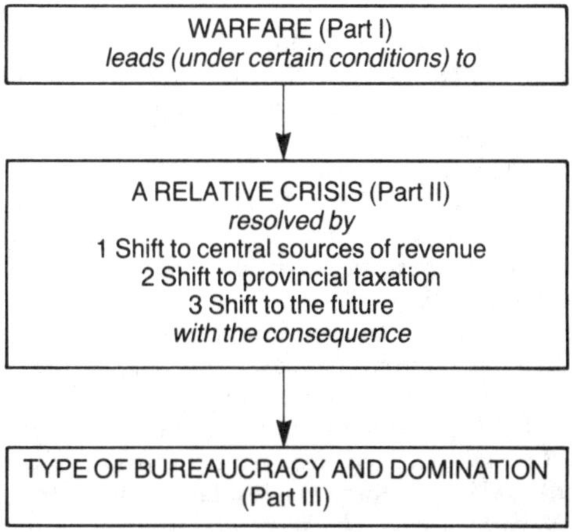

Figure 1.1 Argumentation and sequence of evidence

appeared quite different from the more absolutist and centralized European states.

Notes

1 Geoffrey Parker, *The military revolution. Military innovation and the rise of the West, 1500–1800*, Cambridge, 1988.
2 Paul Kennedy, *The rise and fall of the great powers: economic change and military conflict from 1500 to 2000*, New York, 1989, 70.
3 *Ibidem*, 75.
4 Weber, in the collection H.H. Gerth and C. Wright Mills (eds), *From Max Weber: essays in sociology*, New York, 1958, 160. See also Robert Brown, 'Bureaucracy: the utility of a concept', *Bureaucracy: the career of a concept*, ed. E. Kamenka and M. Krygier, London, 1979, 141.
5 Otto Hintze, 'Wesen und Wandlung des modernen Staates', *Staat und Verfassung*, Göttingen, 1939, 472; George M. Thomas and John W. Meyer, 'The expansion of the state', *Annual Review of Sociology* 10, 1984, 471; Kenneth H.F. Dyson, *The state tradition in Western Europe*, New York, 1980.
6 Norbert Elias, *Über den Prozess der Zivilisation. Soziogenetische und psychogenetische Untersuchungen*, Basel, 1939, 132, 153.
7 Hans Rosenberg, *Bureaucracy, aristocracy and autocracy. The Prussian experience 1660–1815*, Boston, 1958, ix, 9; see also Henry Jacoby, *The bureaucratization of the world*, Berkeley, 1977. S.N. Eisenstadt, *The political system of empires. The rise and fall of bureaucratic societies*, New York, 1963, 371: 'These totalitarian developments [into a monolithic state structure] are not inevitable results of the evolution of modern political systems. However, their emergence is potential; the possibility is innate in

the growing social differentiation [. . .] and in the increasing interdependence between differentiated, non-embedded institutional spheres.'

8 Rosenberg, *Bureaucracy, aristocracy and autocracy*, 12; see also Martin Krygier, 'State and bureaucracy in Europe: the growth of a concept', *Bureaucracy: the career of a concept*, London, 1979, 1.

9 Barrington Moore Jr, *Injustice. The social bases of obedience and revolt*, White Plains, N.Y., 1978, 508. For a treatment of the concepts of authoritarianism and totalitarianism see Juan J. Linz, 'An authoritarian regime: Spain', *Mass politics. Studies in political sociology*, ed. E. Allard and S. Rokkan, New York, 1970.

10 Cf. Stein Rokkan's stimulating interpretation of Barrington Moore's coalition-building theory, in his *Citizens, elections, parties. Approaches to the comparative study of the process of development*, New York, 1970, 55.

11 Cf. Hans Daalder, 'Moderne politieke wetenschap en het nut van de geschiedenis', *Bijdragen en Mededelingen betreffende de Geschiedenis der Nederlanden* 90, 1975, 236; Karel Davids, Jan Lucassen and Jan Luiten van Zanden, *De Nederlandse geschiedenis als afwijking van het algemeen menselijk patroon*, Amsterdam, 1988.

12 Parker, *Military revolution*; James D. Tracy, *A financial revolution in the Habsburg Netherlands. Renten and renteniers in the County of Holland, 1515–1565*, Berkeley, 1985.

13 Immanuel Wallerstein, *The modern world-system. Mercantilism and the consolidation of the European world-economy* I, New York, 1980, 162, 355, 145; II, 61, 113. The Dutch state was one of the few states in Europe possessing considerable internal and external strength and offered merchants maximum advantages. *Ibidem* I, 211–13; II, 60.

14 Simon Schama, *The embarrassment of riches: an interpretation of Dutch culture in the Golden Age*, New York, 1987, 8, 567-8. His concept of nationalism could best be compared to Benedict Anderson's definition of a nation as being 'an imagined political community': *imagined* 'because the members of even the smallest nation never know of their fellow-members, meet them, or even hear them, yet in the mind of each lives the image of their communion': Benedict Anderson, *Imagined Communities. Reflections on the origin and spread of nationalism*, London, 1983, 15. Max Weber had defined a nation as a 'community of sentiment', comprising 'especially all those who think of themselves as being specific "partners" of a specific "culture" diffused among the members of the polity'. *From Max Weber*, 172, 176.

15 Johan Huizinga, *Dutch civilisation in the seventeenth century and other essays*, London, 1968, 14–15; cf. also S. Groenveld, 'Natie en nationaal gevoel in de zestiende-eeuwse Nederlanden', *Nederlands Archievenblad* 84, 1980, 372–87.

16 Jonathan I. Israel, *Dutch primacy in world trade, 1585–1740*, Oxford, 1989, 36, 95, 410.

17 Following Theda Skocpol, 'Bringing the state back in. Strategies of analysis in current research', *Bringing the state back in*, ed. P. B. Evans *et al.*, Cambridge, 1985, 28.

18 John A. Hall and G. John Ikenberry, *The state. Concepts in the social*

sciences, Milton Keynes, 1989, 1–2.

19 This state may be a city-state, a territorial state or a composite state: Wim P. Blockmans, 'Princes conquérants et bourgeois calculateurs. Le poids des réseaux urbains dans la formation des états', *La ville, la bourgeoisie et la genèse de l'état moderne*, Bielefeld/Paris, 1988, 169. The Dutch Republic was a composite state, to some degree centralized and formally coordinated in The Hague, under the 'rule' of the States General.

20 Elias's work on the *Civilizing process* showed that state formation on the one hand and the self-restraint of individuals on the other were two developments which were strongly interwoven and interdependent. Elias, *Prozess der Zivilisation*, especially his concluding chapter. On the problem of authority and superego control, see Cristopher Lasch's criticism, 'Historical sociology and the myth of maturity. Norbert Elias's "very simple formula" ', *Theory and Society* 14, 1985, 716. Cf. the question of obedience and growth of citizenship as described by J.G.A. Pocock, *The Machiavellian moment. Florentine political thought and the Atlantic republican tradition*, Princeton, N.J., 1975, 551: 'The ideal of virtue is highly compulsive; it demands of the individual, under threat to his moral being, that he participate in the *res publica*.'

21 William H. McNeill, *The pursuit of power. Technology, armed force, and society*, Chicago, 1982.

22 Eisenstadt, *Political system of empires*, 361–362.

23 In his 'On taxation [1885]', *Classics in the theory of public finance*, ed. R.A. Musgrave and A.T. Peacock, London, 1967, 28, Lorenz von Stein wrote: 'Taxation is the economic expression of the individual's cohesion with the nation.'

24 Joseph A. Schumpeter, 'The crisis of the tax state [1918]', *International Economic Papers* IV, 1954, 17. Peter-Christian Witt put it even stronger in his recent 'Introduction. The history and sociology of public finance: problems and topics', *Wealth and taxation in Central Europe*, ed. P.-C. Witt, Leamington Spa, 1987, 5: 'Thus it is impossible to analyse the emergence of the modern state without raising the question of public finance'. See also I.A.A. Thompson, *War and government in Habsburg Spain, 1560–1620*, London, 1976, 67: 'the history of a state's finances is almost a history of the state itself'. John Brewer's *The sinews of power. War, money and the English state, 1688–1783*, New York, 1989, and Michael Mann's *The sources of social power* I, *A history of power from the beginning to A.D. 1760*, Cambridge, 1986, used public finance as an indicator of state functions and of the relationship with various social groupings.

25 Charles Tilly, *Coercion, capital, and European states, AD 990–1990*, Oxford, 1990, 5.

26 On the concept of shifting the burden of taxation: R.A. Seligman, *On the shifting and incidence of taxation*, Baltimore, 1892; also Otto von Mering, *The shifting and incidence of taxation*. Philadelphia, 1942, and Fritz Karl Mann, 'Ueberwälzung der Steuern', *Handwörterbuch der Staatswissenschaften* VIII, Jena, 1928, 336–62.

Part I

The context of the problem

1

The Dutch Republic: united in contrasts

From the early beginnings of the newborn state, disparity and discord were to rule the Netherlands provinces which united against Spain.[1] They lacked a consistent geography. The coastal region of the Dutch Republic consisted of polders and islands, and was traversed by broad river deltas, extensive marshes, and canals. Inland, the sandy soil regions were intersected by the fertile banks of major rivers. The provinces did not even share a common history. Holland and Zeeland had lived under the domination of the Counts of Holland and Dukes of Burgundy. Utrecht had been the centre of a bishopric for ages. In the north, Groningen, Friesland and part of the Northern Quarter of Holland (West Friesland) had belonged to the 'Frisian freedom'. Gelderland had been a duchy of the German Empire. Also, parts of Overijssel claimed allegiance to the Holy Roman Emperor. Only in the sixteenth century were these provinces incorporated in the Habsburg Empire. And even in union they remained a conglomeration of accidental partners with widely differing outlooks and traditions.

Diversity in economy and urbanization

History had been somewhat capricious in rendering Holland the core of the new state. In the early sixteenth century no one could have foreseen the dominant role of Holland during the century to come. In the late Middle Ages, the cities in the eastern provinces had experienced prosperity while the towns of Holland were still a backwater. Utrecht's bishop had been a major figure in the region and stood for a powerful tradition. Even the source of Friesland's wealth differed from Holland's: it was based upon agricultural trade dating from the early medieval period. At the time of the revolt, the driving force of the economy was still located not in Holland but in the southern provinces of Flanders and Brabant, with its great city Antwerp.

Yet in the later decades of the sixteenth century, opportunities arose as trade routes shifted from land to sea. Baltic grain came to be indispensable to the stagnating Mediterranean and new resources were developed in the colonies. The Holland merchants managed to grasp a disproportionately large role in international trade, thanks to a strong tradition of shipping that initially had been based upon the herring fisheries. As a result, this 'area made up of moors, grass-land, water reaches and fields' developed a culture 'that radiated across much of Europe and constituted a highlight in the spirit of the age'.[2]

As agriculture became commercialized and large amounts of grain came to be imported, the population grew 'far beyond their natural resources'. By 1500, the area of the Dutch Republic was already thickly populated, at around 1 million inhabitants. A century later they numbered about 1.5 million, and by 1700 some 1.9 million. Most growth was concentrated in the west, in the province of Holland, whereas in the other provinces population density increased but little or even declined. By 1650, about 48 per cent of the population resided in Holland. At the same time, urbanization proceeded. The percentage of the population living in cities increased to as much as 42 per cent in 1675.[3] These large numbers of city dwellers proved surprisingly literate for their time and were hungry for prints, poems and polemics.[4]

Although by comparison small in territory, population, and natural resources, the Dutch Republic came to dominate the world carrying trade:

> As of 1670, the Dutch owned three times the tonnage of the English, and more than the tonnage of England, France, Portugal, Spain, and the Germanies combined. The percentage of Dutch-*built* ships was even larger.[5]

Trade expanded, at least up to 1650, as is shown in Table 1.1. By all means, in the first half of the seventeenth century the economy seemed to expand fast enough to absorb the enormous increase in population. Wages rose, and stagnated only after 1650 or 1675. In the meantime, the costs of daily nutrition did not rise at similar rates. Moreover, the years in which grain prices rose out of proportion were mitigated by favourable employment conditions. The incidence

Table 1.1 *Average annual value of Dutch trade in million guilders, selected years, 1624–1670*

years	*value*
1624–1625	225–275
1641–1650	300–400
1651–1660	225–275
1661–1670	200–250

Source: Johan de Vries, *De economische achteruitgang der Republiek in de achttiende eeuw*, Leiden, 1968, 27. See also Jan de Vries, 'The decline and rise of the Dutch Economy, 1675–1900', *Technique, spirit and form in the making of the modern economies. Essays in honor of William N. Parker*, New York, 1984, 46.

of famine was reduced as the density of trade relations almost always secured imports of foreign grain.[6]

It was the diversity of the economy that gave the Dutch staying power. If one branch collapsed, another was able to take over. Several urban centres were able to coordinate major activities, although Amsterdam, of course, stood out. This city came to replace Antwerp after the latter's fall in 1585. It became the entrepôt for the Baltic trade. Grain, significantly, was called the 'mother trade' of Dutch wealth. Also, Amsterdam was to take the leading role in commerce with the Mediterranean. And after the establishment of the Bank of Exchange (*Wisselbank*) in 1609, the city achieved a dominant position in the international bullion trade, and became the world's financial centre. Another advantage for Amsterdam was the ease of access to the arms and ammunition trade.[7]

Yet Amsterdam was by no means the only centre of trade. By the time of the revolt, Middelburg (situated in the province of Zeeland) was able to compete with the might of Amsterdam. Together with Rotterdam, it shared the bulk of Dutch trade with England and France. In the Northern Quarter of Holland, major towns like Hoorn and Enkhuizen concentrated on fisheries and the northern trade. Dordrecht, the oldest of the major Holland cities, was the main entrepôt for riverine trade. And despite the fact that several new industries were developed in Amsterdam, the city of Leiden remained the most important industrial city of the Republic. Leiden also housed the first Dutch university from 1575. Haarlem, for long the largest Holland city, was famous for finishing cloth and as such a major industrial centre too. Rotterdam was first and foremost a fisheries centre but when it took up river and sea trade as well, it became one of the competitors of Amsterdam in the later seventeenth century. Other cities such as Alkmaar, Gouda, Delft, and Utrecht were major inland markets, while relying on brewing and some branches of the textile industry.[8]

Early political structures

Owing to the decentralized nature of economic growth, power relations were by no means clear at the start of the war of independence. Amsterdam may have been an economic and financial centre, yet Leiden housed the central university. Amsterdam's trade could not chase out the specialized trade of several other Holland towns, and its industry was never dominant. Also, there was no religious centre, as the Reformation had done away with church centralism. The bureaucratic centre did not coincide with the economic centre either, as The Hague came to be chosen as seat of the government. No single city constituted a centralizing force: the towns constrained each other in inter-city rivalry. Even Amsterdam was prevented from assuming a leading position because of combined opposition from other towns. Amsterdam's prolonged support of the Spanish king in the 1570s also rendered that city unacceptable as a bureaucratic centre.

In the course of the revolt, the urban-based Holland elite came to surpass all other Dutch elites. The province of Holland dominated national politics, where the other provinces had 'to make do with a supporting role or even the part of audience in the drama of national life'.[9] However, despite the gravitation towards the maritime west of the nation, Holland could not do without the support of the inland provinces. Also, within Holland itself, no single economic or urban elite emerged as rulers, owing to the wide differentiation in commercialization and the constant bickering of factions.

Moreover, a strong dislike of centralizing policies had been inherited from the beginning of the revolt against the Spanish Habsburgs. Philip II had tried to use Catholicism and taxation as unifying and homogenizing policies for his realm. A violent outbreak in 1566 of iconoclastic revolts had been followed by grim repression under the Spanish governor Alva which drove staunch supporters of the Calvinist religion into exile.

The Stadhouder (governor) for the king in Holland, Prince William of Orange, opposed Alva's policies. He left in 1567 for his parental estate in Germany and mobilized an army of his own.[10] Inducements and motives for joining the Prince of Orange in the revolt were various: religious toleration, lower taxation, a greater say for the local authorities in regional politics, or fear of attacks by the lower class Orangists like the *Watergeuzen*. City magistrates who preferred safe seas and public peace at home supported Philip II as long as possible. But they were opposed to his incursions upon local privileges. The new fiscal policy of the Spanish government – having the Low Countries themselves pay for the Army of Flanders – was the last straw. The new tax (Tenth Penny duty) upon all goods sold hurt the trading cities, the merchants, and the commercial farmers alike, and its imposition was all the more resented as it coincided with an economic downturn in 1571–1572. The general hatred of the new tax greatly increased the popularity of William of Orange and rallied widespread support.[11]

In the 1570s, one city after another had declared for the House of Orange. Only a minority of the population were Calvinist, however, and some major cities remained loyal to Spain. Middelburg had to be won over by a siege, whereas Amsterdam joined the revolt only after the *Watergeuzen* had blockaded her trade routes for almost six years (1572–1578). Finally, in 1579, the Union of Utrecht was signed by the northern provinces. It was still a treaty of allied provinces. The early core of the revolt was formed by the provinces of Holland, Zeeland, Utrecht, Friesland, and parts of Gelderland; others like Groningen, Drenthe, and Overijssel joined later. The southern provinces, Flanders and Brabant, at first more outspokenly anti-Habsburg as compared to Holland, had been included in the union of 1579, but were lost again to Spain after the fall of Antwerp in 1585.[12]

Bargaining and coalition-making dominated the republican state machinery. Despite central meetings at The Hague, little of a conscious national feeling emerged. In the end, the Estates General, or Their High Mightinesses as they came to be called, were composed of delegates of the seven northern provinces. They represented their province first, and the Republic only secondarily. The executive power was vested in the Council of State, which was made subordinate to the Estates General. It was composed of three gentlemen from Holland, two from Gelderland, two from Zeeland, and two from Friesland, and one from each of the smaller provinces, Groningen, Overijssel and Utrecht.[13]

With virtually no independent funds for the war against Spain, it was necessary to obtain the willing support of all cities and provinces in order to dispose of the available resources. To secure that support, provinces had to remain sovereign, with autonomous financial institutions. On all important issues, such as war and peace, or taxation, unanimity was required. Within the provinces themselves, several estates obtained voting rights. In the Provincial Estates of the inland and north-eastern regions the votes of the nobility and other rural representatives balanced or slightly outweighed those of the cities, but in the west the cities dominated. In the Provincial Estates of Holland eighteen cities (instead of the former six) had a right to vote, whereas the nobility retained a single collective vote. In Zeeland, the proportion was six city votes against one vote for the nobility.[14]

Each province elected a Stadhouder, the former governor for the king but now an official of the Provincial Estates. The one for Holland, who was Stadhouder for most other provinces as well, became the highest dignitary of the Republic. The House of Orange came to dominate this post. They were 'treated with the respect normally reserved for kings, and often leading his armies in the field'.[15] The Stadhouder could dispose of some 'sovereign' appointment rights such as the selection of city magistrates out of a double or triple list of nominations drawn up by city councils. He held high arbitrary powers and served on ad-hoc juridical committees installed upon the authority of the Estates General and the Council of State. Also, as head of the army and navy, with a significant say as to the occupancy of military posts, he had considerable powers of patronage.[16]

The Stadhouder William I of Orange, now appointed by the rebel provinces, assumed a leading position in the 1580s, but he could not rely upon a Dutch nobility, nor upon a bureaucracy. Following his assassination in 1584, alternative leaders were sought in France (Anjou) or England (Leicester), yet the Estates of the provinces demanded too much influence to render these state-making attempts a success. The new Stadhouder of Holland after William I was his son Maurice (1567–1625). He was simultaneously Stadhouder of Holland, Zeeland, Utrecht, Gelderland, and Overijssel, while his cousin William Louis, Count of Nassau (1560–1620) was Stadhouder for Friesland and Groningen. Maurice was also the supreme commander of the army, admiral general of the navy, and a member of the Council of State.[17]

Frederick Henry (1584–1647) succeeded his half-brother Maurice as Stadhouder in 1625. He became captain general, admiral general, and first noble of Holland. In the northern provinces, his cousin Ernst Casimir from the Nassau branch was appointed. The latter was succeeded by Henry Casimir in 1632, who was replaced after his death in 1640 by his brother William Frederick of Nassau (1613–1664). In the meantime, Frederick Henry's court at The Hague was established in great splendour and showed monarchical ambitions. He ensured the political future of his son, the later William II (1626–1650), by claiming succession rights, and arranged his marriage into the British Stuart family.[18]

Both Maurice and Frederick Henry won excellent reputations as military leaders. Mostly, they knew how to manipulate the balance of power. Often, they found the Council of State on their side.[19] Yet in the years immediately following the Treaty of 1648, William II tried to pursue his policies more forcefully than his predecessors. In 1650, the United Provinces of the Netherlands were actually faced with the threat of a civil war. But the *coup d'état* was short-lived, as the Stadhouder died unexpectedly of smallpox. An heir, William III, the later king of Great Britain, was born eight days afterwards. Yet his mother Mary Stuart had to allow the Dutch regents to reorganize the state without a Stadhouder.[20] This fact alone, accomplished by the Holland Estates and accepted by the Estates General, without any rioting or bloodshed, showed the constraints on a Stadhouder's powers within the Republic. In peacetime particularly, he had to abide by rules set by coalitions of cities and provinces. In wartime, though, his position was enhanced, as a military commander was needed, and William III was restored as a Stadhouder in the Third Anglo-Dutch War (1672–1674).

Other army and navy leaders, though sometimes of great skill, such as the admirals Piet Heyn and Maarten Tromp, remained attached to their war departments and did not proceed to higher positions as rulers in The Hague. A major civil servant of the Estates of Holland by the name of Grand Pensionary (*Raadpensionaris*) did have much more impact. Foreign ambassadors looked upon him as Prime Minister of the entire Union. From the central colleges in The Hague, other top civil servants were the First Clerk of the Estates General, the Secretary of the Council of State, and the Treasurer General of the Council of State. The power of those four top bureaucrats was derived from daily participation in crucial meetings.

Yet their influence was not institutionalized, and whether they really acted as rulers of the state depended upon their own personal ambition.[21]

Continued warfare

The *raison d'être* of those early political structures was Spanish Habsburg politics. Spain's interests were furthered by Philip II, who had inherited the Netherlands in 1555 from his father, Charles V. Philip II was followed by Philip III in 1598, and the latter was succeeded by Philip IV, who assumed power when the Twelve Years' Truce with the Dutch (1609–1621) was about to expire. Their overall policy was to regain the wealthy regions of the *Paises Bajos* which had been lost as a consequence of the revolt of the 1560s.[22]

Critical for Spain was the overland lifeline from the south to the north, the line of communication for the military establishment in Flanders. This 'Spanish Road' was actually a number of parallel roads which allowed Spanish troops to march from Genoa, into Lombardy, across Savoy into Franche-Comté, and from Lorraine to Luxembourg. The life-line was very vulnerable. It was open to French intervention in Franche-Comté and Lorraine, whereas the communications relied upon favourable political circumstances in Cologne and in northern Italy, too. Any local crisis along its length was bound to involve Spain. Eventually, the Thirty Years' War (1618–1648) distracted Spanish attention from the Dutch.[23]

In between, the position of France was crucial. With its population of 20 million it constituted the greatest potential power in Western Europe. Despite fears of being enclosed by the Habsburgs, France abstained as long as possible from the conflict. It was also preoccupied with its own revolts throughout the 1620s. But when Spanish troops invaded Trier, it was dragged into the Dutch-Spanish war in 1635.[24]

As a result of the revolt, the United Provinces were involved in almost every anti-Habsburg coalition. Gustavus of Sweden allied with the Dutch in 1614. The Dutch supported the Bohemian rebels against the Princes of Habsburg in 1618, and the Elector of Brandenburg, John Sigismund, could count upon Dutch assistance in the conflict over the inheritance of Jülich-Cleves. The Elector of the Palatinate, Frederick V, held his court in exile at The Hague. When Spain launched a major offensive in 1625, which resulted in the reconquest of Breda, the Dutch allied themselves in an anti-Habsburg coalition involving Denmark. In 1630 the coalitions included Sweden, though at the expense of Denmark. In 1635, France joined the anti-Habsburg league. This step was undoubtedly a major relief for the Dutch. The latter recovered Breda in 1637 and in 1639 Admiral Tromp held off a major armada in the Downs. In 1646, combined Dutch–French forces caused the fall of Dunkirk, the Spanish naval base in the north.[25]

For the Dutch, a powerful navy was often more decisive than the whole army. Yet a navy was bound to involve conflict with England, with whom relations were only temporarily cordial. It was fortunate for the Dutch that England was absorbed in a civil war in the 1640s which reduced the threat from this potential naval competitor. In the far north, Sweden and Denmark competed with each other for control of access to the Baltic and the territories of north central Europe. Their strife was of great interest to the Holland merchants because of the crucial impact of the Sound tolls in Baltic trade. In the 1640s, the Dutch became deeply involved in the Sound crisis, and they enforced a settlement upon the Danes in the end.

Yet the Dutch–Spanish conflict was not played out in Europe alone. Increasingly, the new worlds were drawn into the war. Spices, silver, salt, sugar and the slave trade yielded promising returns for European merchants. The Dutch became very competitive with their East India and West India Companies (respectively VOC, 1602, and WIC, 1621). These companies were established under a monopoly of the Dutch state for trade in the East and in the West Indies respectively. Their governing bodies were allowed to conclude treaties of peace and allegiance, to wage defensive wars, and to build strongholds in their regions. These chartered companies constituted in fact extra-territorial states within the Dutch Republic, although they remained formally under the supervision of the Estates General.[26]

The commercial competition over colonies was enhanced when Dutch markets contracted in Germany because of the Thirty Years' War.[27] Spain lost markets in northern Europe too, but continued to hold on to its colonies against Dutch attacks. When Portuguese possessions were opened to the Dutch, however, Spain's relative power fell dramatically.

Worse for Spain, overall, was the fact that its forces were seriously hampered by the failure of the state finances to keep pace with expenses. State bankruptcy in 1627 was followed by revolts from parts of the Spanish kingdom itself. Portugal claimed independence in 1640. The Dutch supported the revolt with shipments of arms and ammunition. And just before the termination of war, bankruptcy had to be declared again in 1647.[28]

Yet almost all states in Europe wanted peace after 1640. War continued until 1648 because of competing claims and demands for compensation among the combatants. In 1647 a cease-fire was finally agreed upon by Spain and the Netherlands. By the Treaty of 1648 the Dutch gained formal independence not only from Spain but also from claims by the Holy Roman Emperor upon their eastern provinces and cities. The Dutch did not have to concede guarantees concerning the rights of Roman Catholics, and they were allowed to retain their conquests in the Spanish Netherlands and overseas. Antwerp remained blockaded and the Dutch had greater opportunity to trade freely in the East and West Indies.[29]

However, the Dutch were soon confronted with another war. It was now England which claimed maritime superiority through the Navigation Act of 1651. England came to replace Spain as a serious trading rival, whereas France threatened to replace Spanish military hegemony in Europe. A combined attack by England and France in 1672 was a bleak turning point for Dutch international power. Each successive armed conflict resulted in a weakening of the Dutch military position.[30] Nevertheless, up to the end of the eighteenth century, the Dutch continued to retain their territorial integrity.

The great seventeenth century exception

The successful defence of the Republic was partly due to several advantageous circumstances. Whereas most European powers suffered from the 'crisis of the seventeenth century', the Dutch Republic was a phenomenon of achievement. Trade and industry expanded, population doubled, 'when most others had stagnated or regressed under the onslaught of plague and civil and foreign wars'. They were, to borrow the expression of Simon Schama, 'the Great Seventeenth Century Exception'.[31] Moreover, because of the absence of a powerful nobility, social structures were less rigid as compared with much of Europe. In all, feudal control had been lightened by the dominance of land reclamation, livestock farming and commercial crops.[32]

As a matter of course, warfare hampered Dutch trade, yet the effects were not always merely adverse:

> Even the Spanish and Portuguese threat to Dutch shipping probably produced as many trading benefits as it brought dangers. Thus by 1596, when the Republic had only been in existence for some eight years and Prince Maurice was still busy consolidating the borders by fortification and battle, Amsterdam was able to inform the States-General that the volume of Dutch trade and shipping was far greater than that of England and France. And yet the commercial might of the Republic was then only in its infancy.[33]

In foreign policy, the image of a 'rational' Republic of merchant rulers prevailed. A petition to Cromwell stated:

> It is no wonder that these Dutchmen should thrive before us. Their statesmen are all merchants. They have travelled in foreign countries, they understand the course of trade, and they do everything to further its interests.[34]

At times, indeed, the magistrates of major cities stood more to the forefront of Dutch politics than their counterparts of the central state. The actual government of the Dutch cities was performed by two, three or four burgomasters (rotating annually) with seven or more aldermen, elected by the *vroedschap*, a council whose members were chosen for life by cooptation.[35]

Yet the direct influence of merchants declined in the course of the seventeenth century. City politics became more oligarchic, which restricted social upward mobility. The number of *vroedschappen* was reduced, and with it the number of families admitted to city government. The main occupation of the regents of 1650, then, was no longer trade; they sought to build careers in local government and administration, which entailed a shift from merchant oligarchs to burgher oligarchs. Those holding municipal office became the real ruling class in the Republic.[36]

Though the influence of the nobility was weak, individual nobles were by no means unimportant in politics. In Holland, the College of Nobles (*Ridderschap*, the only non-city vote) had deputies on all major government boards and in the VOC. Their secretary was the Grand Pensionary of Holland himself, who voted for the nobles in the Provincial Estates, from which considerable political influence was derived. They also voted first. In Friesland and Groningen, the rulers were gentlemen farmers. Gelderland was dominated by rural nobles, whereas hedge squires governed in Overijssel and neighbouring Drenthe.[37]

Yet the 'Great Seventeenth Century Exception' did not extend throughout the whole Republic. The inland provinces experienced less favourable conditions as compared with the urbanized and maritime regions of the country. Traditional trade routes of the eastern cities were disrupted because of the shift from overland to seaborne trade. Moreover, their rural hinterlands suffered from long sieges and the attentions of plundering armies, due to the Eighty Years' War and the Thirty Years' War. Obviously, theirs was not a Golden Age. Even in the west itself, several cities were in decline as well. Inter-city rivalry was strong. Almost all were jealous of Amsterdam's achievements. Dordrecht, Gouda and Delft – all on the decline in the seventeenth century – competed vigorously with Rotterdam. Rotterdam, Hoorn and Dordrecht eagerly snatched business from Amsterdam if the opportunity arose. The towns of Zeeland were often at odds with those of Holland. This province lost much of its former economic glory during the seventeenth century due to stagnation in the Antwerp entrepôt.[38]

But the Dutch constitution remained a highly idiosyncratic one within the setting of Europe. The Union of Utrecht, at first a treaty of sovereign provinces with only practical importance, became the ideological foundation of the Republic. As the state had originated more or less by accident, no political theory backed up the Dutch public institutions. In ideology, the monarchical tradition persisted, even at the new University of Leiden. However, there were some distinctive emphases: the rule of law, strict defence of existing property rights and privileges, came to be emphasized by the Dutch. Moreover, Dutch politics were very much 'the art of associating', referring to the theory of Johannes Althusius. In all, 'the state' was regarded as a function of society, a concept different from any elsewhere in Europe, where the state belonged to the monarch. And despite its decentralist tendencies, the Dutch Republic was a state. It controlled a specific territory and used armed forces and taxation to enforce its claims. The confederal state under the direction of the Estates General in The Hague commanded several central institutions which functioned as broker in balancing powers and yielded some bureaucratic force.[39]

The Reformation had removed one of the possible competitors for new state power, and had increased the grip of secular leaders on state and church. A Calvinist orientation was generally a prerequisite for the highest offices. However, the Republic did not become a country of *cuius regio, eius religio*. Typical of Dutch culture was not Calvinism but the humanist tradition and the tolerance of manifold religious sects. As a result, religious factionalism was to play a role in the new balance of power, and was mixed with party factions, pro- or anti-war groups, and pro- or anti-Orange leagues.[40]

The Dutch exception was made possible by the fact that the country's main rivals were in a parlous condition. In the first half of the seventeenth century, the German Empire was paralysed by the Thirty Years' War; France had to emerge from religious wars and a major uprising of the nobility (the Fronde); post-Elizabethan England was increasingly dissipating her strength in a constitutional struggle; and mighty Spain failed to recover from the Portuguese, Catalonian and Dutch revolts. In addition, the Dutch were able to profit from population increase, economic growth, trade and industrial advantages, and the immigration of wealthy entrepreneurs from the less fortunate parts of Europe.

However, many Dutch political and economic advantages were fading by the second half of the seventeenth century. Both France and England followed a more forceful mercantilist policy and imposed high tariffs. Indeed, the continuing pressure of wars kept the provinces willing to continue their Union. Yet almost every armed involvement that was to come ended with a weakening of the Dutch position. The Anglo–Dutch Wars were one long success for the British, whereas the constant threat of French invasion did materialize in 1672 and 1795. The Dutch republican state managed to survive until the end of the eighteenth century, but it was to play only a secondary role in European politics after 1713. The wars with England and in particular the War of the Spanish Succession after the turn of the seventeenth century broke the Dutch as a great naval and land power. Also in economic respect, the Dutch declined relative to the British.[41]

In all, war had a major impact on the formation of the Dutch state. Chapter Two stresses the role of the Eighty Years' War in consolidating the Republic. It was only at enormous military expense that this essentially decentralized state defended its interests against some significantly larger competitors.

Notes

1 In accordance with E.H. Kossmann, *The Low Countries 1780–1940*,

Oxford, 1978, 1: 'Dutch' points to the region of the present-day Netherlands, whereas 'Low Countries' designates the area of the Netherlands and Belgium together.

2 Huizinga, *Dutch civilisation*, 14.

3 B.H. Slicher van Bath, 'Historical demography and the social and economic development of the Netherlands', *Daedalus* 97, 1968, 609–10; A.M. van der Woude, 'Demografische ontwikkeling van de Noordelijke Nederlanden 1500–1800', *Algemene Geschiedenis der Nederlanden* V, 1980, 134–7; Jan de Vries, 'The population and economy of the preindustrial Netherlands', *Journal of Interdisciplinary History* 15, 1985, 664–6; Simon Hart, *Geschrift en getal. Een keuze uit de demografisch-, economisch- en sociaal-historische studiën op grond van Amsterdamse en Zaanse archivalia, 1600–1800*, Dordrecht, 1976, 121, 136; J.G.C.A. Briels, *Zuid-Nederlanders in de Republiek, 1572–1630: een demografische en cultuurhistorische studie*, Sint-Niklaas, 1985. Holland's numbers increased partly through immigration from the other provinces and especially through the exodus of Calvinists from the southern Netherlands. Outmigration through labour in the navy and the West and East India Companies was considerable too, but the Dutch Republic was on the whole a net recipient of migrants.

4 Schama, *Embarrassment of Riches*, 4–7; see also Wayne TeBrake, *Rebels and rulers. The revolutionary world of an eighteenth-century Dutch city*, Cambridge, 1989.

5 Wallerstein, *Modern world system* II, 46; see also Israel, *Dutch primacy*, 12.

6 Except for maybe 1630 and 1647 as difficult years. Leo Noordegraaf, *Hollands welvaren? Levenstandaard in Holland 1450–1650*, Bergen, 1985, 172; Jan de Vries, *The Dutch rural economy in the Golden Age, 1500–1700*, New Haven, 1974, 185; J. A. Faber, *Dure tijden en hongersnoden in preïndustrieel Nederland*, Amsterdam, 1976, 7–9; Alexander van der Capellen, *Gedenkschriften, [...] beginnende metten Jaare 1621 [...] gaande to 1654* II, Utrecht, 1777, 584. Inflation was restricted during 1620–1650: De Vries, 'Decline and rise', 174–6; J.H. Stuyvenberg and J.E.J. de Vrijer, 'Prices, population and national income in the Netherlands 1620–1978', *Journal of Economic History* 11, 1982, 699. For another interpretation of the period 1620–1650 see Israel, *Dutch primacy*, 121–96.

7 Geoffrey Parker, 'The emergence of modern finance in Europe', *The Fontana History of Europe* II, ed. C. M. Cipolla, Glasgow, 1974, 573; Sidney Homer, *A history of interest rates*, New Brunswick, N.J., 1977, 174; J.G. van Dillen, 'Amsterdam's role in seventeenth century Dutch politics and the economic background', *Britain and the Netherlands* II, Groningen, 1964, 382; M.G. Buist, 'The sinews of war: the role of Dutch finance in European politics *c.* 1750–1815', *Britain and the Netherlands* VI, The Hague, 1977, 125; Froukje Breedtvelt-van Veen, *Louis de Geer 1587–1652*, Amsterdam, 1935, 223; P.W. Klein, *De Trippen in de 17e eeuw. Een studie over het ondernemersgedrag op de Hollandse stapelmarkt*, Assen, 1965; cf. discussion in P.W. Klein, 'De wereldhandel in edele metalen 1500–1800: centraliteit of polycentrisme?', *Tijdschrift voor Geschiedenis* 100, 1987,

185.

8 Gerald L. Burke, *The making of Dutch towns*, New York, 1960; H. Brugmans, *Opkomst en bloei van Amsterdam*, Amsterdam, 1911, 152; R. Bijlsma, *Rotterdam's welvaren 1550–1650*, The Hague, 1918; C.C. Hibben, *Gouda in revolt. Particularism and pacifism in the revolt of the Netherlands 1572–1588*, Utrecht, 1983.

9 Huizinga, *Dutch civilisation*, 108; see also Marjolein 't Hart, 'Cities and state making in the Dutch Republic, 1580–1680', *Theory and Society* 18, 1989, 663–88.

10 After Egmont and Horne were beheaded by Alva, Oranje was the only major noble left. H.F.K. van Nierop, *Van ridders tot regenten. De Hollandse adel in de zestiende en de eerste helft van de zeventiende eeuw*, Amsterdam, 1984, 31; on juridical centralization under the Habsburgs: A.H. Huussen, 'Moderne staatsvorming en wetgeving van het begin van de nieuwe tijd', *Etat et religion aux XVe et XVIe siècles*, ed. W.P. Blockmans and H. van Nuffel, Brussels, 1986, 50.

11 Kossmann, *The Low Countries*, 11; J.J. Woltjer, 'De vrede-makers', *De Unie van Utrecht*, ed. S. Groenveld and H.L.Ph. Leeuwenberg, The Hague, 1979, 69; F.H.M. Grapperhaus, *Alva en de tiende penning*, Zutphen, 1984, 305; J. Craeybeckx, 'Alva's tiende penning: een mythe?', *Bijdragen en Mededelingen van het Historisch Genootschap* 76, 1962, 15.

12 Drenthe had signed early too, but was reconquered by Spain; it joined again in the 1590s. The southern Netherlands were economically more advanced regions. They also experienced sharper class contradictions, which might have weakened the class coalitions against the Spanish monarchy. Guido Marnef, *Het calvinistische bewind te Mechelen 1580–1585*, Kortrijk, 1987; J.J. Woltjer, *Kleine oorzaken, grote gevolgen*, Leiden, 1975; J.C. Boogman, 'De overgang van Gouda, Dordrecht, Leiden en Delft in de zomer van het jaar 1572', *Tijdschrift voor Geschiedenis* 57, 1942.

13 A.Th. van Deursen, 'De Raad van State onder de Republiek 1588–1795', *Raad van State 450 Jaar*, The Hague, 1981, 47–92; M.E.H.N. Mout, 'Ni prince, ni état', *Pouvoirs et institutions en Europe au XVIème siècle*, Paris, 1987, 122; for a general overview: Robert Fruin and H.T. Colenbrander, *Geschiedenis van de staatsinstellingen in Nederland tot aan de val der Republiek*, The Hague, 1922.

14 Woltjer, 'Vredemakers', 86; J.W. Koopmans, 'Drie kleine steden in de Staten. De verschijning van Schoonhoven, Woerden en Oudewater in de Hollandsche Statenvergadering', *Heemtijdingen* 21, 1985, 109–14.

15 Huizinga, *Dutch civilisation*, 32.

16 S.J. Fockema Andreae, *De Nederlandse staat onder de Republiek*, Amsterdam, 1975, 6; A.J.C.M. Gabriëls, *De heren als dienaren en de dienaar als heer*, Amsterdam, 1990, 56.

17 H. de Schepper, 'Raad van State', *Raad van State 450 Jaar*, The Hague, 1985, 37. The nobility of the Netherlands had traditionally been concentrated in the south. Van Nierop, *Ridders tot regenten*, 48.

18 I.H. Gosses and N. Japikse, *Handboek tot de Staatkundige Geschiedenis van Nederland*, The Hague, 1927, 469; J.J. Poelhekke, *Frederik Hendrik: Prins van Oranje. Een biografisch drieluik*, Zutphen, 1983;

Maarten Prak, 'Republiek en vorst. De stadhouders en het staatsvormingsproces in de noordelijke Nederlanden, 16e-18e eeuw', *Amsterdams Sociologisch Tijdschrift* 16, 1989, 30.

19 Van Deursen, 'Raad van State onder de Republiek', 90.

20 Which reinforced provincial separatism in 1651; G.W. Kernkamp, *Prins Willem II, 1626–1650*, Rotterdam, 1977, 97; Gosses, *Staatkundige geschiedenis*, 502; G. de Bruin, 'De souvereiniteit van de Republiek: een machtsprobleem', *Bijdragen en Mededelingen betreffende de Geschiedenis der Nederlanden* 94, 1979, 33.

21 Huizinga, *Dutch civilisation*, 29; Van Deursen, 'Raad van State', 47; J.G. Smit, 'De ambtenaren van de centrale overheidsorganen der Republiek in het begin van de zeventiende eeuw', *Tijdschrift voor Geschiedenis* 90, 1977, 385.

22 The southern Netherlands provinces, which had continued to recognize Habsburg rule or which were recovered by Spain, were governed from 1596 by the Archdukes Albert and Isabel in Brussels in the name of the Spanish king.

23 Geoffrey Parker, *The Army of Flanders and the Spanish Road, 1567–1659*, Cambridge, 1975, 80ff.

24 David Maland, *Europe at war 1600–1650*, Towota, N.J., 1980, 147.

25 *Ibidem*, 68, 147, 155. J.V. Polisensky, *War and society in Europe 1618–1648*, Cambridge, 1978, 88–91.

26 C.R. Boxer, *The Dutch seaborne empire, 1600–1800*, London, 1965, 20, 24, 46; J.G. van Dillen, *Van rijkdom en regenten. Handboek tot de economische en sociale geschiedenis van Nederland tijdens de Republiek*, The Hague, 1970, 127; Joh. E. Elias, *Schetsen uit de geschiedenis van ons zeewezen* I, The Hague, 1916, 73–4. The VOC shares yielded rich returns. The WIC proved far less successful as compared to the VOC: W.R. Menkman, *De West-Indische Compagnie*, Amsterdam, 1947, 44; Jonathan I. Israel, *The Dutch Republic and the Hispanic world, 1606–1661*, Oxford, 1986, 134, 200, 332.

27 Peter Limm, *The Thirty Years' War*, London, 1984, 10.

28 In the sixteenth century, Spain had failed several times as well. J.H. Elliott, *Richelieu and Olivares*, Cambridge, 1984, 69; Thompson, *War and government*, 274.

29 Israel, *Dutch Republic and Hispanic world*, 375.

30 Johan Aalbers, 'Het machtsverval van de Republiek der Verenigde Nederlanden 1713–1741', *Machtsverval in internationale context*, ed. J. Aalbers and A. van Goudoever, Groningen, 1986.

31 Schama, *Embarrassment of riches*, 223–4.

32 Jan de Vries, *The economy of Europe in an age of crisis 1600–1750*, Cambridge, 1976, 70–1.

33 Huizinga, *Dutch civilisation*, 21.

34 Quoted by Jacob de Liefde, *Great Dutch admirals*, Freeport, N.Y., 1972, 82.

35 Guilds and burgher militias exerted little influence on everyday politics, although magistrates had to consider their feelings as they were able to mobilize support. See Paul Knevel, 'Onrust onder schutters. De politieke

invloed van de Hollandse schutterijen in de eerste helft van de zeventiende eeuw', *Holland* 20, 1988, 158–74; E.A.M. Eibrink-Jansen, *De opkomst van de vroedschap in enkele Hollandsche steden*, Haarlem, 1927, 21, 56.

36 D.J. Roorda, 'The ruling classes in Holland in the seventeenth century', *Britain and the Netherlands* II, Groningen, 1964, 46–8; Maarten Prak, 'Geschiedschrijving van het Nederlands Ancien Régime', *Tijdschrift voor Sociale Geschiedenis* 14, 1988, 133–59; Boxer, *Dutch seaborne empire*, 34; Cees Schmidt, *Om de eer van de familie. Het geslacht Teding van Berkhout. Een sociologische benadering*, Amsterdam, 1986, 65–9. Democracy is a misnomer here as lower classes were never given a voice in representation.

37 Van Nierop, *Ridders tot regenten*, 127, 221; Van Dillen, *Van rijkdom en regenten*, 285.

38 J.L. van Zanden, 'Prijs van de vooruitgang? Economische modernisering en sociale polarisatie op het Nederlandse platteland na 1500', *Economisch en Sociaal Historisch Jaarboek* 51, 1988, 89; B.H. Slicher van Bath, *Een samenleving onder spanning. Geschiedenis van het platteland van Overijssel*, Assen, 1957, 154, 534–47; W.S. Unger and J.J. Westendorp Boerma, 'De steden van Zeeland. Middelburg', *Archief Zeeuwsch Genootschap*, 1954, 60.

39 J.C. Boogman, 'The Union of Utrecht: its genesis and consequences', *Bijdragen en Mededelingen betreffende de Geschiedenis der Nederlanden* 94, 1979, 377, 389; Johannes Althusius (1557–1638) was an East Frisan magistrate; see *The politics of Johannes Althusius*, ed. F.S. Carney, Boston, 1964, 12; Hans Daalder, 'Consociationalism, center and periphery in the Netherlands', *Mobilization, center–periphery, structures and nation-building*, ed. Per Torsvik, Bergen, 1981, 182; Mout, 'Ni prince, ni état', 117.

40 Heinz Schilling, 'Calvinismus und Freiheitsrechte', *Bijdragen en Mededelingen betreffende de Geschiedenis der Nederlanden* 102, 1987, 434; Daalder, 'Consociationalism', 205; Gosses, *Staatkundige geschiedenis*, 454; Huizinga, *Dutch civilisation*, 48.

41 Johan Aalbers, 'Holland's financial problems (1713–1733) and the wars against Louis XIV', *Britain and the Netherlands* VI, The Hague, 1977, 93; Charles Wilson, 'Taxation and the decline of empires, an unfashionable theme', *Bijdragen en Mededelingen van het Historisch Genootschap* 77, 1963, 10–23; see also De Vries, *Economische achteruitgang*, 177; A.M. van der Woude, 'De contractiefase van de seculaire trend in het Noorderkwartier nader beschouwd', *Bijdragen en Mededelingen betreffende de Geschiedenis der Nederlanden* 103, 1988, 373; J.L. van Zanden, 'De economie van Holland in de periode 1650–1850: groei of achteruitgang', *Bijdragen en Mededelingen betreffende de Geschiedenis der Nederlanden* 102, 1988, 608; Boxer, *Dutch seaborne empire*, 118.

2

The costs of warfare

The Dutch were at war most of the time in the late sixteenth and seventeenth centuries. It was the period of the 'military revolution', which entailed profound changes in the tactics, strategy, scale and size of armies. Feudal warfare had been replaced by hired troops. The number of soldiers increased enormously, both in permanent armed forces and in additional temporary troops for campaigns. Professionalization proceeded and armaments improved. Campaigns were frequently decided by sieges. Siege warfare depended in large measure on organization: troops could not live off the land any more, so finance had to be regulated. Not only armies but also navies felt the impact of professionalization and modern war finance. Vessels were built specially for warfare and drilled soldiers were assigned to assist the sailors. The net result of the military revolution was an overall increase in the power of the early modern state. True, not all countries experienced such a military revolution. Yet, generally, those that failed to modernize were crushed on the battlefield and became absorbed into others.[1]

For an increasing number of men, warfare became a permanent trade. The larger the armed force, the greater the possible impact upon state formation. Sweden and Spain maintained huge armies, while Prussia was the outstanding model for the eighteenth century. These countries had to hire many men in relation to their respective populations. This could even cause a militarization of the civil service, as in the case of Sweden and Prussia. The tax-collecting agency in Prussia typically came to be called the General War Commissariat. France had an enormous force too, yet by comparison with its population the impact was smaller. The Dutch Republic, though, maintained a large army relatively to its tiny population throughout the seventeenth century.[2]

By this time, some armies were only recently professionalized. In England, a standing army came into being during the Cromwellian period, although a standing navy had been established in the sixteenth century. The navy was of limited importance to France (eighteen warships in the 1660s) by comparison with its massive army. But the French army was professionalized only after 1660. It was an arduous task to find men willing to serve, and in the 1670s France even had to resort to a compulsory levy of forces.[3]

In general, for recruitment of the troops, the paymaster(s) would award a commission to a (preferably wealthy) officer as *overste* or colonel, stipulating the number, the pay and other conditions of recruitment. The colonel contracted captains, who were assigned particular companies or vessels, and a date and place would be set for the troops to convene. The captains sent out sergeants, supported by a drummer, who would hire men at market places and inns. Often, they had to travel to distant villages. The soldier or sailor brought his own clothes, armour, and arms. Captains could provide these items too, in return for a soldier's pay. At the first muster day, the regiment was formed. Officers were introduced to the troops, oaths taken, the articles of war read, and sermons might be heard.

Such initial recruitment was a costly business and could fail, merely because of shortage of cash – in such a case, all the monies spent were lost. Cash shortages could occur during campaigns as well. Regular pay constituted a major problem for all early modern states, despite any military revolution. Spanish troops mutinied and deserted in 1607 on a large scale. French armies refused to cross the Rhine until they had received pay in 1638. Even the Swedish army of Gustavus Adolphus, one of the major architects of the military revolution, mutinied in 1633 over pay arrears.[4]

Again and again, the population of the war-torn territories had to pay through contributions. Armies, friend or enemy, always constituted a considerable burden for a region, the more so if there was no permanent provision of a garrison. Semi-official exactions like 'safeguards' (in return for the promise of the troops not to sack) were an important source of revenue for companies, though they seldom appeared in official budgets.[5]

Despite the impact of the military revolution, voluntarism persisted. In the sixteenth and seventeenth centuries, mercenary troops dominated. Their commanders acted as military entrepreneurs willing to sell their services to the highest bidder. In Spain, through contracts or *asientos*, private financiers took care of the whole supply and distribution of war funds in the 1630s. In England, too, the victualling of the fleet was organized by means of a private contract in 1655–1660. In France, Colbert established government shipyards, but after his death shipbuilding reverted to private hands again. Generally, the manufacture of shot, armour and small arms, and the provisioning of both armies and navies, continued to be carried out by contractors.[6]

There was a significant advantage for countries with predominantly naval concerns over others having to maintain huge land forces. Armies tended to be more costly than navies. At the end of the seventeenth century, the English fleet comprised 35 per cent and the troops 40 per cent of the state's budget.[7] But whatever the nature of the costs, warfare always weighed heavily on the state budgets of early modern Europe. After 1600, wars spread over larger regions, involved more states, a larger number of soldiers, and incurred greater losses than before. All states, even the most rudimentary and peripheral ones, were affected by the emergence of larger state units.[8]

In this chapter the costs of war will be followed for the Dutch army and navy. The military revolution had its impact on both, although private interests remained large. Subsequently, wartime increases during the Eighty Years' War are analysed and a Dutch 'budget' of expenses is reconstructed.

The military revolution in the army

The first regiment of the Dutch army to last longer than a couple of campaigns was formed in 1572. Four years later more companies were added, and a standing army came into being. It was an army of the Republic, the highest authority being the Estates General. The Council of State supervised the finances, discipline, recruitment, budgeting, pay, fortifications, commissions and oaths. The right to review the instructions of the Council of State was vested in the Estates General and the provinces. The conduct of war was supervised by the Estates General, sending deputies with the army in the field. The Stadhouders Maurice and Frederick Henry obtained the highest commanding office, but only the latter was made captain-general of the Union.[9]

Since the provinces were the paymasters, furnishing the funds for the troops in this army, they had special rights with regard to marching orders, the appointment of middle-ranking officers, and discipline. Strictly speaking, the 'monopoly of violence' of the central state was not well advanced, since each city, and each province, was sovereign in the recruitment of troops. But in reality the only standing army was that of the Estates General, and decisions as to recruitment and disbanding had to be taken in their meetings. Disputes arose, though, concerning appointments and marching orders, in particular when troops were paid by one province but stationed in another, or when one company was paid jointly by two provinces.[10]

Added to the standing army were the extraordinary troops contracted for specific campaigns (*veldleger*) and the contracts with military entrepreneurs. These forces were outside the control of the individual provinces. Within the provinces, the chartered cities had burgher militias, defensive corps called *schutterijen*. In a case where the *schutters* could not be trusted by the magistrates, special temporary troops could be hired. They were called *waardgelders* and were under the command of the city magistrates as a kind of extraordinary militia. Amsterdam had these *waardgelders*, and so did Dordrecht and Gorinchem.[11]

No regular conscription took place under the Dutch Republic, despite the fact that the Union of Utrecht (in article VIII) had made it the duty of every Dutchman to serve in the army. Only in 1629, under severe threat by Spanish troops, was a general levy under discussion. Then, in fact, Holland did raise conscripted forces. Mostly, though, the soldiers were of foreign origin. Serving the army had little to do with nationalist feelings or religious sentiment. Many troops were Catholic. A minority of the Republic's troops spoke Dutch, while most were of French, Walloon, German, Swiss, Danish, Irish, English or Scottish origin.[12]

Yet despite the multitude of languages, the Dutch army was relatively well organized by seventeenth-century standards. The last major mutiny under the Republic dated back to 1588. In the 1590s, the Stadhouder Maurice introduced innovations such as better drill and exercising. Troops came under stricter discipline. Garrisons relieved the local population of undisciplined soldiers. The control of the state increased, and negotiations about contributing by way of taxation, rather than exactions by force, were embarked upon. Still, the threat of minor mutinies remained. In 1622 soldiers at Goch (district of Cuyk in Brabant) mutinied, though actual marauding was avoided by sending funds quickly. More serious were raids by Zutphen soldiers, in 1624, who had not been paid. They burnt a house and killed three children, fifteen cattle and many more sheep.[13]

Yet in general the payment of the troops improved, and during the Truce of 1609–1621 the Estates' army even gained a good reputation among soldiers. As Michael Howard has written:

> there was, in western Europe, one great exception – the armies of the United Provinces; and they were exceptional for the very simple reason that they were regularly supplied and paid.[14]

Furthermore, the army of the Estates General had the reputation of being quite 'modern' for the time. The latest methods of warfare were applied more consistently than in other armies. Dutch infantry and cavalry formations were less deep (no more than five horsemen no more than ten foot soldiers deep), tactical units were reduced, weapon designs were standardized (cannon restricted to four calibres), and soldiers were drilled.[15]

The commanders of the Republic's army, Maurice, William Louis, and Frederick Henry, acquired excellent reputations as army leaders. The study guide of the first European military academy, created in Siegen in 1617, referred to Maurice's successes:

> Und solches zwar auf eben die weisz
> welch heut vor andern hat den preisz,
> dasz sie die best und nützlichtst sei,
> wie man die erfahrung had hirbey,
> und auch Prinz Moritz hogh gebohren
> Ihm diese weisz had ausverkohren.[16]

Artillery was moved more quickly into position, musketeers riflemen learned volley shooting, siege tactics were copied from the Italian and Spanish. Moreover, the Dutch had the advantage of easy access to a flourishing industry and trade in arms and ammunition.[17]

Older soldiers were more sought after than young men. Personal experience was highly valued. Within each company, twenty of the best and eldest soldiers were 'appointees', a position entailing better pay and exemption from duties such as night watch. New recruits always became arquebusiers: they were the younger, novice soldiers. Musketeers had heavier guns and were better drilled. Pikemen were the elite core of the infantry, because of their coordinated manoeuvres. They were the most disciplined and best paid.[18]

The cavalry likewise had its distinctions. Lowest were again arquebusiers (or carabineers) who were lightly armed. Cuirassiers with heavy armour and better pistols rated above them in pay. Lancers, the soldiers by profession, often of noble birth, ranked between the light and heavy cavalry. They were regarded as the elite troops. To these horsemen Maurice added companies of dragoons or 'mounted infantry', who were equipped to fight on foot as well.[19]

Each infantry company consisted of a fixed number of junior officers: one captain, one lieutenant, one ensign (cornet), two sergeants, three squad masters, one clerk/victualler, one barber (and doctor), one officer of justice (*provoost*) and two drummers. For each company of 100 soldiers there were 113 men to pay. The cavalry's direct commanding officers were the captain of the horse and a lieutenant. They were supplemented by an ensign, one quartermaster, two buglers, one clerk/victualler, and a farrier.[20]

During the Truce of 1609–1621, the actual number of men per company was decreased. It was raised in 1621 with the resumption of war, but reduced again when hostilies moderated in the 1640s and was brought to a minimum level in 1650. The cavalry company, likewise, varied in number.[21] On paper, its averages (including the junior officers) were as shown in Table 2.1. To all companies a couple of gunners (*canonniers*), engineers, and sappers were added. Moreover, there was a civil bureaucracy, made up of wagon masters, ammunition masters, controllers of the army in the field, clerks for the fortifications, provision clerks, magazine clerks, some doctors, and a couple of schoolteachers and ministers.[22]

These men were paid separately, like the senior commanding officers. The latter constituted a class apart. The highest-ranking

Table 2.1 *Average number of men in each company of cavalry and infantry, selected years, 1618–1650*

years	*cavalry*	*infantry*
1618	80	89
1621	105	152
1643	78	116
1650	55	63

Source: ARA CoA *Staten van Oorlog*; J. W. Wijn, *Het krijgswezen in den tijd van Prins Maurits*, Utrecht, 1934, 29.

commanders of the army, as well as the governors of garrisons and fortresses, were nominated by the Estates General. Officers from captain to colonel were appointed by the paymaster provinces. Many officers of the army, though, were foreign noblemen with little influence in the Dutch body politic. Only Friesland restricted its appointments to native citizens, whereas Gelderland showed a preference for republican nationals as well.[23]

A semi-private category of officers were *solliciteurs-militair*. They were private financiers, who lent money to the captains at interest in advance of the provincial pay. Provinces were generally too slow in providing the sums, and these financiers virtually prevented mutinies in the army.[24]

The captains themselves were semi-private entrepreneurs as well. They received the funds from the provincial paymaster. Because any smaller number of men than that officially assigned yielded significant additional income, captains were reluctant to replace those who died or who had defected. The full number were only present on muster days, those missing partly replaced by passers-by (*passevolanten*) who were prepared to act as soldiers during the muster – on payment, of course. Several attempts to introduce strict payment by head were never put into effect and the captains continued to act as entrepreneurs within the military system. Moreover, they could replace payment in cash by payment in kind, such as food and clothing.[25]

An example of a major abuse was the company of the French captain Parsoureux. When mustered in 1640, it was found that of the 120 men only sixty were effectively in service. During the investigation the number even declined to 50: several *passevolanten* had run away and a couple of soldiers had died.[26] To combat such abuses, the captains were allowed to receive the pay of soldiers who had died (*mortepayen*). It was regarded as a premium for the captains, to defray the cost of interest incurred with the *solliciteurs-militair*. Especially during years of high mortality, such as 1622 and 1625, the actual strength of the army was much lower than on paper. Moreover, it was allowed to have fewer soldiers serving during winter, while full company pay continued.[27]

Because of siege tactics, much expenditure went on fortifications. Many cities improved their defensive barriers on their own account, but frontier cities obtained support from the Estates General for building walls and fortresses. The area comprising Holland, Zeeland

and Utrecht became the redoubt, the core of the Republic. Policy was aimed at protecting this redoubt. It was relatively safe from the south, with the sea arms of Zeeland and the major rivers of the Rhine and Meuse delta. Weakest was the east: at many places the river IJssel was shallow, and the Council of State was very concerned about improving this border. In the far north-east, extended peat bogs defended the northern provinces from attack from Germany. Open to intervention, then, were the provinces of Overijssel and large parts of Gelderland. They suffered most from the direct burdens of war: enemy troops, forced financial contributions and undisciplined soldiers.[28]

The standing navy of the five admiralties

Not only did the Republic have a standing army, it also maintained a standing naval establishment. It was at times more crucial for the defence of the Dutch Republic than the army. The organization was delegated to five admiralties: three in the province of Holland (Rotterdam, Amsterdam, Hoorn/Enkhuizen), one in the province of Zeeland (Middelburg) and one in Friesland (Dokkum, later Harlingen). How they came into being is a complex story of inter-city and inter-provincial rivalries.

In the sixteenth century, cities had taken care of their naval vessels themselves. Apart from a central court in Veere for prizes, no formal coordination existed. In 1576 the provinces of Holland and Zeeland decided to combine their forces to constitute a fleet of 100 ships for convoys, the collection of revenue, and privateering. This fleet was put under command of the Prince of Orange, the Stadhouder of Holland as well as of Zeeland. At the time of the Union of Utrecht in 1579, the navy was still regarded as belonging to the two provinces of Holland and Zeeland alone, as no mention was made of the navy in the Act at all.[29]

As the admiralty role expanded, the Council of State assumed supervisory tasks. Centralization proved to be hard, though, because of animosities between Holland and Zeeland over trade and convoys. Holland was preoccupied with the Baltic trade, neglecting convoys to the rest Europe; Zeeland, by contrast, was heavily engaged in trade with the Southern Netherlands, which was regarded by Holland as trade with the enemy. In a reorganization of 1588 the Estates General tried to resume the supervision from the

Council of State and vested it in a new central institution: the College of Superintendence. The college existed only until 1593, as Zeeland refused to send deputies, regarding it as too Holland oriented.[30]

Rotterdam was pre-eminently suited to housing a central admiralty, because of its role in fisheries and shipping, and because of its central position near the sea and the main rivers. Amsterdam's harbour was not easily accessible and the disloyal attitude of Amsterdam during the revolt was still remembered by the others. But when the central government installed the navy board in Rotterdam, Zeeland refused to submit to an admiralty in Holland. It mistrusted any generality institution in that province, and demanded the right to create one of its own. In rank, though, the Rotterdam admiralty remained first among the four others, which meant that it was allowed to speak and vote first.

At the same time, rivalry existed in Zeeland itself between the cities as to the site of the admiralty. Flushing had developed a major harbour, while there was some reason to install the admiralty in Veere, because of its court of jurisdiction. Middelburg had the largest capital resources and was keen on cutting the influence of its neighbours. In the end, it did obtain the seat. The province's governing deputies became at the same time the councillors for Zeeland in the admiralty, which resulted in a curious amalgamation of the two administrations.[31]

In Holland, too, local patriotic feeling took its toll, and the central establishment in Rotterdam was consequently weakened.[32] The government decided to locate a separate generality board in Hoorn, in order to obtain cooperation from the Northern Quarter. The city, however, refused, claiming the right to organize its own West Frisian admiralty. As a temporary measure, the Board of Admiralty was moved to Amsterdam. When the Northern Quarter finally decided it would be better-off accepting the generality board, Amsterdam refused to move, and kept it within the city boundary. The seven Northern Quarter towns were furious, fearing domination by Amsterdam. They exerted pressure for a new institution, and the result was the setting up of a fourth admiralty in 1593. But now inter-city rivalry accounted for the fact that it was to move every three months between the cities of Hoorn and Enkhuizen.[33]

In the meantime, there had been problems in the collection of customs in Groningen in 1594 and 1595. Partly to increase control, and partly because of claims by Friesland that scorned the authority of the Northern Quarter of Holland over Frisian territory, a fifth admiralty was set up in Dokkum in 1596. The seat was moved to Harlingen in 1645 as this latter port was more accessible.[34]

Thus, with the settlement of 1597, termed 'provisional' but nevertheless permanent up to 1795, no fewer than five admiralties existed, ranging from the powerful Amsterdam board to the tiny Friesland establishment. Their task was to protect Dutch interests at sea, and to collect the customs for their upkeep. Coordination was poor. Some incidental meetings at The Hague, called *Haagsche Besognes*, tried to impose supervision, yet they became regular only after 1648. Central command over the warships was, in theory, delegated to the admiral-general, usually the Stadhouder of Holland and Zeeland. A College of Superintendence or something like it was proposed in 1610, 1629 and 1648, but was never created.[35]

At the same time, as in the army, the monopoly of force by the central state was not complete, since cities and merchant companies had the right to send out their own fleet of armed vessels. In 1619, for example, Rotterdam sent a couple of ships armed with guns to threaten nearby Dordrecht during a conflict over duties (*stapelrecht*) on the Meuse.[36]

Each admiralty was originally assigned seven councillors: four from the province itself, three from the other provinces. In practice, though, the number of councillors came to range from eight to twelve. The highest officers were appointed by the Estates General, the junior civil servants by the boards.[37] One of the board members, the Advocaat Fiscaal, was a crucial figure: his main duties were to observe the regulations of the central government and to supervise the receiver and the acts of the councillors, with his private property as bail.[38]

Other officers of the admiralties were: a Receiver, a Secretary, a couple of clerks for the secretary, an Auction Master for the prizes and confiscated goods, two to four Equipment Masters for the warships, a head officer of justice and some assistants, and usually two ushers or housekeepers and some messengers. Each customs office had a receiver (Convoy Master), a controller who had to keep a shadow administration of the receipts, and some checkers for the actual search of arriving vessels (and wagons in the inland regions). Over time, these custom offices increased: in 1600 they numbered sixty-seven, in 1650 ninety-one, and in 1700 127.[39]

The Estates General supervised the admiralties through the

Advocaat Fiscaal and the Chamber of Accounts (*Generaliteitsreken-kamer*), and five to six commissioners general of the customs who oversaw the customs collection in their region through controllers.

Yet the admiralties were prone to local oligarchization. Almost all the higher posts of the admiralties were linked to the local commercial elite. Many regents had ties with the world of shipping, and the same persons could be found in the offices of admiralties and the large merchant companies.[40] An anonymous pamphleteer wrote about the East India Company (VOC):

> For, they say, if we complain to the regents of the VOC and the magistrates of the towns, there sit the directors, [. . .] if to the admiralties, there are the directors again. If to the Estates General, we find that they and the directors are sitting there together at the same time.[41]

The upper echelons of the navy were, though, not attractive for ambitious Dutch leaders. As in the army, the posts of the officers and captains were typically reserved for members of the nobility. But it was hard to find candidates, with the result that the navy was commanded by many more 'common' men than the Dutch army, which included several (foreign) noblemen.[42]

The sailors were contracted by the captains, who also provided the food on board. Ship's crews consisted of fifty to ninety men on the smaller and 100 to 300 men on the larger vessels. On the rivers, smaller ships counted crews of twenty to thirty men. Among the sailors, foreigners were numerous. Pay was bad and minor mutinies were recurrent. In 1626, the captains of the vessels on the rivers complained that they had not received money for years. In 1631, Rotterdam sailors claimed forty to fifty months' pay. Some seamen went to The Hague. In front of the hall of the Estates General they demonstrated. They even broke in and asked each of the members for money.[43]

Demands for constructive reforms came from able commanders like Piet Heyn and Maarten Harpertsz Tromp. Heyn argued that the captains should not provide the food on board, but there should be a separate purveyor, so as to reduce the arbitrariness of captains, who stood to gain by skimping. Most improvements came with the supervision of Tromp in the late 1630s: the quality of guns was improved, their number decreased, and the bore standardized, which reduced the load of cannonballs aboard.[44]

An overall increase in pay by the admiralties was accomplished in

1641, but only the sailors serving the admiralty of Amsterdam noticed the difference. At the other navy boards the higher pay only resulted in a 900,000 guilder increase in the arrears. As for provisions, these were put on a better footing in the 1640s by allowing seven stuyvers per sailor a day. Yet the merchantmen of the semi-private VOC and WIC were generally better equipped than the navy, even as compared to those vessels of the Amsterdam board.[45] And as conflict intensified during the Eighty Years' War, additional regulations were indispensable for the protection of Dutch interests.

Debating the number of troops

The number of troops was decided upon in the Estates General. The Council of State constructed a proposal with a forecast for the near future. This petition was presented in a war budget, the *Staat van Oorlog*, which listed the necessary expenses, allocated to the seven provinces.

The standing army (that is, excluding temporary troops, the navy musketeers, the troops of mercenaries like Ernst von Mansfeld, but including *waardgelders*) increased in number from some 21,000 troops in 1588 to 32,000 in 1598. In the course of the Eighty Years' War, new men were added to the Dutch standing army, as can be observed in Fig. 2.1. Up to 1607, the increases even exceeded the 60,000 mark. At this point, the Republic's army was almost as large as the Spanish Army of Flanders. For a population of just under 1.5 million, this represented a large burden indeed. Of course, actual numbers were lower than the official figures, because of the abuses of *mortepayen* and *passevolanten*. Yet this was not a specially Dutch problem: other European armies suffered from fraud by captains too.[46] And in any case, whether fraudulent or not, the sums had to be provided by the provinces.

The Truce of 1609–1621 resulted in a cut in the forces by half, to 30,000 in 1609. According to Fig. 2.1, they remained so with few additions up to 1620. With the resumption of hostilities in 1621, new companies were added and older companies were increased in size. The 55,000 men constituted a considerable force, but in 1621–1625 the first four years of renewed warfare were aggravated by a successful offensive by the Spanish. It was not the only setback for the Dutch. They had also supported the troops of Duke Christian of Brunswick and Count Ernst of Mansfeld in the Thirty Years' War,

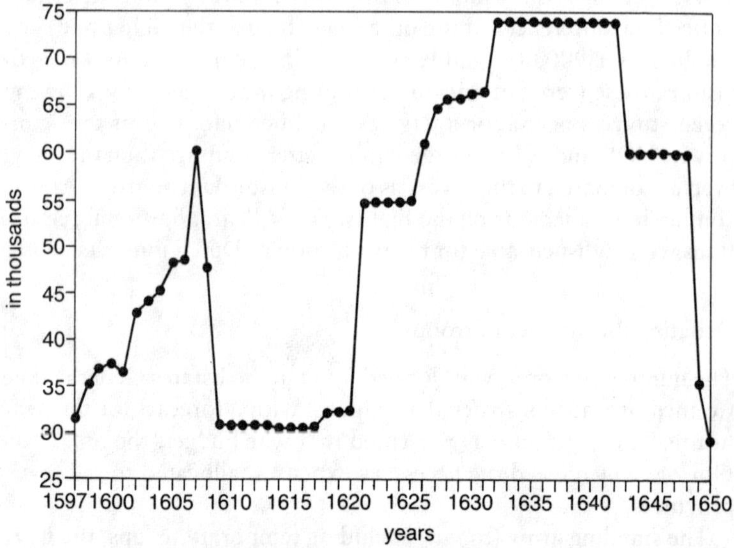

Figure 2.1 Number of Dutch troops in standing army, 1598–1650
Source: F.J.G. Ten Raa, F.de Bas and J.W. Wijn, *Het Staatsche Leger*, The Hague, 1911; ARA CoA *Staten van Oorlog*.

but both commanders suffered considerable losses against the combined forces of Tilly and Wallenstein, in the service of the Catholic League. In all, Dutch prospects were gloomy in 1625 as Breda fell to Spain. To crown misfortune the commander-in-chief of the army, Stadhouder Maurice of Orange, died the same year.

But the years 1626–1633 were the years of the Dutch counter-offensive. Spain concentrated its forces at sea, while the Dutch gambled on land warfare. They built up their army, first to over 65,000. The recapture of Oldenzaal and Grol by Frederick Henry, the direct threat of Spinola's forces within the *redoubt* in 1628, and the successful siege of Den Bosch in 1629 made the provinces more willing to furnish new troops. Significant extensions were voted for in 1628 and 1629.[47] In addition, Holland called for conscription. The city soldiers, *waardgelders*, were brought into the garrisons of Heusden and Steenbergen, releasing the troops there for actual expeditions. From the West India Company 1,200 troops, initially destined for an expedition against Brazil, marched in the Dutch campaigns as well. In all, the Dutch could temporarily dispose in 1629 of a wholly unprecedented total of 128,877 men, of which almost 68,000 in the standing army.[48]

In the meantime, the anti-Catholic League forces were on the whole unsuccessful: the armies of Denmark, of Christian of Brunswick and of Ernst of Mansfeld were defeated. A second major increase in the number of troops occurred in 1632, while Frederick Henry managed to recapture fortresses in the Upper Quarter of Gelderland. It rendered the Dutch standing army one of the largest in Europe: 75,000 men. Taking into account extraordinary troops, it was even larger. Then a decrease was voted in the 1640s, coinciding with a reduction in hostilities over land, and after the peace of 1648 the number of men declined to 30,000 soldiers, which was roughly the size of the Truce period.

Spain also waged economic warfare. Dutch fisheries and seabourne trade suffered seriously from Spanish piracy. On the continent, trade between the southern and northern Netherlands was interdicted in 1625 by a river blockade. Butter and cheese prices in Holland fell markedly, along with those of wine and herring. But prices in Flanders and Brabant, on the other hand, soared, which was eventually the reason why Spain lifted the blockade again in 1629. And when Den Bosch, Wesel, Rheinberg, Lingen and Orsay were lost between 1629 and 1634, the Spanish position in the land war had weakened considerably as compared with the early 1620s.[49]

Increases in the number of troops were only accomplished after laborious deliberations. In 1628, Holland at first resisted the decision, because new companies implied new officers, and those new officers were likely to support the Stadhouder's policies. Holland preferred to enlarge the old companies by adding men, leaving the officer corps the same. Augmentation was accepted in the end, however, because of the seriousness of the Spanish threat. As a result, the Prince's power was growing indeed: following Maurice's death in 1625, Frederick Henry's authority was more and more firmly established.[50]

The Council of State was annoyed by the increases, not because it opposed a strengthening of the forces, but because it had been kept out of the decision process. The Estates General with the Stadhouder had decided on the augmentation, whereas the councillors complained that they had been informed about the changes by rumour only (*straatgerugt*).[51] This complaint typified problems in the highest colleges within the Republic, which competed with one another over the weakly defined rights and duties of the central government.

Many of the extraordinary companies of 1628–1629 came to be incorporated into the structure of the standing army by 1632. Yet decision making was seriously hampered by protracted debates about whether negotiations should be embarked upon with Spain or not. The three 'war provinces' (Zeeland, Groningen and Friesland) stood against the three 'peace provinces' (Gelderland, Overijssel and Utrecht (except the city of Utrecht)). Holland itself was divided over the matter. In that province, the 'war cities' were – among others – Leiden, Haarlem, Gouda, Hoorn and Enkhuizen (supported by Utrecht), whereas the 'peace cities' were Amsterdam, Rotterdam, Dordrecht, Alkmaar, Delft and some smaller towns. The nobility were peace-minded, too, whereas the Stadhouder shifted from a slightly pro-war position to a pro-peace standpoint.[52]

A major part of the dilemma could be explained by the different interests of the urban elites. The textile industry in general feared the industry in the southern Netherlands, whose products were safely kept out because of the high wartime custom duties. Therefore, Leiden (with its cloth industry) and Haarlem (renowned for its finishing and bleaching of textiles) were mostly the core of the war party, against Amsterdam. The latter, together with others having their main interests in trade, generally regarded war as harmful.

But the conflict was not simply a matter of trade versus industry. Some trading cities joined the anti-peace party as well. There was a contrast between the European carrying trade and river trade on the one hand and the colonial trade on the other. The first two suffered heavily from trade restrictions imposed by Spain, Portugal and the Republic, whereas the raids of privateers at sea were particularly damaging for vessels on the North Sea. The colonial trade, however, gained from the opportunity to attack Spanish and Portuguese possessions in the Far East and in the Americas, in particular through privateering.[53]

In Amsterdam, the factions representing the European carrying trade came to dominate municipal policy. They were also stronger in Rotterdam and Dordrecht. The wealth of the latter was based upon the river trade and its connections with the German and Southern Netherland cities. The river trade group was composed not only of Rotterdam and Dordrecht, but also of the inland cities in Overijssel and Gelderland. In Hoorn and Enkhuizen, on the other hand, as well as in Middelburg, the colonial interests ousted the influence of the factions of the European carrying trade, which explains their position in the war party.[54]

Antwerp was another factor to be reckoned with. If peace were contracted at this stage, that glorious city would never again become part of the Netherlands. The Stadhouder Frederick Henry and cities such as Utrecht and Middelburg would welcome a city with enough financial power to outweigh Amsterdam. It was very much in Amsterdam's interests, on the other hand, to keep this possible rival out.[55]

Apart from such deliberations, Holland consequently tried to reduce the number of troops. Complaints were voiced about the *mortepayen* and *passevolanten*. Reductions in troops, it was argued, would not immediately result in a weakening of forces, but only cut back abuses. Frederick Henry, however, reminded Holland about the treaty with France of 1635, which had stipulated the Dutch contribution in the war against Spain. Yet the influence of the Stadhouder was weakening. In 1640, several companies that were to receive their pay from Amsterdam had to be paid by the generality because of the blunt refusal of the city to provide the funds. This antedated a major revision of 1643, in which expenses for land forces were cut significantly. It was widely regarded as a victory for Amsterdam over the Prince. The French ambassador D'Estrades wrote: 'Son authorité se diminue beaucoup.'[56]

Also, in 1645 Holland was prepared to vote for land campaigns, but only in exchange for a naval expedition to Denmark. Then, with the prospect of peace in 1647, Holland demanded retrenchment and started to cut the pensions and pay of the officers. In 1648 a general reduction followed. Yet the Estates of Holland, heavily in debt, demanded that the army should be reduced further. But in 1649, supporters of the army and the Stadhouder's court in the Estates General resisted such proposals. Moreover William II, the new Stadhouder since 1647, refused to agree to Holland's demands. To enforce the payment of troops by the city of Amsterdam, he marched on the town secretly with an army in order to replace the sitting magistrates. This problem of army politics was as critical as the disbanding of the Queen of Sweden's regiments in Germany, or the case of the army in England after 1646. It raised the question of sovereignty in the state. But the coup misfired as the Stadhouder died of smallpox shortly thereafter.[57]

The province of Holland, though, was not the only province acting high-handedly upon the army of the generality. In 1623 the Council of State had to warn Overijssel and the Quarter of Zutphen that they were not allowed to reduce the Union troops which were on their allocation. Three years later a similar dispute followed with Zeeland. In that province, a reduction in the size of its companies had been ordered to 100 men. In 1630, Friesland disbanded its eight companies of extraordinary troops voted for in 1628, bringing about excited debates in The Hague. And in 1643, similar disputes arose with the companies of the Veluwe, one of the three districts in Gelderland. In the face of these moves, the position of the central state as worded by the Council of State ('The Hague') remained clear: the troops were generality troops (*generaliteits krygsvolk*) and to reduce them without central consent would break the spirit of the Union.[58]

Such moves were understandable, as the payment of troops consumed by far the largest proportion of ordinary war budgets. Therefore, any possible reduction in the number of men was welcome to the paymaster provinces. Table 2.2 shows the breakdown of expenses of the land forces for 1620–1650. This distribution varied only slightly over time. In all, the amounts spent on officers increased from 9.2 per cent in 1620 to 13.6 per cent in 1650. These amounts included the senior officers and the sappers, engineers, and gunners, and pointed to growing professionalization in the army. Yet this trend did not entail centralization, which was reflected in the

Table 2.2 *Ordinary army budgets, 1620–1650, percentage distribution*

pay for cavalry	14.9
pay for infantry	57.7
salary for officers	7.3
lodgings	5.4
transport	1.4
magazines/ammunition	3.9
fortifications	1.9
pensions	0.7
other	6.8
total	100.0
[annual average: 9,682,324 guilders]	

Source: ARA CoA *Staten van Oorlog.*

paymastership of those officers. Up to 1600, most officers had been paid by Holland, whereas subsequent increases were generally taken care of by the other provinces. Local bureaucratization of the army, therefore, increased, as can be observed in Table 2.3.

Looking at the figures for 1650 in Table 2.3, it is obvious that the end of hostilities in 1648 was not followed by discharges of the officers. Those who profited most from the army increases were the senior officers. In comparing the establishment of 1617 with that of 1650, the number of officers in the higher army command had actually trebled in the last three decades of the Eighty Years' War. Lower rates of increase (around 150 per cent) were noted among the army constables and among the clerks for provisions, lodgings, and ammunition. But the number of ministers and schoolteachers, the medical doctors, the muster commissioners and the sappers hardly increased at all.[59]

Additional war costs were incurred by the administration of reconquered regions. The Republic as a whole controlled several areas won back from Spain, the most important being parts of northern Brabant, parts of Flanders, Overmaze in Limburg, and Wedde with Westerwolde in Groningen. Eventually, they came to be called generality lands. Most of these funds had to be spent on fortifications and military provisions, as shown in the breakdown of the expenses of generality lands in Table 2.4. In 1642, during time of war, military expenses exceeded all other items in the generality lands. After peace was signed in 1648, direct payments in the generality lands declined overall. Yet in the post-war era, relatively more was spent on administration and debt service, despite the fact that the bureaucratic apparatus introduced was only slight. Much of the administration of the garrisons and fortifications in the generality lands came to be delegated to the local magistrates.[60]

Table 2.3 *Number of higher officers and civil servants in the land forces of the Republic*

year	*total number*	*paid by Holland*
1598	98	98
1617	363	163
1621	381	162
1643	541	272
1650	597	293

Source: ARA CoA *Staten van Oorlog.*

Table 2.4 *Expenses of generality lands, 1642 and 1648, percentages*

item	*1642*	*1648*
fortifications	31.6	46.8
military provisions, lodgings	32.5	6.6
local administration	25.5	32.9
debt charges	7.0	11.0
miscellaneous	3.2	2.7
total	100.0	100.0
[in guilders:	969,701	615,143]

Source: ARA CoS 2157; RAZH Van Slingelandt 247; RAZH Jacob Cats 77.

Paying for military provisions and fortifications was an item for the general wartime budget too. It was remarkable that in the *Staat van Oorlog* (see Table 2.2) the expenses for logistics such as lodging and transportation of troops, the maintenance of magazines and ammunition, remained largely the same over time. Pensions, too, were contained. The only item that increased after peace was signed were fortifications, which coincided with the still predominant tactic of siege warfare.[61] Yet before we can analyse the overall increase in war budgets, the costs of naval warfare must be taken into account.

The reluctant consent to new naval vessels

The standing navy establishment was constituted by the five admiralties providing warships and sails for convoys of fishery and private merchants's vessels. Regular convoys were arranged for ships bound for Bordeaux and Bayonne. Similarly, there were regular escorts to England and Scotland. Costs for the colonies and the convoys of the VOC and WIC were carried by the companies themselves, at least, in principle. Inland, the admiralty of Rotterdam provided for the vessels that guarded the major rivers. Several vessels followed the army inland for transport and provisions. The Stadhouder, as admiral general, could dispose of his own ship too.

From time to time, the navy establishment was extended with men-of-war to guard the North Sea, to blockade the Flemish coast, to provide additional convoys for the merchantmen and herring fisheries, and for special expeditions such as to the Iberian coast or in support of the West India Company in Brazil. Mostly, for those extensions, ships were hired from merchants.

The early seventeenth century had been marked by a deep crisis for the Dutch navy. Mutinies broke out in 1600 and 1601. The Truce with Spain of 1609–1621 alleviated the burden for the admiralties. The number of ships was reduced and salaries were curbed. However, piracy at sea continued to threaten Dutch trade, and as Spain strengthened her naval forces at Gibraltar a Dutch fleet was sent to the Mediterranean to protect the merchants. As a result, the admiralties were still in poor financial condition when war resumed in 1621.[62]

And war did resume, because Spain preferred hostilities to the 1609 Truce settlements. The latter left Antwerp blockaded to Amsterdam's advantage, and allowed the Dutch to dominate the north–south carrying trade and to expand in the East and West Indies. By the summer of 1621, the Dutch navy included only forty-six warships. The Estates General decided to increase the number to 105, sixty-four for the open sea with eighty sailors each and the remainder for the inland rivers with thirty sailors each. New ships had to be hired. Yet the owners of the vessels increased their charge, and some ships had to be bought, which was a pressing time for the admiralties. The whole scheme failed and only a few additional ships sailed out. Many vessels destined for the blockade came to be used by the admiralties for the protection of 'their own' trade, i.e. for convoys of the city's merchants, because the degree of safety in their harbours was a higher priority than the threat of some distant armada.[63]

The greatest harm to Dutch shipping was done by Dunkirk privateers, where the Spanish crown had concentrated its North Sea armada. As a result, Dutch freight and insurance charges soared. Dunkirkers attacked herring busses in particular. For example, in 1625, as many as eighty-four ships of the Meuse herring fleet were sunk, the crews taken prisoner, and the convoys put to flight. The navy boards, moreover, did not succeed in improving the escorts. Cash shortages were chronic, and when the Enkhuizen herring fleet was attacked the escorts proved powerless in the face of the much faster privateers.[64]

The Estates General decided on a more coordinated policy. For the years to come, thirty-five men-of-war, each of 240 to 300 tons, with twenty-two to fifty guns, and thirty musketeers aboard in addition to the crew of sailors, and five yachts and five frigates, forty-five ships in all, were to be added to the fleet to curb the Dunkirk threat. According to the plans, which were basically the same throughout

1627–1633, almost 200 vessels should have been in use by the navy. They were divided over eight tasks, their costs being represented in Table 2.5.

Table 2.5 *Number of ships, average and annual costs, according to the budget of the Dutch navy in 1631*

	no. ships	*avg. cost*	*annual costs*
blockade of Flemish coast/North Sea	45	21,038	946,701
defence of Dutch coast	6	11,084	66,506
convoys, herring fisheries	13	10,259	959,730
convoys, small fisheries	6	16,320	
convoys, Baltic trade	4	10,111	
ordinary convoys	53	12,981	
defence of inland rivers	65	7,120	462,796
army vessels	7	7,094	49,658
total	199	12,489	2,485,391

Source: ARA Adm 3399.

In all, 12,730 men were to serve on these ships.[65] The budget showed that average costs for the men-of-war to cruise the Flemish coast were almost twice as high compared to the other vessels. Moreover, they had to be used the whole year round, whereas some other tasks, such as the convoy for the Baltic trade, could do their service for seven months only. The expenses were equally divided over the special men-of-war and the convoys for the trade, both comprising almost 40 per cent (about 950,000 guilders), as Table 2.5 shows.

To say that plans entailed in the budgets were badly executed would be an understatement. In reality, few vessels set sail, and the Dunkirk threat remained. The task of the convoys was carried out much better than the general blockade against the Dunkirkers, as it was in the direct interest of the harbour itself to protect the traditional trade routes. Threats remained: for the year 1632 alone, the Dutch lost 200 vessels against Dunkirk's only fifteen.[66]

At the bureaucratic centre of The Hague, in the meantime, the power of the Stadhouder had gained as a result of his successes in the land war. To increase the quick-wittedness of the Dutch at sea, a daring new proposal was put through: a new centralized navy board at Hellevoetsluis. This place was a small port south of Brielle, near Rotterdam, at the Haringvliet in the Meuse delta. It grew into a centre for provisioning the Dutch men-of-war on the Flemish coast and the North Sea. A fleet was assigned to it in 1632, but Zeeland refused to contribute ships and the plans were delayed. Four years later, the design was revived with new enthusiasm. The admiralties were to send warships to Hellevoetsluis, after which Jan Simonsz Blauhulck, who had been an equipment master in the Northern Quarter as well as in Amsterdam, was granted a salary of 1,600 guilders for the supervision of the whole project. His staff consisted of a clerk, an officer of justice, and some constables. The admiralties continued the operation of the escorts for trade and theirs would also remain the jurisdiction over prizes. The Estates General were divided over the matter, though, and instead of the forty-five ships demanded by the Council of State, only thirty-two vessels were voted.[67]

The central navy board started off with some improvements. The sailors of Hellevoetsluis were to receive better pay than formerly. Their food was provided not by the captains, but by special victuallers. Each province had to send one supply master (called *directeur*, *aannemer* or *beleider*), who was to receive the funds from his province and who would take care of one or more ships. The number of sailors and soldiers was projected at 3,100 or 3,200: for each large vessel there would be ninety sailors and twenty musketeers. The annual costs were budgeted at 1,108,870 guilders. And despite the fact that the number of vessels was reduced by the Estates General, the arrangement was still regarded as an improvement over the former plans when many vessels had existed on paper only.[68]

Again, it failed. First of all, the establishment itself had several shortcomings. Funding from the provinces did not materialize soon enough. Cash was a chronic problem. Instead of influential merchants, as on the other navy boards, a handful of common civil servants had to provide the purveyance. They did not have the connections necessary to lease the ships and find the credit. The small town did not have sufficient provisions, and they were easily spoiled in the lengthy and costly transportation. But most crippling was the boycott by Zeeland and Amsterdam.[69]

The Zeeland admiralty never sent any ships at all to Hellevoetsluis. Amsterdam did, but on condition that it was a temporary expedient only. The city subsequently imposed restrictions upon its director at Hellevoetsluis. After disputes over customs with the central government had come to a head in 1639 (see Chapter Four), it withdrew its support altogether. The Northern Quarter admiralty quickly followed the Amsterdam protest. The only one left was thus Rotterdam with its relatively poor background: not much to build a forceful centralization policy upon. The project was dismantled. Frederick Henry retained the formal authority over the warships, but the administration and fitting out were left once more to the admiralties and their semi-private purveyors.[70]

In the years to come, central control failed, the more so because no regular budgets of expenses existed. In order to provide the delegates with some overview, a special commission of the Estates General examined the expenses incurred by the navy boards in the early 1640s. They based themselves upon data from Amsterdam, Rotterdam and the Northern Quarter (all 1641–1642), and Friesland (1638–1640). In Table 2.6. data from Zeeland (1640–1642) are added and an annual average of *c.* 1641 is reconstructed.

Pay and food for the sailors absorbed about half the costs for the five navy boards. The equipping of the vessels took over a quarter. The latter included the costs of hiring ships from private shipping companies. The dockyards, representing repairs and the effort to build new warships, comprised almost 7 per cent. Yet most new ships were built in Amsterdam's docks only, and in general the majority of the men-of-war were still leased or bought from merchants direct.

Additional costs for the admiralties were incurred in obtaining the subsidies and funds from provinces or cities, who were often in arrears with their payments. Clerks had to be paid substantial fees for this work.[71] Yet overall, despite the costs connected with the maintenance of five separate boards, expenses for administration seemed contained.

Table 2.6 *Annual expenses of Dutch navy, c. 1641, percentages*

pay and food	47.9
equipment	27.1
administration	8.1
dockyards	6.8
debt service	5.1
other	5.0
total	100.0
[annual average: 4,007,978 guilders]	

Source: ARA CoA 950–952; SG 12561.98.

In all, the long-term policies of the Estates General for the seas failed throughout the Eighty Years' War. Now and then, they reacted with ad-hoc forces. The decisions to expand the navy in the Estates General, thus mainly providing extraordinary vessels, are displayed in Fig. 2.2. The largest peak appeared in 1639, the year of the major sea battle in the Downs. At first, the Dutch Admiral Tromp could dispose of thirty ships only. His successful attack, though, on some Dunkirk privateers brought about a surge of support in Holland. Within a couple of weeks, the admiral could dispose of over 100 vessels, from merchant companies and individuals alike. His fleet's success against a Spanish armada saved the Dutch for the time being.[72] The year 1645 (the other peak in the graph) constituted the expedition for the Sound toll crisis.

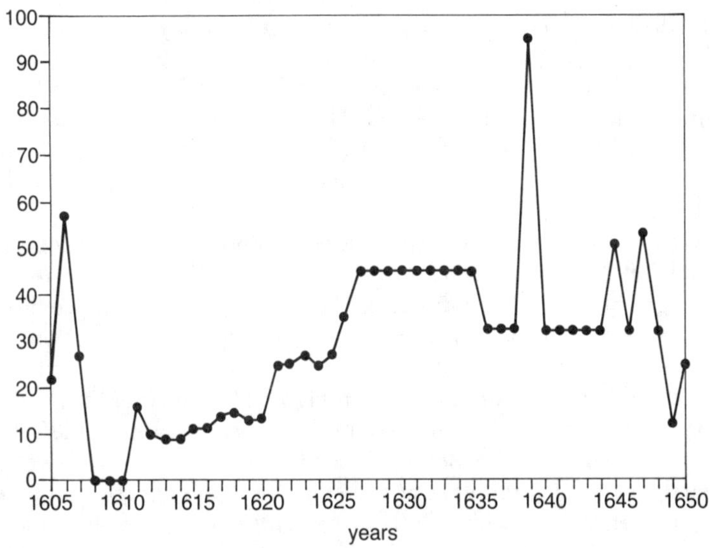

Figure 2.2 Number of extraordinary vessels approved for the navy by the Estates General, 1605–1650
Source: 'Aanwijzing hoe de extraordinaris vloten . . . 1605–1652', in GAA 5030 portef. 60; J.C. de Jonge, *Geschiedenis van het Nederlandsche Zeewezen* I, The Hague, 1833, 478; J.J. Hartsinck, *Overzigt der geschiedenis van het Zeewezen in Nederland en voornamelijk van de Admiraliteit te Amsterdam van de vroegste tijden tot 1648*, The Hague, 1763 [Manuscript ARA Adm 1.01.47, XLVII, 2], 105.

But in general, the warfare at sea concentrated on indirect methods. The vessels of Fig. 2.2 were used mainly for protecting Dutch merchantmen with men-of-war, blockading the Flemish coast, convoys for the larger fisheries, and for privateering. From time to time, support was voted for colonial policies: such as in 1606 (viz. the first peak in the graph) and 1624 (both for the VOC, the Dutch East India Company), and in particular in 1647–1650 for the West India Company (WIC) policy in Brazil.[73]

Although both VOC and WIC were responsible for warfare in the colonies, the Estates General came to subsidize the WIC heavily. The VOC was in a stronger position and did not need the same amount of government support. The focal point in the 'West' came to be Brazil. In 1637, the WIC captured this rich sugar-producing region. Slave ports on the Gold Coast of Africa were taken over too. Slaves were shipped to Brazil to expand production while in Amsterdam sugar refining on a large scale began. The trade in gold from Guinea enriched a small number of merchants considerably, and each year the company shipped 20,000 slaves from Angola. All these profits were made with help of the navy. But the expeditions of the WIC turned out costlier than expected. The company's debt amounted in 1631 to 19 million guilders. And when the WIC vessels were damaged in a storm in 1640, the Estates General had to vote for yet another subsidy.[74]

The inland provinces were not keen on supporting colonial policies at all. But Zeeland pressed for support for the WIC in the later 1640s, since many Zeelanders had invested heavily in the WIC. The province opposed peace negotiations with Spain as it might lose some colonies. The trade with Spain and Portugal, on the other hand, had been concentrated in Amsterdam, which favoured a quick peace. In the end, the provinces agreed to Zeeland's proposal to support the WIC with an expedition to Brazil, to send 6,000 troops, with twelve warships of the admiralties at a cost of 600,000 guilders, and nine frigates of the company. Holland consented only in exchange for Zeeland's approval of a peace treaty with Spain and its support for the Sound policy. The whole expedition proved ill-fated, though, and had a negative effect upon the admiralties' finances. Apart from Amsterdam, all other navy boards saw their debts increase.[75]

In the meantime, the Dutch navy failed regularly in protecting trade. The value of all vessels captured, excluding those sunk, was estimated at 23 million guilders between 1626 and 1646. Ransoms added to these costs. They ranged from 100 to 200 guilders per sailor, and from 2,000 to 3,000 guilders per vessel. In 1635 the Dunkirk raids even evoked an uproar in Enkhuizen, as the losses had involved almost every single inhabitant of the city. Two naval captains were thrown into the sea and the house of Admiral Quast was pillaged. Lesser disturbances occurred in Rotterdam and Goes.[76]

Merchants and shipowners, therefore, looked for other solutions. Semi-private fleets came into being, sometimes for a couple of years only. A separate board had existed since the sixteenth century for the herring fisheries, called *Grote Visserij*, with deputies from Rotterdam, Delft, Schiedam, Enkhuizen and Brielle. It coordinated the voyages and was subsidized by the Estates of Holland and by the admiralties of Rotterdam and the Northern Quarter.[77]

Other new *directies* were proposed. In 1625, a Board of Directors for the trade in the Levant was under the control of the cities and admiralties. The ships had to be armed with a certain number of guns. Voyages had to be made with the minimum of forty vessels. In 1628, Amsterdam proposed to organize ten to twelve men-of-war, especially for the Baltic trade, and to pay for them all by itself. This was not approved because other cities feared exclusion from the project. But in 1631, in response to the collective and continued request of merchants in the cities of Amsterdam, Hoorn, Enkhuizen, Edam, Medemblik, and Harlingen, the Estates General authorized another semi-private organization to be set up, specially for defending the trade to the Baltic and Norway.[78]

Another project of Amsterdam the same year was to create a so-called Company of Assurance. It was calculated that about sixty warships were needed for the protection of the Dutch European trade. To defray the costs, the company was to gain a monopoly of trade in the Mediterranean and Africa. Most of the inland provinces liked the idea, as it would relieve them of the payment of a subsidy for the navy. But non-Amsterdam merchants of the seafaring provinces of Holland and Zeeland opposed the scheme. Southern Europe and Africa belonged to the last parts of the world in which free trade was still possible, other routes being already monopolized by the chartered companies, and the plans were not approved.[79]

The idea re-emerged in 1634, this time promoted by Frederick Henry, though it had changed considerably in substance. Supervision was not to be by the cities, as Amsterdam had proposed, but by the Estates General. The Company of Assurance should take over the separate Boards of Directors and organize all convoys for the merchantmen, as well as supervise the payment of the premiums for privateers. Together with the plan for Hellevoetsluis, all responsibilities of the admiralties were to be taken over by two centralized institutions. Opposition was strong, therefore, especially from Amsterdam this time, and the idea was left to languish.

As an alternative, Holland put forward another scheme of having the provinces of Holland and Zeeland take care of the navy on their own, leaving the army and other responsibilities to the inland provinces. The resistance of Leiden was overcome by offering that manufacturing city a seat on the new directorate. However, the Stadhouder did not like the idea. An army without the support of the wealthiest province must have seemed to him a very unpromising project indeed.[80]

Yet after new and exceptional losses in 1640, a large group of the principal merchants of Amsterdam, supported by the Estates of Holland, urged the Estates General to give them permission to organize their own semi-private fleet. They wanted 'to clear the seas' of pirates themselves. They even threatened to withhold the contribution of the city in the provincial quota. The protest was successful: in the end, the cities of Amsterdam, Rotterdam, the Northern Quarter and some Zeeland merchants sent sixteen to twenty-four cruisers to the North Sea and to the coast of Flanders in 1643.[81]

These semi-private vessels were partly financed by public funds (see Chapter Four). The organization also showed an overlap with the East and West India Companies and the admiralties. The relationship was not always cordial, however. At one point in Hoorn (Northern Quarter) the directors used two of their ships to break into the warehouse of the admiralty in order to lay hands on some sails and other necessities, which had been refused them by the navy board. Inter-city rivalry, moreover, remained strong, as the semi-private boards added to the competition in trade since merchants from other cities could be excluded from the scheme.[82]

Thus the boards of admiralty and the semi-private navies both tended to favour the policies of the city they were based in. Of all the navy boards, Amsterdam came to outstrip the others, even the central board in Rotterdam. In that city the magistrates gave priority to Baltic matters. In 1645, at their insistance, a fleet was sent to keep the Danish Sound open during the war between Sweden and Denmark. In 1649, again on the initiative of Amsterdam, the permanent redemption of the Sound tolls was being negotiated with the Copenhagen government. By contrast, the Stadhouder, who had dynastic interests in England – his son William had married Mary

Stuart in 1641 – tried to organize a fleet to help his in-laws in the English Civil War, but he could not get the support of the admiralties.[83]

The year 1648 was followed by major cuts in the navy. The number of inland vessels was reduced to eleven. Seagoing vessels were reduced in number as well. Whereas England was building up a powerful navy at this time, the Dutch were selling their former equipment and ships in order to provide for sailors' pay. Of the 125 ships on the wartime strength, only a few were left by 1648. It was decided to keep only sixty men-of-war. Even this modest figure was reduced to forty by Holland in 1649. The running costs of the navy boards were spared, though, and not reduced. In the meantime, Dutch trade was still being hurt by privateering, although the threat from Dunkirk had disappeared. There were the French from Calais, Boulogne, La Rochelle, Biscay and Toulon; the English royalists from Jersey and Sorlings; the Algerians; and the Irish from Waterford and Wexford.[84]

The first Anglo-Dutch war of 1652–1654 proved fatal for the relaxed policy of the Dutch. Their navy was decisively defeated. The admiralties debt charges jumped from 5 to 16 per cent of all expenses. In the budget of 1654, the policy of selling ships of the later 1640s was clearly reversed: 20 per cent of the navy's budget was now devoted to the building of new ships as opposed to leasing.[85] Yet it was all of little avail. At sea, the Dutch were gradually loosing to the English. The latter had reorganized their navy more efficiently. They were able to mobilize resources on a bigger scale because of the centralization of state institutions, coupled with favourable developments in their economy and population.

Increases during the Eighty Years' War

Although the seven United Provinces had been extremely reluctant to vote for extensions of the navy and army, the Eighty Years' War against Spain resulted in an unprecedented increase in expenses. The first year that a regular *Staat van Oorlog* was presented was 1586, consisting of an ordinary part of 2.4 million guilders, and an extraordinary part of 0.5 million guilders for temporary troops (*veldleger*). This war budget always covered the standing army expenses, but the navy was included in the later budgets only.

Figure 2.3 charts a threefold increase in this war budget for the standing army up to the Twelve Years' Truce. The decrease during

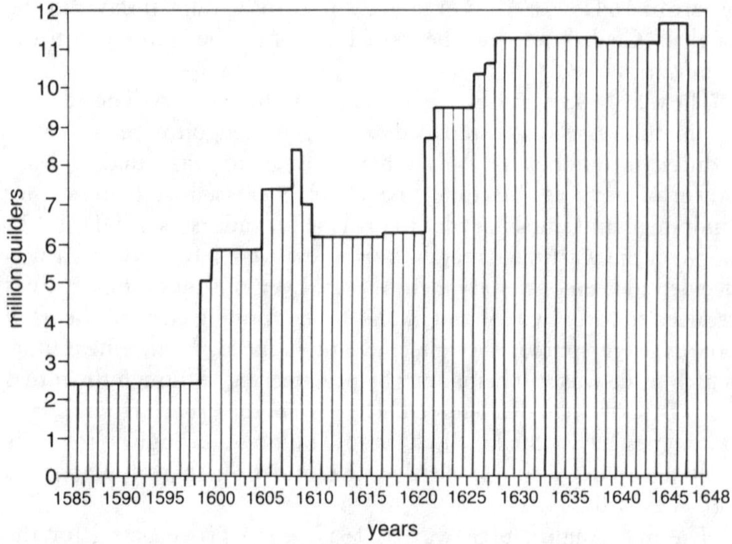

Figure 2.3 Ordinary costs, standing war establishment (excluding navy), 1586–1648
Source: ARA CoA *Staten van Oorlog.*

the interlude of 1609–1621 was only minor, and when war was resumed in 1621 the pressure intensified again. In addition, the temporary 'extraordinary' appropriations which were necessary are represented in Fig. 2.4. These amounts constituted about one-third of all war expenses voted by the Estates General since the start of regular petitions by the Union.

A sharp rise occurred up to 1604. Some of those expenses were absorbed into the ordinary establishment, as in Fig. 2.3, which allowed the extraordinary costs to decline up to 1609. During the Truce, votes of ordinary funds remained at the same level. Yet the extraordinary costs increased. Dutch intervention among others in the Palts, J?(lich-Cleves, and Bohemia proved costly. After 1621, both ordinary and extraordinary funds were raised. The spurt of expenditure in 1628–1630 coincided with the major counter-offensive of the Dutch against Spain. A peak was reached in 1633. Thereafter, expenses diminished, in particular after 1641, as actual hostilities were reduced.

Extraordinary sums appropriated for the navy increased dramatically after 1623. As the ordinary income of the admiralties was

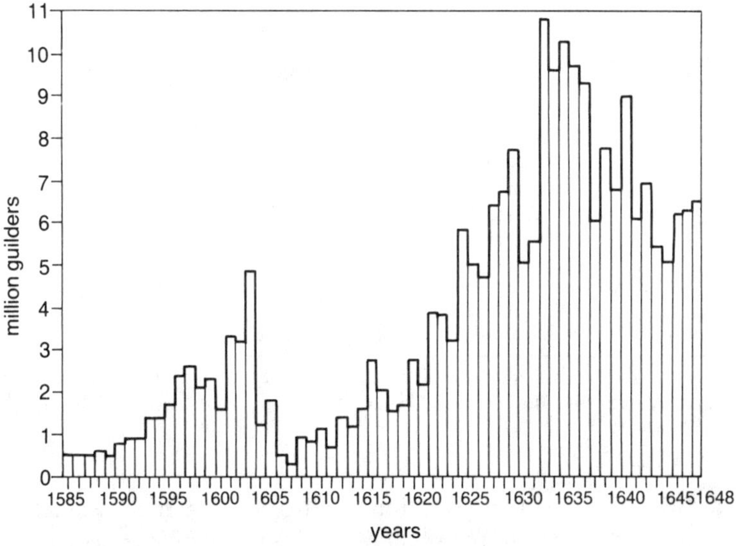

Figure 2.4 Extraordinary war expenses (including navy), 1586–1648
Source: ARA CoA 90: *Staat van alle petitiën.*

insufficient to meet their costs, additional subsidies were necessary. The debates in the Estates General as to this shift will be dealt with in a subsequent chapter.

It was difficult to observe the overall impact of war expenses on the Union, as there was no regular overview of all expenses. Yet a reconstruction was possible, using the ordinary war budget, the extraordinary votes for war, the lists of costs incurred by the navy, the administration of the central government boards at The Hague, the administration over conquered areas, and the debt charges. Table 2.7. presents the distribution of all these items in an annual average for 1641.

The Dutch army proved almost twice as expensive as the Dutch navy. In all, taking into account the fact that most pensions were for officers and soldiers temporarily out of military service, as much as 89.5 per cent of expenses were devoted to war purposes alone: army, navy, pensions and fortifications. Diplomacy (including foreign subsidies, envoys and embassies) took up about 1 per cent of the total. Charges upon contracted debts were almost as high as administration costs. Most of those debts had been incurred because of the war again (see Chapter Six). Despite the fact that five navy boards existed,

Table 2.7 *Reconstructed annual budget of expenses of the Dutch Republic (c. 1641), in percentages*

army	51.5
navy	26.0
pensions	3.3
fortifications	8.7
diplomacy	1.0
administration	4.6
debt service	4.4
miscellaneous	0.5
total	100.0
[annual average: 23,696,505 guilders]	

Source: ARA CoA *Staten van Oorlog*; ARA CoS extraordinaris consenten; RAZH Van Slingelandt 47; RAZH Jacob Cats 77; ARA SG 12561.98; ARA CoA 950–952.

the overall costs of administration were restricted, as much was left to local government – responsibilities such as police, justice, assistance to the poor, and church affairs (see Chapter Seven).

The debates about extensions and cuts in the army and navy had throughout reflected an extraordinary high degree of control by local oligarchies. Next to the conduct of the war, conflicting issues centred in particular on state finances, the Sound toll policy, trade with Flanders ('trade with the enemy'), grain duties, policy towards the Stuarts in England, and support of the WIC in Brazil. To enforce decisions, coalitions shifted, and there were compromises; for example, Zeeland signed the peace in 1648 in exchange for support of the WIC. Throughout, Amsterdam was able to exert more direct pressure upon naval policy than on army policy. The metropolis promoted the Amsterdam admiralty as well as semi-private convoy boards operating within its district. It was significant that the centralizing project at Hellevoetsluis was soon cut back. In this regard, a complaint by Admiral van Dorp is illustrative: he had so many masters – the Prince, the Estates General, the Estates of Holland, his admiralty board – that he did not know who or how to serve.[86]

Professionalization and privatization had occurred both in the army and in the navy. The Dutch did not differ from most other European countries in this respect. *Sollicituers militair*, captains, directors of semi-private fleets figured alongside an increasing number of specialist canonniers, sappers and the more disciplined sailors of Admiral Tromp. In the long run, professionalization seemed stronger in the army, while privatization took a larger toll in the navy with the establishment of manifold semi-private convoy boards. In all, mercantile warfare gained ample opportunities in the setting of the Dutch Republic.

The costs of warfare, though, were enormous for the small population of the United Provinces. Shifting this burden on to society was a complicated matter, which involved widespread political debates again. It revived the federalist tendencies within the Republic, as will be described in the following chapters.

Notes

1 Michael Roberts, *The military revolution 1560–1660*, Belfast, 1955, 16; Michael Duffy, *The military revolution and the state, 1500–1800*, Exeter, 1980, 1; Parker, *The military revolution*, 1.

2 Based upon figures relating to standing armies. See Tilly, *Coercion, capital, and European states*, 79; Duffy, *The military revolution and the state*, 3; André Corvisier, *Armées et sociétés en Europe de 1494 à 1789*, Paris, 1976, 126; W. Brulez, 'Het gewicht van de oorlog in nieuwe tijden', *Tijdschrift voor Geschiedenis* 91, 1978, 398; Limm, *Thirty Years' War*, 87.

3 N.A.M. Rodger, *The Admiralty*, Lavenham, 1979, 15; Duffy, *The military revolution and the state*, 49–85; Corvisier, *Armées et sociétés in Europe*, 60; Daniel Dessert, *Argent, pouvoir et société au Grand Siècle*, Paris, 1984, 156.

4 Pierre Goubert, *The Ancien Régime. French society 1600–1750*, New York, 1974, 79; Parker, *Army of Flanders*, 20.

5 Myron P. Gutmann, *War and rural life in the early modern Low Countries*, Princeton, 1980, 33; Goubert, *Ancien régime*, 125; Corvisier, *Armées et sociétés en Europe*, 192–3.

6 Thompson, *War and government*, 99, 282–4; Corvisier, *Armées et sociétés en Europe*, 55.

7 Brian R. Mitchell and Phyllis Deane, *Abstract of British historical statistics*, Cambridge, 1971, 389.

8 Thomas and Meyer, 'Expansion of the state', 464; Thompson, *War and government*, 1: 'war was by far the severest test that faced an early modern state'; Brulez, 'Gewicht van de oorlog', 381.

9 J.W. Wijn, *Het krijgswezen in den tijd van Prins Maurits*, Utrecht, 1934, 20, 29, 533; Van Deursen, 'Raad van State onder Republiek', 74; H.L. Zwitzer, 'The Dutch army during the Ancien Régime', *Revue Internationale d'Histoire Militaire* 58, 1984, 31; see for the general history of the Dutch army F.J.G. ten Raa, F. de Bas and J.W. Wijn, *Het Staatsche Leger*, The Hague, 1911.

10 See Elias, *Prozess der Zivilisation*, 215; Zwitzer, 'Het gezag van het leger in de tijd der republiek der Verenigde Nederlanden', *Mededelingen van de Sectie Militaire Geschiedenis van de Landmachtstaf* 6, 1983, 14; C.M. Schulten and J.W.M. Schulten, *Het leger in de zeventiende eeuw*, Bussum,

1969, 27.

11 Simon van Slingelandt, *Staatkundige geschriften* IV, Amsterdam, 1784, 149. On the *schutterij*: J.C. Grayson, 'The civic militia in the county of Holland, 1561–81: politics and public order in the Dutch Revolt', *Bijdragen en Mededelingen betreffende de Geschiedenis der Nederlanden* 95, 1980, 35–63; Knevel, 'Onrust onder schutters', *passim*.

12 A.Th. van Deursen, *Het kopergeld van de Gouden eeuw* III, Assen, 1979, 80; F.C. Spits, 'Unie en militie', *De Unie van Utrecht*, ed. S. Groenveld and H.L.Ph. Leeuwenberg, The Hague, 1979, 82; J.R. Bruijn, 'Personeelsbehoefte van de VOC overzee en aan boord, bezien in Aziatisch en Nederlands perspektief', *Bijdragen en Mededelingen betreffende de Geschiedenis der Nederlanden* 91, 1976, 11. According to two samples of 1622 and 1637, 58 and 68 per cent of the soldiers were foreigners.

13 Gutmann, *War and rural life*, 32, 60, 63; Barry N. Nickle, *The military reforms of Prince Maurice of Orange*, University of Oklahoma Press, 1975, 72, 100; Van der Capellen, *Gedenkschriften* I, 139, 191, 245, 323, 523.

14 Michael Howard, *War in European history*, London, 1978, 37.

15 The Dutch may not have been the inventors of the military revolution, yet they were successful in applying it. Limm, *Thirty Years' War*, 80; Roberts, *Military revolution*, 7.

16 Wijn, *Krijgswezen*, 77–8.

17 Klein, *De Trippen*, 205–6, notes that it was not Amsterdam which was the centre of this trade: Hamburg, Lübeck and Bremen were equally important. Nevertheless, access to these markets was relatively easy for the Dutch.

18 Wijn, *Krijgswezen*, 175; Roberts, *Military revolution*, 9.

19 Wijn, *Krijgswezen*, 149.

20 Schulten, *Het leger*, 42.

21 Schulten, *Het leger*, 36 and 42; *Resolutiën der Staten-Generaal. Nieuwe Reeks, 1610–1670*, ed. A.Th. van Deursen, J. Roelevink and J.G. Smit, The Hague: 21 October 1619, 29 July 1620.

22 Apart from altering the number of men per company or disbanding whole companies, a reduction in the expenses might be established by increasing the number of days in the 'month', the unit of payment being a month's service. Zeeland had months of thirty-nine days at the beginning of the seventeenth century. After the Truce the regular month in the army was fixed at forty-two days. See also Algemeen Rijksarchief (ARA) Staten-Generaal (SG) 12548.272.

23 A.F. van Ommen, 'Het ambt van officier en het nederlanderschap', *Mededelingen van de Sectie Militaire Geschiedenis Landmachtstaf* 5, 1982, 62.

24 Van Deursen, 'Raad van State onder de Republiek', 75.

25 Nickle, *Military reforms*, 92.

26 The captain was arrested. Van der Capellen, *Gedenkschriften* II, 25.

27 H.J. Kann, *De militie en het militair bestuur gedurende het tijdvak der Unie van Utrecht 1579–1795*, Leiden, 1874, 15, 52; Van der Capellen, *Gedenkschriften* I, 120, 365.

28 Van der Capellen, *Gedenkschriften* I, 191; J.C.P.M. van Hoof,

'Fortifications in the Netherlands', *Revue Internationale d'Histoire Militaire* 58, 1984, 104; Brulez, 'Gewicht van de oorlog', 395.

29 J. de Hullu, *De archieven der Admiraliteitscolleges*, The Hague, 1924, 4; Elias, *Schetsen*, 3, 17. Neither did the Union refer to customs on foreign trade.

30 On Zeeland versus Holland: J.H. Kernkamp, *De handel op den vijand, 1572–1609* I, Utrecht, 1931, 210.

31 Both employed the same receiver general, who did not get his commission from the generality (Estates General) like the other admiralty receivers but from the Provincial Estates. Harold E. Becht, *Statistische gegevens betreffende den handelsomzet van de Republiek der Vereenigde Nederlanden gedurende de 17e eeuw (1579–1715)*, The Hague, 1908, 112; J.J. Hartsinck, *Overzigt der geschiedenis van het Zeewezen in Nederland en voornamelijk van de Admiraliteit te Amsterdam van de vroegste tijden to 1648*, The Hague, 1763 (Manuscript ARA Admiraliteiten (Adm) 1.01.47, XLVII, 2), 284.

32 Dordrecht was the main competitor for the seat. On the Rotterdam admiralty: H. de Jong, 'De "Admiraliteit van de Maze" te Rotterdam', *Marineblad* 58, 1948, 232–44.

33 De Hullu, *De archieven*, 20; J.L.F. Engelhard, *Het generaal-plakkaat van 31 juli 1725 op de convooien en licenten en het lastgeld op de schepen*, Assen, 1970, 248; C.T.F. Thurkow, *De Westfriese admiraliteit*, Enkhuizen, 1946, 25; J.R. Bruijn, 'De vaart in Europa', *Maritieme Geschiedenis der Nederlanden* II, Bussum, 1977, 215: Hoorn was the more volatile port, Enkhuizen greatly dependent upon herring fisheries.

34 Kernkamp, *Handel op den vijand* II, 166: in 1638, when the whole Friesland administration was revised, there had been plans to abolish this navy board altogether. See also Elias, *Schetsen*, 38. Cornelis J. Guibal, *Democratie en oligarchie in Friesland tijdens de Republiek*, Assen, 1937, 56: the move to Harlingen involved some bargaining with Groningen (Harlingen being more distant from that province). The latter agreed after it was allowed to send four councillors instead of two.

35 Van Slingelandt, *Geschriften* IV, 316–17; De Bruin, 'Soevereiniteit in de Republiek', 31.

36 P.H. Engels, *De belastingen en de geldmiddelen van den aanvang der Republiek tot op heden*, Utrecht, 1862, 16.

37 Appointments in Zeeland, however, were provincial even among the highest ranks, because of the curious amalgamation of admiralty and provincial government.

38 Engelhard, *Generaalplakkaat*, 267.

39 Becht, *Statistische gegevens*, 186.

40 J.R. Bruijn, 'Scheepvaart in de Noordelijke Nederlanden 1550–1650', *Algemene Geschiedenis der Nederlanden* VII, Haarlem, 1980, 141; M.G. De Boer, 'Een kwarteeuw admiraliteitsleven', *Tijdschrift voor Geschiedenis* 56, 1941, 126. Some examples in ARA Generaliteitsrekenkamer (Council of State: CoA) 94: 10 July 1632; 9: 15 February 1642.

41 Quoted by Boxer, *Dutch seaborne empire*, 45.

42 Elias, *Schetsen*, 94; De Liefde, *Dutch admirals*, 50, 66.

43 ARA Adm 3399 on the early 1630s. Engelhard, *Generaalplakkaat*, 258; Boxer, *Dutch Seaborne Empire*, 79; G.J.A. Raven, 'That expensive asset. A short history of Netherlands naval personnel', *Revue Internationale d'Histoire Militaire* 58, 1984, 167. On the early eighteenth century see J.R. Bruijn, *De admiraliteit van Amsterdam in rustige jaren, 1713–1751. Regenten en financiën, schepen en zeevarenden*, Amsterdam, 1970, 139–44.

44 De Liefde, *Dutch admirals*, 65; Joh. E. Elias, *De vlootbouw in Nederland in de eerste helft der zeventiende eeuw 1596–1655*, Amsterdam, 1933, 50; Jan Lucassen, 'Zeevarenden', *Maritieme Geschiedenis der Nederlanden* II, Bussum, 1977, 141.

45 Elias, *Schetsen*, 95–6; F. Graefe, *De kapiteinsjaren van Maarten Harpertszoon Tromp*, Amsterdam, 1938, 92.

46 Goubert, *Ancien Régime*, 127; M.E. Mallet and J.R. Hale, *The military organization of a Renaissance state. Venice c. 1400 to 1617*, Cambridge, 1984, 488; Nickle, *Military reforms*, 184.

47 The composition of the new troops was confusing. The fifty new extraordinary companies of 1628 consisted of 200 men during the summer; they were reduced to 100 men in the same year, but in 1629 augmented to the larger size. In addition, forty other companies were increased by 125 men on average, fifteen new companies were recruited of 200 men, and 3,000 Scots were contracted (in all, 16,000 troops in infantry). Moreover, new *waardgelders* were appointed temporarily, and 12,000 Danish soldiers were added to the army establishment. But in November of the same year, the fifty companies of 200 men were reduced again to 100. In the years following, they became companies of 150 or 120 men. ARA SG *Staten van Oorlog*; Van Slingelandt, *Geschriften* IV, 149; Van der Capellen, *Gedenkschriften* I, 486, 500, 540, 559.

48 Israel, *Dutch Republic and Hispanic world*, 177.

49 J.I. Israel, 'The States General and the strategic regulation of the Dutch river trade, 1621–36', *Bijdragen en Mededelingen betreffende de Geschiedenis der Nederlanden* 95, 1980, 471, 489.

50 The Guelders stateman Van der Capellen wrote in his diary: 'Ondertussen komt d'autoriteyt in militaire saken allenskens aen den Prints . . .', *Gedenkschriften* I, 456.

51 Van Slingelandt, *Geschriften* IV, 148.

52 J.I. Israel, 'The Holland towns and the Dutch–Spanish conflict, 1621–48', *Bijdragen en Mededelingen betreffende de Geschiedenis der Nederlanden* 94, 1979, 50.

53 *Ibidem*, 55–6.

54 *Ibidem*, 64–6.

55 The Amsterdam regents condemned Frederick Henry's determination to liberate Antwerp as a self-seeking ploy to provide the House of Orange with an independent principality. Finally, in the Peace of 1648, Antwerp would stay out of the Republic, whereas access to Antwerp's harbour could still be hindered by the north. Israel, *Dutch Republic and Hispanic world*, 256, 374; Maland, *Europe at war*, 177.

56 Frederick Henry had even established a committee in the Estates General whose members were bound by oath to him in divulging information to their own provinces. But after 1643 the Estates of Holland forbade this oath to their delegates. Israel, *Dutch Republic and Hispanic world*, 317. Because of the treaty with France, the Dutch had to furnish at least 25,000 infantry and 5,000 cavalry for the extraordinary expeditions. Their costs were calculated at 1,600,000 guilders, half of which was paid by a French subsidy. See also Van der Capellen, *Gedenkschriften* II, 14–16; Maland, *Europe at war*, 151.

57 The premature death of the Stadtholder settled the issue to the advantage of Holland. Kernkamp, *Willem II*, 57. For the *Staat van Oorlog* in 1650, the Estates of Holland voted for the following: fifty-five infantry companies had to be disbanded (1,750 men), the 202 companies of seventy men were reduced to sixty; twenty cavalry companies were disbanded, and the thirty-eight companies of sixty men had to become fifty (1,340 horsemen). Only the two companies of Stadtholder William II and the company for the Stadtholder of Friesland were to remain intact. Military salaries were reduced if successors were appointed; the sitting officers were to keep the same pay. Some officers, the lieutenants in the cavalry and infantry, were not to be reappointed (in case of succession) in the future. Van der Capellen, *Gedenkschriften* II, 266, notes different figures: sixteen cavalry companies instead of twenty and a reduction in the infantry companies to sixty-five instead of to sixty.

58 Van Slingelandt, *Geschriften* IV, 151. On 1643: Van der Capellen, *Gedenkschriften* II, 51; see also I, 220–2. ARA Raad van State (Council of State: CoS) 1905: 1 November 1623; 9 February 1626.

59 In addition, officers in the service of the Council of State (mainly accountants and clerks) numbered fifty-three in 1640. Rijksarchief in Zuid-Holland (RAZH) Jacob Cats 77 and 8.

60 ARA CoA *Staten van Oorlog*; RAZH Van Slingelandt 247.

61 J.R. Hale, *War and society in Renaissance Europe, 1450–1620*, London, 1985, 234.

62 Elias, *Vlootbouw*, 33; *Resolutiën* SG: 18 December 1600, 14 November 1603; F. Snapper, *Oorlogsinvloeden op de overzeese handel van Holland 1551–1719*, Amsterdam, 1959, 56.

63 Israel, *Dutch Republic and Hispanic world*, 87; Elias, *Schetsen*, 90, 98. See also *Resolutiën* SG: 21 October 1622.

64 Israel, *Dutch Republic and Hispanic world*, 116, 192–3.

65 The actual number of men was probably lower, though, as this was largely a paper plan. Lucassen, 'Zeevarenden', based on J.C. de Jonge (*Geschiedenis van het Nederlandsche Zeewezen* I, The Hague, 1833), estimated the navy sailors to have numbered 8,000 during 1630–1649, but he excluded those on the rivers inland. According to Lucassen, the VOC and WIC had 9,000 and 4,000 men respectively, and the remainder of the Dutch sea-borne trade 29,000. The warships for Flanders and the North Sea were distributed as follows: Rotterdam nine, Amsterdam eighteen, Zeeland nine and the Northern Quarter nine; see ARA Adm 3399.

66 Maland, *Europe at war*, 138.

67 Graefe, *Kapiteinsjaren*, 93; S.W.P.C. Braunius, 'Oorlogsvaart', *Maritieme Geschiedenis der Nederlanden* II, Bussum, 1977, 338; ARA CoA 94: 30 December 1636.

68 See ARA CoA 94, 30 December 1636; Elias, *Schetsen*, 106–10.

69 Graefe, *Kapiteinsjaren*, 103.
70 *Ibidem*.
71 Engelhard, *Generaalplakkaat*, 265.
72 Israel, *Dutch Republic and Hispanic world*, 269.
73 On the distinction between piracy and privateering: J.Th.H. Verhees-van Meer, *De Zeeuwsche kaapvaart tijdens de Spaanse successieoorlog 1702–1713*, Middelburg, 1986, 7–9, 29–30. On the VOC and WIC expeditions: Israel, *Dutch Republic and Hispanic world*, 203, 273, 278.
74 Snapper, *Oorlogsinvloeden*, 77, 84; Van der Capellen, *Gedenkschriften* II, 39.
75 Menkman, *West-Indische Compagnie*, 127; Snapper, *Oorlogsinvloeden*, 82; Boxer, *Dutch seaborne empire*, 88–9.
76 Israel, *Dutch Republic and Hispanic world*, 265, 288; A.P. van Vliet, 'Kapers op de kust: Maassluis en de Duinkerker kapers', *Tijdschrift voor Zeegeschiedenis* 6, 1987, 4; Van Deursen, *Kopergeld* III, 90, 119.
77 Transformed into the Directie Grote Visserij in 1635. A. Bijl Mz., *De Nederlandse convooidienst. De maritieme bescherming van koopvaardij en zeevisserij tegen piraten en oorlogsgevaar in het verleden*, The Hague, 1951, 64, 78.
78 *Ibidem*, 74; Bruijn, 'Scheepvaart in de Noordelijke Nederlanden', 140; Becht, *Statistische gegevens*, 149; *Groot Placaet Boeck vervattende de placaten, ordonnantiön ende edicten van de Staten-Generaal der Vereenigde Nederlanden*, ed. C. Cau, The Hague, 1644, I, 1000, 2572, 2574.
79 Bruijn, 'De vaart', 204; Van der Capellen, *Gedenkschriften* I, 476.
80 Elias, *Schetsen*, 122–7.
81 W.F.H. Oldewelt, 'De scheepvaartstatistiek van Amsterdam in de 17e en 18e eeuw', *Jaarboek Amstelodamum* 45, 1953, 118; Pieter de la Court, *Interest van Holland, ofte gronden van Hollands welvaren*, Amsterdam, 1662, 189–91; Elias, *Schetsen*, 141; Israel, *Dutch Republic and Hispanic world*, 271.
82 W.F.H. Oldewelt, 'De Hoeffijserse schuld (1616–1681)', *Jaarboek Amstelodamum* 51, 1959, 40; *Groot Placaet Boeck* I, 2174; ARA CoA 9: 26 May, 15 September 1645.
83 Van Dillen, 'Amsterdam's role in the seventeenth century', 143; P. Geyl, *The Netherlands in the seventeenth century 1648–1715*, New York, 1964, 165; John J. Murray, *Amsterdam in the Age of Rembrandt*, Norman, 1967, 37.
84 Elias, *Vlootbouw*, 74.
85 J.R. Bruijn, 'Mercurius en Mars uiteen. De uitrusting van de oorlogsvloot in de zeventiende eeuw', *Bestuurders en Geleerden*, ed. S. Groenveld *et al.*, Amsterdam, 1985, 100–2; Elias, *Vlootbouw*, 86.
86 M.G. de Boer, *Het proefjaar van Maarten Harpertsz Tromp*, Amsterdam, 1940, 131.

Part II

The relative crisis

3

Shifting the burden of war

In fighting the Spanish Habsburgs, the newborn Republic could maintain its integrity only at the expense of high military costs. This part deals with the shift of that financial burden of the Eighty Years' War onto Dutch society. In Chapter Two, those costs have been calculated at an annual average of 24 million guilders in the last three decades of the war.

In the history of warfare in early modern Europe, the military revolution had monetized that burden with the increased use of hired troops. The burden of war had to be shifted onto the population within the territorial boundaries. Obviously, financing each war resulted into a political crisis of some sort, as taxation always involved conflict. State agents had to find funds, draft proposals, and make decisions amidst manifold exemptions and traditional privileges.[1] This kind of political crisis is labelled 'relative' when alternative options were available within the given economic and political structure:

> A crisis of the tax state is 'relative', if a majority rejects a proposed fiscal policy package, but if there exist other fiscal policy packages that find a majority in the given framework [. . .].[2]

An absolute crisis, on the other hand, entailed a change of government, a civil war or even a revolution. Any crisis, no matter how acute, could be rendered relative by trying to find a new majority consensus. Such consensus was established by bargaining with the groups who could either provide funds, or who could prevent social unrest if the burden was to be shifted onto the lower echelons of society. Bargaining was always easier given the existence of a representative institution, such as the Estates General and Provincial

Estates in our case.[3] Also, the burden was less likely to evoke a crisis of an absolute sort if there was some other favourable condition, such as economic development, that could reduce the direct incidence of impositions. Expenses for a 'just' war were also a favourable condition owing to the legitimacy of the burden, as in a war against an incursion on privileges or because of religious issues. The legitimacy of the state was always likely to raise the 'political ceiling of taxation':

> Taxation will reach its practical limit when the political and social resistance by taxpayers becomes so serious that the government is prevented from imposing an additional burden. The upper limit, which may be called the political ceiling on taxation, depends upon the tax structure besides many other factors.[4]

As bargaining usually diminished the autonomy of the power holders, solutions were favoured which were independent of major social groupings. Shmuel Eisenstadt wrote:

> There are two basic manifestations of [the] exercise of power: the holders of power are able (1) to use various resources for the implementation of different goals and (2) to mobilize human resources at will – those who exercise power (the 'rulers') can impose their will on others. Thus to analyze the ways in which the political system may tend to stress or evolve its own autonomy, we must examine the ways in which political power can develop without being encumbered.[5]

A state's autonomy was reflected by whether rulers could dispose of various resources, whether they were free in choosing which factions they would support, and whether they were not bound by the consent of a single economic or ideological elite. Historical conditions and previous decisions set limits to autonomous measures as well. Wallerstein noted rightly:

> A state machinery involves a tipping mechanism. There is a point where strength creates more strength. The tax revenue enables the state to have a larger and more efficient civil bureaucracy and army which in turn leads to greater tax revenue – a process that continues in spiral form. The tipping mechanism works in the other direction too – weakness leading to greater weakness. It is in this arena that the skills of particular managerial groups make a difference.[6]

A state based upon a previous princedom commanded more traditional autonomous power, by extracting revenue from Crown lands and feudal prerogatives. Also, the development of state monopolies and state enterprises widened the freedom of operation of rulers.

In all, the policies of shifting the financial burden could be divided into three major alternatives: central means, taxation, and loans. The first option for shifting the burden onto society was the extraction of means under direct control of the state agencies (see Chapter Four). Generally, it was the preferred solution, as it circumvented pressure from societal groupings. The agencies of the state were directly responsible for the distribution of the burden and the collection of the revenue.

The second major option was taxation through intermediaries or local rulers (see Chapter Five). Society was drawn into this means of shifting the burden in a most direct way. In early modern Europe, taxes were a relatively new phenomenon. In the Middle Ages, public authorities had relied upon such devices as feudal duties, church tithes, tolls, and domain income. Direct taxes (impositions bearing upon property or revenue, such as land and crop taxes) had evolved out of feudal and church duties (tithes); indirect taxes (upon trade and consumption, such as excises and customs, thus avoiding a direct charge upon the taxpayer) were levied in the tradition of tolls and certain feudal prerogatives, like the monopoly of grinding corn (taxes upon grain consumption). If state agents could not collect the funds with their own appointed officers, bargaining with societal groupings was necessary.

The third major option to resolve the relative crisis was the shift to the future (see Chapter Six). Loans relieved direct demands, although the service charges upon the debt had to be raised through taxes again. In early modern Europe, the charges upon the debt could easily rise disproportionately, because of high interest rates and short-term contracts. A major step forward in this respect was the gradual move towards long-term arrangements with low interest rates, in which loans were only repaid over the very long term; they might even be made permanent. Such a development, which could only have been sustained by permanent and stable taxation to pay for the interest charges, has been labelled the 'financial revolution in the state'. This public debt made political stabilility possible even in times of severe war pressure and reduced the degree of insecurity for the state.[7]

Whether the shift was made by central means, taxation, or loans, a recurrent problem for many early modern states was the absence of a regular budget. It was highly desirable to know how much was spent and received each year. Waging war was becoming increasingly expensive, yet no established mechanism existed to bring the revenues up to the level of the expenditures. Information was secret, or data were simply lacking. In France, the *Compte Rendu* was a kind of budget for the king, but always irregular and inconsistent in arrangement and scope. In Spain, royal officials never really attempted to construct a budget, for neither the revenue nor the expenditures could be estimated with any accuracy.[8]

However, a budget was of prime importance for bargaining, in rendering the crisis at hand only relative. It facilitated the consent of representatives from cities and the countryside. In return for the consent, control over resources was required. In South Brabant, for example, the main function of the Estates was fiscalist. In England, Parliament took over control of the customs in 1641, and in the years thereafter, it imposed excises. Bargaining in England, though, was very different from continental Europe as there was only one major Parliament and there were no provincial Estates, as in the Netherlands or France. Such bargaining at the centre, in general, reduced the danger of revolts. In France, the fact that no Etats Généraux were convened after 1614 (until 1789) contributed to the recurrence of tax revolts throughout the seventeenth century. In Sweden, on the other hand, a well organized Riksdag represented even the peasants. It made the Riksdag an accomplice in state policy, reduced the danger of revolts, and facilitated the consent to taxation.[9]

Although public finances in the Netherlands were less surrounded by secrecy than in other principalities, no overall budgets existed. The initial shift occurred in a quota system. Revenues were voted for in the Estates General upon request of the Council of State, listing the ordinary expenses in the *Staat van Oorlog*. This chapter describes the failed attempts to impose unified taxes over the whole territory of the Dutch Republic. A distribution of quotas was necessary. Unexpected and extraordinary expenses required additional voting, in particular for the navy, as provincial taxes had not been intended to pay for warfare at sea. Finally, with the available data from the archives, a budget of revenues is reconstructed, showing the possible options and alternatives for the bureaucrats of the Dutch central state machinery.

Attempts at unified taxation

From former Habsburg rule the Dutch Republic inherited no unified tax system over its territories. Though the provinces had consented to taxes before through their respective Estates, these impositions had always been temporary and restricted to certain regions. Such permanent taxation as did exist was administered by the cities, rural quarters and provinces themselves. The latest tax reforms of 1568 by the Spanish government had entailed the introduction of a hundredth upon property, a twentieth penny on death duties and the sale of fixed property, and a tenth penny upon all sales of movable property, which was actually a kind of general excise. Yet even this policy was applied separately to the 'new' regions and the 'old' ones. The territories acquired recently were allowed to buy off the tenth: Gelderland, Friesland, Overijssel with Drenthe, Groningen and Lingen. But the patrimonial provinces – Flanders, Brabant, Holland, Zeeland and Utrecht – were forced to accept the measures. Redemption of taxes was always advantageous, as it prevented any prying into local privileges and rules. In addition, with the lapse of time, redeemed sums almost always declined in value. Moreover, the tenth was designed to be permanent, a crucial change over previous regulations. Although the tax was never imposed in reality, the protest against it was furious and constituted a major motive for the revolt.[10]

During the revolt, fiscal autonomies were re-established. Tax structures differed according to socio-economic composition. Holland, Zeeland and Utrecht shared a more or less common social and historical background. Yet even within this maritime western part of the country, centrifugal forces existed. Holland itself was divided into two quarters, the Southern and the Northern, each with its own administration. At times West Frisian separatism in the Northern Quarter threatened Holland's unity. Zeeland was closest in history to Holland and shared the highest juridical courts. Yet the province was generally strongly Calvinist and pro-war, and because of its different trading interests it was often sharply opposed to Holland's influence on the finances of the Union. Utrecht had been characterized as the centre of an age-old bishopric. In the Republic, its country dwellers were regarded with suspicion because as Catholics they had long continued to support the Spanish king.[11]

Urban–rural dichotomies were particularly strong in the other provinces. In Groningen, both the city and the countryside had their own sovereign administration. From of old, the city had much power over the countryside owing to market staple rights (*stapelrecht*), and its attempts to maintain or extend its power frequently clashed with the rural representatives (the *jonkers*). The Fries language, distinct from Dutch, extended from Friesland into the countryside of Groningen and East Frisia. Friesland did have one central provincial administration, but it was divided into four collective votes, according to its four quarters: the three rural ones, Oostergo, Westergo, and the poorer Zevenwouden, and one quarter of the eleven cities combined. The right to vote within the Frisian quarters was, for the time, quite extensive: about 10,000 persons were allowed to elect their representatives. Within the Republic, Friesland was one of the largest provinces, with an advanced agricultural economy, and numbering roughly 150,000 inhabitants at that time. Groningen was about half Friesland's size in population.[12]

Some cities in Holland itself were more populous than the whole province of Groningen or any other province or quarter in the east. Overijssel boasted some 65,000 inhabitants, the Gelderland Quarter Veluwe 41,000, and Drenthe 20,000. Links with the neighbouring Holy Roman Empire (Germany) were particularly strong in the inland provinces. The province of Gelderland, because it was the *duchy* of Gelre, stood formally highest in rank in the Republic. Gelderland even came before the *county* of Holland in matters of the Generality, from which significant symbolic power was derived.[13] It was divided into three quarters: Betuwe, Graafschap and Veluwe, each with its own administration, sharing no common provincial administration at all. Voting was repeatedly blocked between the city and the rural (noble) delegates within those quarters.[14]

Likewise, the province of Overijssel often experienced the blocking of votes between city and nobility. It too was divided into three quarters: Salland, Vollenhove and Twente. But at least there was a single administration for the whole province. For long, though, the Estates General regarded Twente as enemy territory. Peasant revolts had occurred there after the Estates' troops had pillaged the countryside in the 1580s and 1590s. The coexistence of a Spanish Overijssel government made matters worse, but all Spanish influence virtually disappeared when Rheinberg fell in 1632. Drenthe, finally, though it had no representation in the Estates General, was a sovereign province, with predominantly rural Estates. The government of the province consisted of a *Drost* and the deputies of the *landschap*, four in number: two from the gentry and two from the independent farmers.[15]

In the first years of the war, the republican armed forces were paid through private investments of the Prince of Orange, through more or less voluntary contributions by city dwellers, through customs levied mainly in Holland and Zeeland, through foreign subsidies from France and England, and through sales of goods of exiled nobles and the Catholic church.[16] However, in particular after the loss of the wealthy regions of Flanders and Brabant, these means were not sufficient for longer periods of sustained warfare.

Common taxes would undoubtedly have constituted the best solution. The idea of a unified taxation system had been embodied in the Union of Utrecht of 1579, the charter of alliance against Spain. Article Five spoke of common taxes that were to be levied in all provinces at the same rate (*eenpaerlick ende op eenen voet*). If necessary, new taxes were to be introduced, upon the consent of all (*bij gemeen advys ende consent*). Article Eighteen specified in addition that no customs should be imposed by the provinces on their own.[17]

Yet by 1583 the prospect of unified taxes had already disappeared. Holland and Zeeland enacted a list of taxes for their territories and did not wait for the agreement of the others. Both declared at a meeting in Utrecht:

> that it was sufficient to have each province bear its part of the general burden and that each province should find the yield out of those means, which they think of as most appropriate, according to their state of being.[18]

It was left to the individual provinces to employ whatever means they judged efficacious to supply their share.

A return to centralized taxes occurred in 1586 under Leicester, who was temporarily appointed as a governor for England. A crucial act stated that costs of warfare had to be defrayed by raising 'common means [. . .] approved by the general states of the provinces [. . .] on one footing [. . .]', in which even a centralized government, centralized taxes, and a centralized Treasury were part of the plans. Duties on salt, soap and beer were indeed imposed. But shortly thereafter, Leicester was accused by the Estates of Holland of usurpation, and he was put to flight. The new instruction of the Council of State of 1588 reflected the emphasis on federate taxes and the limited powers of the council, and each province was assigned a quota for contribution towards the expenses. The duties on salt, soap and beer were reduced again.[19]

Nevertheless, because of the pressure of war, attempts reappeared to install new central taxes. In 1606 the Estates General tried to impose a general hearth tax throughout the Republic, at 1.50 guilders per hearth, after the army had been increased considerably. Some provinces consented, others refused, and the impost was withdrawn.[20] Renewed efforts to introduce general taxation throughout the Republic followed. In 1619, the Council of State proposed to levy general duties on wine, spirits, beer, meat, cattle and crops. In the 1620s a general duty on wine was expected to bring some relief for the Union finances. Most subsequent reforms aimed at a general land tax (*verponding*), based upon the example of Holland, and at the introduction of five crucial excises: wine, beer, salt, soap and cloth. The latter were called the *Vijf Speciën*. The Estates General pointed to the worrying situation in public finances in order to get equalization of taxes voted for, as in a proposal to Overijssel in April 1639:

> one notices the empty coffers of the general offices, and the pressing burden [. . .] of interest which can hardly be paid, the magazines falling short of necessary provisions, fortifications are not being looked after, [. . .] troops remain unpaid, [. . .] the highest colleges are losing their authority [. . .].[21]

At times, these projects of *egalisatie* were even officially voted for in the Estates General, as in 1633 and in 1638–1640.[22] Yet all the plans fell short of actual implementation. Friesland introduced its *Vijf Speciën*, but they were totally different taxes altogether (on horses and hearths!). Obviously, there was no central power to apply persistent pressure and sanctions to get the reforms introduced. Despite republican distress and want, the fiscal autonomy of the provinces was to last until 1795.

The vote in quotas

Most of the funds were to come from the provinces, who were sovereign in fiscal matters. By the Union of Utrecht they commited themselves to hand over sums voted for centrally. In the Estates General, the proposed *Staat van Oorlog* acted as a kind of traditional petition: the Council of State *asked* the provinces to concede the budgeted expenses. The *Staat van Oorlog* was divided into fixed quotas, and the sums voted were called *consenten*. Drenthe, because it was too poor to send a representation, could not vote: the other provinces consented for this *landschap*. In addition, the representatives in the Estates General ratified the customs, the generality salt tax, the generality stamp duties, the passports and all taxes in the generality lands.[23]

The voting upon the *Staat van Oorlog* involved many longwinded debates. The representatives in the Estates General had first to hear their sovereigns, the provincial Estates. In turn, the latter might have to hear the representatives of cities, quarters, colleges of nobles or other rural delegates of the province. The recurrent meetings caused travel costs to soar and delayed decision-making. It was far more efficient for the Council of State if the *Staat van Oorlog* did not differ too much from the preceding one, as this greatly simplified voting behaviour. Minor changes would be noted in the margin of the *Staat* of the preceding year, and the same budgeted expenses were continued for years. One drawback was that underestimates tended to be perpetuated. Moreover, exact control was difficult, as few copies of the *Staat van Oorlog* were similar, owing to all the additions of later years.

Provinces were expected to contribute evenly. Yet as no population figures existed, nor calculations of trade balances, nor estimations of industrial output, equity was an extremely tricky business. The distribution of quotas often caused bitter disagreement. Arguments as to wartime losses, population declines, inundations and other disasters were exploited to the hilt. During 1605–1615 discord rose to such a level pitch that mediation was needed by French and English envoys. It was clear that fixing the quotas would reduce some of the animosities. In 1586–1595, 1596–1604 and since 1616 (until 1672) they had been decided as shown in Table 3.1. Holland, the most wealthy and populous province, took care of more than half of all republican expenses. It was followed by Friesland, the second largest province, with Zeeland third. The smaller provinces, Utrecht, Gelderland and Groningen, were set at almost similar proportions (5.5 per cent), whereas the poorer Overijssel had to pay 3.5 per cent of all expenses. Little Drenthe was obliged to pay 1 per cent above the hundred.

Temporarily, the quotas of Gelderland and Overijssel were lowered when war was resumed in 1621, because their territories suffered recurrent army exactions and contributions. The former situation was restored in 1633 when all direct threats had diminished considerably.[24] These temporary reductions did not affect the

Table 3.1 *Quota distribution as between provinces for the ordinary war establishment*

province	*1586–1595*	*1596–1604*	*1616–1672*
Holland	64.2	59.7	57.7
Friesland	13.3	12.3	11.6
Zeeland	15.8	14.6	9.1
Utrecht	6.6	6.3	5.7
Groningen		6.8	5.7
Gelderland			5.5
Overijssel			3.5
Drenthe			1.0
total	100.0	100.0	100.0

Source: ARA CoS 2115 I 'repartitie'; H. L. Zwitzer, 'Het quotenstelsel onder de Republiek der Verenigde Nederlanden alsmede enkele beschouwingen over de generale petitie, de staat van oorlog en repartitie', *Mededelingen van de Sectie Militaire Geschiedenis Landmachtstaf* 5, 1982, 12.

quotas of the other provinces, as the deficit was shifted to the Receiver General of the Union (the 'generality'), who had to find additional funds from central means.

In the meetings at The Hague itself, provinces watched closely to see whether the others did agree to the sums demanded by the Council of State in the *Staat van Oorlog*. Nevertheless, deficits in the consents were recurrent: provinces repeatedly voted lower sums (*defecten*) than asked for by the Council of State. Such shortfalls had a cumulative effect: any province would readily refuse a sum if another was not prepared to pay either. The *defecten* were passed on to the Receiver General again.[25] Zeeland complained regularly about its share, which was perhaps not totally unreasonable, as it was put at 3.8 per cent in the eighteenth century (as compared to 9.1 per cent in the seventeenth century) when more information as to population and wealth had become available.[26]

To facilitate the transfer of the burden of the war, differences were allowed in the constitution of the quotas. All, of course, had to pay most to the companies of cavalry and infantry, which consumed 73 per cent of war costs during 1620–1650. But garrisons were of particular interest. The stationing of troops provided revenue for the cities from excises and the troops constituted an additional source of power for whoever was the paymaster. The province of Holland paid for the garrison in Harlingen in Friesland because of its interests in the Zuiderzee. Holland tried to extend its control over Steenwijk in

Overijssel too. Administration over the garrison of Coevorden in the *landschap* of Drenthe was disputed by Groningen and Friesland. Friesland controlled the garrisons in the Groningen territory of Zoutkamp and Delfzijl, much to the chagrin of Groningen, of course. Both provinces shared the costs of the Bourtange and Bellingwolde forts at the eastern border of the Union.[27]

In addition, striking differences were noted in the matters of debt service, central bureaucracy and extraordinary ammunitions. By far the most interest on the generality debt was paid by Holland, as much as 96 per cent to 98 per cent in the ordinary budgets from 1621 up to 1647. Also, the bulk of the costs of the generality in The Hague, such as colleges and embassies, was paid by this province: from 88 per cent to 89 per cent of all such expenses. As for stores and ammunition, it proved that much of those came from Holland too: 85 per cent in the 1620s and even 92 per cent in the 1640s. Furthermore, the pay of the Guard and the regiments of the Stadhouder were taken care of by Holland. Many of these costs, evidently, were incurred in the province itself. But all these items were also typically the costs of a central establishment, a central government. Holland's strength secured these vital branches of the state, with the result that they were not endangered by antagonistic attitudes on the part of a peripheral province. In return, the core province paid somewhat less on the other items.[28]

After all, the most effective way of payment was to keep the funds in the province where they had to be spent. A disproportionately large share of billeting and provisions was taken care of by Gelderland and Overijssel. Payments for billeting went straight to the inhabitants, who profited from this opportunity for additional income. It paid well, and the discipline of the men in the Netherlands was generally good enough to make it a profitable business.[29]

Fortifications were paid for by the generality, the provinces and the cities. In Zeeland, fortifications constituted a disporpotionate large part of the quota during the war because of the province's proximity to Flanders. In the 1650 peace budget the provinces of Gelderland, Utrecht and Overijssel were also allowed to spend larger sums on fortifications as compared with the other provinces to strengthen their defences.[30]

Along with the billeting and fortifications, pensions ranked among the more popular items of expenditure, as they were easy to use as an instrument of patronage. They were watched over jealously by the provinces. Most of them were destined for officers and experienced soldiers during periods of non-employment. Highly unpopular items to pay for in the budget were the costs of transport, travel and attendance. Invariably, they were underestimated, and thus mostly paid for in the end by the Receiver General of the Union.

To establish a fair distribution, the Estates General aimed at similar pay rates for officers and soldiers. However, Zeeland had a tradition of paying officers more, which was still evident in the 1621 budget. Furthermore, Zeeland tended to pay sailors and captains more as compared with Holland. Also, the hundredth penny pay cut imposed as a measure of retrenchment upon all soldiers was not applied in Zeeland, nor in Friesland and Groningen. The Estates General strove to get these inter-provincial differences out of the way, and by the budget of 1650 they had indeed diminished.[31]

When a province failed to provide the sums agreed in the Estates General, the Council of State had the right of *executie*, which entailed either the billeting of soldiers or taking representatives from the province as hostages. Non-payment of troops constituted an obvious threat to the Union, yet the *executie* was always highly contested and therefore seldom applied.[32] Overall, despite its shortcomings, the quota system stabilized the shifting of the Dutch burden. It was mortar to the provincial bricks of the new state in that the provinces agreed to a common effort and made the political problems of shifting the burden relative.

Voting extraordinary budgets

But the *Staat van Oorlog* could not pay for all expenses, and the vagaries of war necessitated recurrent additional funds. They were voted for in the Estates General through an extraordinary *Staat van Oorlog*, mostly for temporary troops (*veldleger*), mercenary officers, additions to the navy, or demolished fortifications.[33] As traditional quotas did not necessarily apply, these petitions were contested more than the ordinary *Staat van Oorlog*.

Let us follow an example for the year 1624. The budget for expenses was presented by the Council of State to the Estates General on 23 October 1623. Apart from the ordinary *Staat van Oorlog*, the following was demanded in rounded figures:

1. Payment of all arrears in the *consenten* since 1614.

2. A solution to the problem of the 4,894,000 guilders generality debt.
3. To maintain the extraordinary troops at the frontiers.
4. 687,000 guilders for the French troops on Dutch territory who received no French payment.
5. 247,000 guilders for 250 new carabineers, eleven German companies and one Scottish company.
6. 300,000 guilders for *waardgelders* (city soldiers).
7. 800,000 guilders for the costs of transport, the salaries of new officers and other army costs not provided for by the *Staat van Oorlog*.
8. 300,000 guilders for new fortifications.
9. 50,000 guilders for a gun foundry (*geschut*).
10. 600,000 guilders in subsidy to the admiralties.

As usual, the Council of State had to wait long for the provincial decicions. Only Groningen and Holland responded in the same year: their decisions dated from 18 and 23 December 1623 respectively. Others followed in 1624: Overijssel on 9 March, Zeeland on 21 March, Utrecht on 7 and 8 April (with additions on 17 June), whereas the three Gelderland quarters decided on different dates. Friesland voted only on 10 December 1624, its decision arriving at the Estates General on 4 January 1625. Needless to say, the belated voting had its repercussions on the country's efficacy in actual warfare. Moreover, the consents themselves did not fully conform to the original petition. Some sums were voted under strict conditions that could not always be met.

Little could be done about the *defecten*, these failures or refusals to vote, as *executie* could only be brought about after official consent. Whereas all provinces agreed to the *Staat van Oorlog*, the extraordinary troops at the borders (item 3) and the ordnance (item 9), the other items were either contested or voted under certain conditions. As for fortifications (item 8), most provinces stipulated that their quota should be used for establishments on their own territory. The petition for payment of arrears of previous budgets (item 1) was refused by Zeeland, on the ground that proper regularity had to be established first in the accounting. Gelderland and Utrecht denied any arrears on their part, whereas Overijssel and Groningen omitted to mention this item in their consent. As for the generality debt (item 2), Utrecht refused, Overijssel failed to mention it, while Friesland

and Groningen demanded an investigation into the origin of the debt, as they denied any responsibility for it. Zeeland did not agree to the payment of French troops (item 4), nor did it want to pay for the new German and Scottish companies (item 5). Groningen demanded that these troops should be paid out of contributions from enemy territory and not by the United Provinces. Furthermore, Zeeland voted for only two-thirds of the *waardgelders* (item 6) and was prepared to vote for half the extraordinary army costs only (item 7), as it did not consider them essential. Should the latter turn out to be more expensive in reality, Zeeland would be prepared to consent to the remainder in a future petition.

In this round of voting, Holland was the only province agreeing to the whole petition. Yet a condition was set in Holland's vote as well: the 600,000 guilders for the admiralties (item 10) should be paid by the United Provinces. If necessary, should the other provinces withhold consent, Holland declared that it would simply deduct the 600,000 from its own quota in the *Staat van Oorlog*.[34]

That item, the 600,000 guilders subsidy for the navy, was met with great unwillingness by the inland provinces. Overijssel refused to vote it, and was joined by Utrecht, Groningen and Gelderland, the latter voting 300,000 instead of 600,000. This attitude was typical of the non-maritime provinces. They did not house admiralty establisments, and they did not gain directly from the trade advantages of safe seas.

This subsidy from the inland provinces for the navy constituted a recurrent problem. After all, should not the customs that were collected by the admiralties be sufficient for the upkeep of the fleet? Now the inland provinces were having to levy taxes to pay for a navy which defended the trade of Holland and Zeeland more generally, and as such it was a new counter in the bargaining among the provinces. Utrecht stated explicitly that the navy boards should not profit from the yield of taxes levied inland. Similar difficulties were encountered in England when Charles I tried to spread the burden of the navy around the country. Ships had been paid for by coastal towns, but his ship money levies of 1627 changed the tradition by making inland communities to pay as well. It was one of the things that antagonized the landed elite and prepared the ground for the later civil war.[35]

In the Republic, a partial solution was found by having the provinces pay differing sums. Provincial payments for the Friesland admiralty, voted in 1630–1632, came typically 98 per cent from Friesland itself, the remaining 2 per cent being provided for by its neighbour Groningen. In the Northern Quarter, 93 per cent came from the Northern Quarter receivers of taxes, 7 per cent from the other provinces through the Generality Receiver and a half per cent from the VOC. Zeeland, likewise, was mainly supported by the province itself: 56 per cent, the remainder coming from the Receiver General of the Union, who transferred sums received from the inland provinces. The admiralty at Amsterdam was heavily subsidized by the Estates of Holland, and only 11 per cent came from the city itself. A minor part came from the VOC, only 1.1 per cent, but it was the largest sum spent on the admiralties by this company. Rotterdam differed from the others, in that a minority of the funds came from the host province of Holland: 17 per cent, whereas 83 per cent had to be provided by the other provinces. This fact surely added to the financial difficulties of the Rotterdam admiralty, as inland provinces were notoriously slack contributors to the navy.[36]

Most problems, however, subsided after votes for the navy had become common in the 1630s. They came to average 2 million guilders annually. The amount declined to 1.8 million after 1636. This was in all probability related to distrust of the centralization project of Frederick Henry at Hellevoetsluis. The idea of that project was that the admiralties should keep the customs revenue, while the central establishment would be paid for by provincial subsidies. Frederick Henry supposed that warships provided by a navy board far away from the city cliques of the admiralties would gain the support of the inland provinces. However, his scheme did not work out as planned, and the project failed (see Chapter Two).[37]

A peak in navy subsidies was noted in 1639, the year of the victorious battle of the Downs. After the dismantling of the Hellevoetsluis establishment in favour of the five admiralties, 3,102,000 guilders were approved at The Hague, one-fifth of all sums voted in the Estates General in that year. Another peak occurred around the time of the Sound crisis: 2,406,000 guilders in 1643, followed by 2,033,000 guilders for the three subsequent years.[38]

Yet even after such consents, the funding by the provinces remained problematic. In 1626, the provinces were 1.9 million guilders in arrears to the admiralties. In 1635, the provinces still owed 1.4 million to Amsterdam alone, 1.3 million to Rotterdam and another 1.4 million to the Northern Quarter. The province of Friesland generally lagged behind all others in paying.[39]

A budget of revenues for the Union

The bickering and squabbling in the Estates General over the provincial payments was partly due to the absence of a complete overview of annual revenues. In Table 3.2 a budget of revenues is reconstructed, based on data surviving from 1638–1642, listing all revenues at the central level.

Table 3.2 *Annual budget of revenues of the Dutch Republic (c. 1641), in percentages*

central revenues	0.8
taxes generality lands	5.3
customs	12.2
provincial taxes	81.8
total	100.0
	[22,632,589 guilders]

Source: RAZH Van Slingelandt 147; GAA 5030.60; Harold E. Becht, *Statistische gegevens betreffende den handelsomzet van de Republiek der Vereenigde Nederlanden gedurende de 17e eeuw (1579–1715)*, The Hague, 1908, table 1; ARA CoS petitions.

The annual expenses amounted to 24 million guilders on average (see Chapter Two). Consequently, revenue fell short by 1.1 million guilders, which constituted about 5 per cent of the total budget. This had to be borrowed (see Chapter Six). As for the major part of the revenues (82 per cent), this had to be shifted towards the provinces through direct and recurrent bargaining at the Estates General in The Hague (Chapter Five).

The Dutch Republic commanded few of the autonomous options: in the table the central means amounted to a mere 0.8 per cent. As the revenues from the generality lands and the customs were formally under the control of The Hague (the Council of State and the Estates General respectively) they made up the centralized funds of the Republic next to the autonomous measures. In the first phases of the Eighty Years' War in particular, those funds had been crucial in making the crisis of spreading the burden of war to society generally only relative. Their constitution, and above all their limitations and constraints, are the subject of the next chapter.

Notes

1 James Alt, 'The evolution of tax structures', *Public Choice* 41, 1983, 183. On the opposition to taxation in general: H.J. van de Braak, *Belastingweerstand. Een proeve van fiscale sociologie*, Deventer, 1981. On the shifting of taxation: Seligman, *On the shifting of taxation*; also Von Mering, *Shifting and incidence*, 145.

2 Dieter Bös, 'The crisis of the tax state', *Public Choice* 38, 1983, 235.

3 See also Brian M. Downing, 'Constitutionalism, warfare, and political change in early modern Europe', *Theory and Society* 17, 1988, 8.

4 Sei Fujita, 'Political ceiling on income taxation', *Public Finance* 16, 1961, 183.

5 Eisenstadt, *Political system of empires*, 364.

6 Wallerstein, *World system* I, 356.

7 This concept was introduced to the general public by Peter G.M. Dickson in his book which dealt with the financial settlements after the 1688 Glorious Revolution in England. See his *The financial revolution in England: a study in the development of public credit, 1688–1756*, New York, 1967, 2; Carolyn Webber and Aaron Wildavsky, *A history of taxation and expenditure in the Western world*, New York, 1986, 251; Tracy, *A financial revolution*, 3.

8 R.A. Stradling, *Europe and the decline of Spain. A study of the Spanish system, 1580–1720*, London, 1981, 39; Parker, 'Emergence of modern finance', 560; J.F. Bosher, *French finances, 1770–1795: from business to bureaucracy*, Cambridge, 1970, 44. For a more positive view of French finances: Michel Morineau, 'Budgets de l'état et gestion des finances royales en France au dix-huitième sìcle', *Revue Historique* 104, 1980, 189–336.

9 Paul Janssens, 'De Brabantse statenadel tegenover het absolutisme', ed. F. Vanhemelryck, 185; Gerald E. Aylmer, *Rebellion of revolution? England 1640–1660*, Oxford, 1987, 18; Jean Meuvret, 'Comment les Français voyaient l'împôt', *Etudes d'histoire économique. Receuil d'articles*, Paris, 1971, 298; Michael Roberts, *The Swedish imperial experience, 1560–1718*, Cambridge, 1979, 62, 76.

10 Engels, *Belastingen*, 6; Grapperhaus, *Tiende penning*, 113; J. Craeybeckx, 'Aperçu sur l'histoire des impôts en Flandre et au Brabant au cours du XVIe siècle', *Revue du Nord* 29, 1947, 99, 102; J. van der Poel, 'De Unie van Utrecht, de geboorteklok van een Nederlandsch belastingstelsel', *Tributen aan het Recht*, Deventer, 1971, 31–5.

11 Murk van der Bijl, *Idee en interest. Voorgeschiedenis, verloop en achtergronden van de politieke twisten in Zeeland en vooral in Middelburg tussen 1702 en 1715*, Groningen, 1981, 5; D.A. Felix, *Het oproer te Utrecht 1610*, Utrecht, 1910, 21; Wijn, *Krijgswezen*, 362.

12 I.B.M. Matthey, 'Op fiscaal compas. Een bijdrage tot de economische geschiedenis van het gewest Groningen in de 17e en 18e eeuw, met toespitsing op de dorpen in het huidige Stedum', *Westeremden. Het verleden van een Gronings terpdorp*, Groningen, 1975, 287; W.J. Formsma, 'Jonkers en boeren op de Ommelander landdag in de eerste helft der achttiende eeuw', *Groningse Volksalmanak. Historisch Jaarboek voor Groningen*

1974–1975, 1975, 79; J.A. Faber, *Drie eeuwen Friesland. Economische en sociale ontwikkelingen van 1500 tot 1800*, Wageningen, 1972, 344–6, 562; John Grever, 'The States of Friesland: Politics and society during the 1660s', Parliaments, Estates, Representations IX, 1989, 1; Van der Woude, 'Demografische ontwikkeling', 102.

13 If a Gelders man was on a committee he was likely to be the first president; on the signing of Treaties (like 1648) Gelderland came first. Yet Holland claimed some symbolic power from the decision that the members of their Estates were called the *Edel Groot Mogenden* (Honourable Great Mightinesses) whereas those of all six other provinces were addressed as *Edel Mogenden* only.

14 In all, Gelderland politics have been labelled 'European' rather than 'Holland'. J.J. Poelhekke, '1609–1672', *Geschiedenis van Gelderland* II, Zutphen, 1975, 158; Van der Capellen, *Gedenkschriften* I, 158–60.

15 Richard Reitsma, *Centrifugal and centripetal forces in the early Dutch Republic. The States of Overijssel*, Amsterdam, 1982, 302; Wijn, *Krijgswezen*, 361; S. Zijlstra, *Des lieven geldes isser an alle oorden gebrek*, Assen, 1983, 2.

16 Flemish Calvinists had put forward the plan in 1566 to buy off freedom of religion from the Spanish king for 3 million golden guilders. As for initial war finances: H. Enno van Gelder, *'s-Gravenhage in zeven eeuwen*, Amsterdam, 1937, 99; W.E. van Dam van Isselt, 'De geldmiddelen onzer Republiek voor den veldtocht van 1599', *Bijdragen voor Vaderlandsche Geschiedenis en Oudheidkunde* V-2, 1920, 9–56; J.H. van Dijk, 'De geldelijke druk op de Delftsche burgerij in de jaren 1572–1576', *Bijdragen voor Vaderlandsche Geschiedenis en Oudheidkunde* VII-5, 1935, 180–1.

17 Simon Groenveld, 'Die originale Unie metten acten daernaer gevolcht', *De Unie van Utrecht*, The Hague, 1979, 32, 36.

18 Quoted by Engels, *Belastingen*, 21.

19 *Groot Placaet Boeck* I, 1596.

20 *Groot Placaet Boeck* I, 1534; *Resolutiën* SG 12 March, 25 April 1606.

21 April 1639, Estates General to Overijssel; Van der Capellen, *Gedenkschriften* II, 40–1; see also ARA SG 12548.205, letter of 23 October 1638.

22 *Resolutiën* SG 21 October 1619, 15 December 1620, 7 October 1621, 26, 27 October, 2 December 1623; ARA SG 205: 'Stukken betreffende egalisatie'; F.N. Sickenga, *Bijdrage tot de geschiedenis der belastingen in Nederland*, Leiden, 1864, 114.

23 On the character of the budget, A.Th. van Deursen, 'Staat van oorlog en generale petitie in de jonge Republiek', *Bijdragen en Mededelingen betreffende de Geschiedenis der Nederlanden* 90, 1976, 44 ff; H.L. Zwitzer, 'Het quotenstelsel onder de Republiek der Verenigde Nederlanden alsmede enkele beschouwingen over de generale petitie, de staat van oorlog en repartitie', *Mededelingen van de Sectie Militaire Geschiedenis Landmachtstaf* 5, 1982, 22; Sickenga, *Bijdrage*, 81.

24 ARA CoS 2115 I 'repartitie'; ARA SG 12548.208 'Stukken betreffende quotas 1635'; Engels, *Belastingen*, 22.

25 *Resolutiën* SG 20 August 1621; Van Deursen, 'Staat van Oorlog', 50.

26 W. Dircksen, 'Enige opmerkingen over de belastingheffing in de Republiek der Verenigde Nederlanden in de 17e en de 18e eeuw, in het bijzonder over inkomstenbelastingen in Zeeland', *L'impôt dans le cadre de la Ville et de l'Etat. Collection Histoire* 13, 1966, 240; *Resolutiën* SG 30 March 1621.

27 Kann, *De militie*, 51.

28 Based on ARA CoA *Staten van Oorlog.*

29 Wijn, *Het krijgswezen*, 126.

30 Based on ARA CoA *Staten van Oorlog.*

31 Elias, *Schetsen*, 63; ARA CoA 91: 6 May 1625; CoA 8: 12 October, 9 December 1630; CoA 9: 14 November 1641; CoA *Staat van Oorlog* 1650.

32 Van Deursen, 'Staat van Oorlog', 54; Zwitzer, 'Quotenstelsel', 29. In 1639, the provinces voiced a general protest against the 'execution' of the Council of State, which was confirmed after 1651: H. Lamens, 'De Unie van Utrecht en de landelijke heffingen', *Fiskaal* 1979, 487.

33 Zwitzer, 'Quotenstelsel', 35.

34 All voted for the customs upon the condition that a quarter of the revenue should be farmed out, in order to combat fraud, but not the provinces of Holland and Zeeland. On the 1624 petition: ARA CoS 2225 Propositie en consenten 1624 (23 October 1623, 11 November 1624); CoS 2253 Res SG 4 January 1625 (Friesland's consent); *Resolutiën* SG 23 October 1623, 3, 26 October 1624.

35 Aylmer, *Rebellion or revolution*, 6; *Resolutiën* SG 6 February 1623; Snapper, *Oorlogsinvloeden*, 196; Elias, *Schetsen*, 92; Van der Capellen, *Gedenkschriften* I, 477.

36 Based on the figures in ARA Adm Vd Heim XXXVII 79; CoA 950–952 accounts Zeeland.

37 ARA CoA 8: 16 March 1638; ARA SG 12561.98, 3 November 1640; GAA 5030/60; Hartsinck, *Overzigt*, 95; Graefe, *Kapiteinsjaren*, 92–3, 103.

38 ARA Adm XLVII 30 memorie van de subsidien; see also: CoA 94 'Reason why the admiralties should be subsidized'.

39 Control over the subsidies from the provinces was poor. In 1641, it appeared that the admiralty of Rotterdam had never received a 153,096 guilder subsidy from Holland. The Estates had accounted for these sums themselves elsewhere. ARA CoA 9: 3 May 1641.

4

The first shift: centralized means

For spreading the costs of war, centralized sources of revenue were the solution nearest to hand. To the decision makers in the highest state councils they were a preferred option, as they circumvented pressure upon state policies from societal groupings. Examples of those more or less autonomous measures were: reforms and retrenchment in state institutions; loans from a foreign body or person; developing state domains and enterprises; and exploiting colonies and conquered areas. Also, the burden could be shifted to the revenues that were controlled centrally. These were constituted by minting and monetary policies, tolls, feudal rights, and the sale of monopolies (on mining or the sale of grain, salt, or spirits). In addition, customs were frequently regarded as 'royal' (and hence central) revenues. Furthermore, centralized means were those taxes which were collected by the central state agencies. In such cases, when the vote of representative bodies was required the voting was mere ratification and did not entail actual control over the funds.

Some states had great internal resources and autonomous revenues. The English around 1600, for example, could count for 30 per cent upon royal domains. In addition, customs were regarded as crown revenue, with no need for recurrent consent by Parliament. When trade developed, the power of the Crown subsequently increased too. Later in the century, customs rates were increased considerably, up to fivefold, which constituted again a significant addition in revenue for the Crown.[1]

Domains and feudal prerogatives were important for continental states as well. In Poland and Sweden, royal domains had been the base for the crown's fiscal policies, while in Hesse 52 per cent of the revenue was derived from domains in 1694–1704. In Denmark, domains constituted 67 per cent of the state income in 1608.[2]

Domains were an inheritance from the past. Yet sometimes states were in a position to pursue an active policy developing internal state strength. For example, Russia built up a system of state granaries that collected and disbursed taxed grain, a kind of state monopoly in food supply. Salt and spirits, likewise, came to be exploited under a state monopoly. Revenues could be derived from granting individual merchants a monopoly of trade in and sales of certain products, as in England, where monopolies were granted in the early 1640s on wine, salt, oil, soap, starch, hats, bricks, tiles, and cloths. France had built its state around the tax farm of the *gabelle*, the salt monopoly. The monopolists became tax farmers for the state. In general, such policies tended to increase the autonomous power of the monarch. On the other hand, they also antagonized the merchant community: while one obtained a monopoly, the other was excluded.[3]

Sweden's state power was based not only upon domains, but upon several other autonomous resources as well. Its customs were levied without parliamentary consent, as in England, and during the course of the seventeenth century the influence of the Estates was reduced when land rents on the royal domains were increased. Moreover, Sweden managed to get the new conquered territories to pay for the war through an imposition called *satisfactio*. In 1630, the Swedish taxpayer had to find 1,800,000 silver daler for the German war, but by 1633 the amount had dropped to 128,000 owing to local war contributions. The system worked as long as there were victories. In addition, Sweden's role as a supplier of copper in Europe provided a means of paying for all its armies, another expedient reflecting that state's autonomy.[4]

Spain could reckon on substantial revenues (silver!) from the colonies too, in particular during the sixteenth century. However, these funds were declining in the first decades of the seventeenth century. Monetary policies, such as devaluation, were an other option for autocratic governments. Spain resorted to minting debased copper currency. The result was a severe monetary crisis in 1626, and the *vellon* was restamped at three times its value in 1636. France also used the sale of coins to cover its deficit. The tsar Peter the Great issued copper at higher rates in Russia, as his predecessor had done in 1656.[5]

In this chapter the centralized and autonomous options open to the Dutch state are analysed. The mint policy, domains, and colonial revenues will be discussed. They are followed by the remaining central means, revenues from conquered areas, and the generality customs, amounting to 1 per cent, 5 per cent and 12 per cent respectively of all Union revenue in the last decades of the Eighty Years' War.

Central options

For the Dutch state, some of the more autonomous options did exist, but only to a limited degree. Mint manipulation was unlikely to be approved of in a society where commercial interests dominated such a large part of the body politic. In the revolt against the Spanish Habsburgs, each of the provinces had acquired the sovereign right to mint. Holland even had two mints, one for each of its quarters. In addition, six towns in the east still owned a traditional right to mint.[6]

The multitude of mints hampered any central policy. In particular the trading provinces of the west were much concerned with the stability of the rates. One of the main tasks of the Bank of Amsterdam (1609) was to fix rates of exchange for the manifold coins which were circulating. Several varieties of small change were declared bad money. However, the mints on the eastern periphery continued to mint them, as minting small change was a profitable business for the mint masters, and much in demand at local markets. Deventer, Kampen, and Zwolle, the three mint cities of Overijssel, refused to observe the central declaration on minting. In the debates that followed in the Estates General, they claimed to have obtained the right of mint from the Holy Roman Empire ('Germany') and not from the generality or from a former overlord of Holland. When improvements did not come about and bad double stuyvers continued to be coined, Holland acted high-handedly in prohibiting gold and silver exports to the other provinces in 1621. The move caused uproar among the inland mints. The eastern provinces found themselves suddenly short of bullion, and they were subsequently forced to ratify the mint proclamation. Commercial interests in the maritime west, obviously, managed to safeguard Dutch money standards to a satisfactory degree. Despite all these different mints and coins, Dutch money made a relative coherent impression among foreign powers, a major achievement for such a decentralized state.[7]

Domains were virtually absent. They had yielded 146,200 Flemish pounds in 1551 (about 900,000 guilders), but many had been sold because of the hazardous financial policies of Philips II in the later 1560s.[8] The domains that were left contributed to the Stadhouder's and the provincial coffers. Colonial revenues had been sold as part of the monopolies of trade to the VOC and WIC. No state mines or enterprises existed. Finally, subsidies could be had from foreign states like France and Venice, but these were mostly spent directly on troops and were not controlled by the Estates General.[9]

The regular funds at the direct disposal of the central colleges, then, were composed of a generality salt tax, a generality beer tax, a generality soap tax, passports and safeguards, and the generality stamp duty (*klein zegel*). In all, they probably yielded about 180,000 guilders per year.[10]

The generality taxes on beer and soap were levied temporarily before the Truce. They had been imposed specially to pay off a loan from England. The salt duty had a less temporary character. It was imposed first in 1584, along with the taxes on soap and beer. In 1588 the rate was reduced significantly. This was the year of a strong decentralist tendency, after Leicester's centralizing governorship, and the Estates wished to curb any independent fiscal power of the central governnment as much as possible. The tax lasted until 1680 after being reduced in 1676.[11]

It was the only generality tax which was imposed over a longer period of time. From this tax there was no exemption for any person, rank, class or trade within the Republic. The tax was collected in six tax districts, and sold to the highest bidder for a lease of one year. This method of collection is called tax farming. The tax farmers were vested with far-reaching powers of investigation and used their own checkers. The salt trade was already under strict control because of the high standards required in the herring fisheries, but through the salt tax it was regulated even more. Transport, barrelling, measurement and the sale of salt all required specific bills of the tax farmers and sworn-in measurers and secretaries.[12]

Unfortunately, few accounts of the tax survive, preventing an analysis of the yield. Yet in all probability the revenue declined. The price of the lease of the salt tax, farmed out in the Northern Quarter during 1618 to 1621, was 21,000 guilders a year. By 1650 it was a mere 12,000, while for the Southern Quarter a yield was reported of 13,350 guilders only.[13]

Another permanent central tax was the *klein zegel* of the generality. This duty dated from 1635, levied in a stamp upon officially recognized documents. It was copied from a Holland tax which had been introduced in 1624. The collection of the revenue was farmed out to a commissioner, who resided with his office in The Hague. The revenue increased slightly from 9,273 guilders on average in 1635–1640 to 13,953 guilders in 1641–1645, yet it declined again to 12,773 guilders on average in the five years following.[14]

A highly irregular species of central revenue was constituted by the generality passports. The money was collected by the customs officers (convoy masters), the receivers of the admiralty, the senior civil servants at The Hague, the receivers of the provinces and the secretary of the Stadhouder. They had to hand over their funds to a clerk of the Council of State, Johan van der Haer, the general receiver for passports. The yield averaged roughly 50,000 guilders in 1620–1648.[15]

In all, the amount of direct central measures was restricted. Despite an extension of functions in the central colleges, due to accumulated warfare, no significant increase was noted in the central receipts. Probably, the yield of the central duties even declined in the last decades of the Eighty Years' War. Obviously, these central institutions offered few opportunities indeed for any expansion of bureaucratic power (or 'monopoly of taxation') at The Hague.

The revenue from conquered areas and generality lands

As the conquered regions were directly administered by the Council of State, some opportunity existed here to strengthen central government's power. The term generality lands came into official use after 1648 for the areas reconquered from Spain. These were, for most of the period of the Republic, the northern part of Brabant with the city of Grave and the district of Cuyk and the northern part of Flanders. In the 1630s the Upper Quarter of Gelderland (Venlo) and parts of Limburg (Overmaze) were added. Regions of Walloon Brabant, Namur and Luxembourg were obliged to pay contributions for a certain period up to 1648 as well. In the province of Groningen near the German border, Wedde and its district of Westerwolde were also considered a generality land throughout the seventeenth century.

The peace settlement of 1648 resolved the differences and disagreements between the Netherlands and Spain over these regions. To the Republic went a northern strip of Flanders (now called

Zeeuws Vlaanderen) with the cities of Sluis, Hulst (conquered in 1645) and the fortification of Sas van Gent. Also, the territory of Northern Brabant came under Dutch control: the cities of Den Bosch ('s-Hertogenbosch or Bois le Duc, conquered in 1629), Breda (republican from 1590 to 1625, then Spanish but reconquered in 1637), Bergen op Zoom and Steenbergen, the district of Den Bosch (*Meierij*), the district of Breda (*Baronie*) and the district of Bergen op Zoom (*Markiezaat*). On the border of Gelderland, Grave and Ravestein and the Land of Cuyk became Republic territories as well. Parts of Limburg, conquered in the 1630s, remained 'Dutch' at the Treaty of 1648: the city of Maastricht (with Vroenhove) and the Land of Overmaze with the villages of 's-Hertogenrade, Valkenburg, and Daalhem.[16] To the Spanish the Upper Quarter of Gelderland was ceded, as well as the Quarters of Antwerp and the remaining Quarters of Brabant. On the whole, at the peace settlement of 1648 the Dutch Republic gained in territory as compared with the Truce of 1609–1621.

Yet central government control through the Council of State was already limited by the fact that surrender treaties often contained stipulations as to the previous administration. In the case of Den Bosch in 1629, for example, it was stipulated that former officers were allowed to remain in their posts. Accounts up to 1629 were not to be audited by the new rulers, but were to be transferred to the government in Brussels. Some old taxes were continued. The new taxes (excises and land taxes) were levied at reduced rates only. Most of the tax funds were spent in the region itself, never reaching The Hague at all.[17]

As a matter of course, the revenue of the generality lands fluctuated, as some areas were lost whereas others came under the domination of the Republic. The loss of a city always counted significantly. City populations contributed relatively most to taxation, and cities were crucial to control over revenues from the surrounding rural districts. Increasing taxes in the countryside was always difficult and took longer to materialize as compared to levies in cities.

Taxation naturally linked up with the problem of sovereignty, as the sovereign over an area had the right to impose taxation. But this question was far from resolved. Republic tax farmers encountered serious difficulties as rural dwellers claimed to have paid the Spanish overlords already. Evasion was easy, as borders were ill defined. A solution was to have the rural excises redeemed, as in the districts of Den Bosch, Breda, Bergen op Zoom, and partly in Cuyk. Usually, a redemption became an allocation on top of the existing property taxes of the area, and thus increased land and hearth taxes or grinding duties. It was remarkable that during most of the Eighty Years' War Spain could farm out its taxes in the countryside of Brabant, whereas the Dutch Council of State could only agree to a redemption. Up to 1648, Dutch rural levies frequently looked more like contributions to the enemy than taxation. By contrast, the Brussels government levied the *beden*, four excises (wine, beer, bread and meat) and customs in the district of Den Bosch up to the Peace of Westphalia. Claims by The Hague that this area belonged to the Republic after 1629 failed to yield any actual taxation.[18]

Not only excises, but also land taxes were hard to impose in the newly acquired regions. A house tax in the cities seemed more feasible, and in the 1620s and 1630s the 'land' taxes from the cities were more remunerative as compared with the rural districts. In 1635 the Holland land tax (*verponding*) was extended to the generality lands, but was apparently applied to newly acquired areas in northern Flanders only.[19]

In Maastricht and Overmaze the traditional *beden* were levied. No new taxes were demanded at all by the Republic government. *Beden* were levied in Brabant as well. They were imposed as of old, and used to pay off the former loans of this province. Originally the *beden* had been a direct tax: an assessment by hearths. Uniquely in the city of Den Bosch a beer excise furnished the sums for the city quota. Later, other items were included, such as duties on salt, wine, beer, dice, playing cards, and wheat. In some places, it was even converted into a capitation tax. The *beden* registers were also used to levy additional taxes.[20]

Apart from the taxes mentioned above, such as the excises, the stamp duties, the land taxes and the *beden*, two other sources of ordinary revenue existed: the domains of Brabant and the income from church property in the area. One of the major domanial revenues was the *houtschat*, a duty of 16 per cent upon felled trees. Another revenue source was a toll: the *Groote Brabantse Swijgende Landtol* in Bergen op Zoom, which taxed the major trade routes between southern Brabant and the Republic. It had belonged to the Republic since 1630.[21] Other tolls were imposed with the acquisition of the Upper Quarter, on the rivers Rhine, Meuse and

Waal, in 1640.[22]

In all, the regular part of the generality lands yielded almost 900,000 guilders. Table 4.1 shows a breakdown of the ordinary revenue in the 1640s. The first column represents averages over the five years 1637–1642; the second column gives data from 1648, after the conclusion of the peace. Comparing columns 1 and 2, the revenue declined 6 per cent, despite the inclusion of the newly incorporated areas in Flanders. Apart from the domains, church property and the district of Wedde and Westerwolde the yield from all other cities and their districts decreased.

Table 4.1 *Annual ordinary revenue from the generality lands, 1637–1648*

region or city	*averages 1637–1642*	*1648*
Brabant		
Den Bosch city	162,932	134,479*
Breda city	48,228	46,659
Bergen city	57,336	58,739*
Steenbergen	17,989	13,765
Den Bosch District	219,468	203,953
Breda District	134,720	54,000
Bergen District	23,177	18,164
Grave, Ravestein, Cuyk District	49,603	29,460
Flanders		
Sluis	117,301	90,599
Hulst	(Sp.)	36,992
Sas van Gent	(Sp.)	25,483
Overmaze		
Maastricht and Overmaze District		47,623
Groningen		
Wedde and Westerwolde	26,731	33,487
Other ordinary revenue		
Domains	12,237	17,117
Church property	26,832	33,032
total	896,554	843,552

Source: RAZH Jacob Cats 29 and 77; Van Slingelandt 247; ARA CoS 2517, 2423. *Den Bosch 1648: including the land tax of Grave (about 3,000); *Bergen 1648: including the land tax of Steenbergen (about 1,000).

In proportion, the cities contributed less as the war went on: cities had provided 55 per cent of the generality land revenue in 1639, 38 per cent in 1648 and 22 per cent in 1657.[23] In part, this tendency was due to a general decline in trade. However, with the cessation of enemy activities, the power of the cities over their districts probably increased too, resulting in a shift of more of the burden onto rural dwellers. In addition, some cities had obtained favourable regulations as to taxation. After Den Bosch had been forced to introduce new taxes (mainly stamp duties) in 1635, Breda was more careful. Its capitulation treaty of 1637 promised exemption from land taxes and *beden*, while the rates were not to be increased in the future at all. The city, as a result, was relatively undertaxed.[24]

Apart from the ordinary revenue, there was a more irregular element, consisting of contributions, confiscations and extraordinary *beden*. Confiscations resulted from the declaration of war and were mostly levied in Flanders. As for contributions, an army could levy them on any community in war-stricken areas unable to resist its demands. The Council of State used the local army detachments or special troops, mostly cavalry, to certify and extend the amount of a contribution. In the event of defaults in paying the contribution, some inhabitants might be taken hostage.[25] The rural population feared armies and, for that reason, were quite willing to enter into negotiations with the enemy over monetary payments.

The extraordinary funds yielded in 1637–1642 on average about half the proportion of the regular revenues, about 400,000 guilders. Table 4.2 shows a breakdown of the different areas paying contributions and confiscations. On the other hand, contributions had to be paid on the republican side too. When troops of Hendrick van den Bergh, the Stadhouder for Gelderland of the government in Brussels, invaded the Betuwe in Gelderland, farmers in 't Gooi, to the southeast of Amsterdam, tried to get in touch with him to talk about contributions. The Estates General opposed these attempts and imposed fines to the amount of four times the payments. Nevertheless, during 1620–1650 considerable parts of the Republic paid contributions to Spain: Drenthe, Overijssel and Gelderland (Betuwe in particular), the generality lands, such as the districts of Den Bosch and Cuyk, and also inhabitants of villages in southern Holland and Zeeland during 1637 to 1640.[26]

In all, the revenue from the generality lands consisted of the items presented in Table 4.3. Around 1641 land taxes contributed only a small part of the whole. The sum of taxes upon consumption was highest: 58.5 per cent, although rates of excise duties were low as compared with those in the United Provinces.[27] War exactions

Table 4.2 *Extraordinary annual revenue from generality lands and conquered areas, 1637–1642*

region	*annual average 1637–1642*
Brabant	
Quarter Antwerp	114,535
Other Flemish Quarters	44,004
Walloon Quarters	23,529
Flanders	
Districts	81,910
Limbourg	
Maastricht/Overmaze	78,977
Gelderland	
Upper Quarter	57,992
total	400,947 guilders

Source: RAZH Jacob Cats 29 and 77; Van Slingelandt 247.

(contributions and confiscations) amounted to 33.4 per cent. This element disappeared totally when peace was signed with Spain. Revenue from domains and church property was limited to only 3.2 per cent. And as the expenses in the generality lands (fortifications, the army, local administration) amounted to 969,701 guilders in 1642 few generality lands' funds were transmitted to the central government at all.[28]

Table 4.3 *Annual revenue, generality lands, c. 1641, by item, percentages*

item	%
land and house taxes	4.7
excises and stamp duties	58.5
domains	1.0
church property	2.2
contributions	30.5
confiscations	2.9
total	100.0
[in guilders: 1,197,600]	

Source: see tables 4.1 and 4.2.

Pressure to impose heavier taxes came typically from the maritime provinces of Holland and Zeeland. After a request from Brabant for the existing burden to be reduced, representatives of the Estates of Holland even declared in the Estates General in 1649:

That Hollanders were ready to move to Brabant, if they could live there more cheaply, and that Staats-Brabant had to reconcile itself to the wishes of its present overlord and pay the same duties as those levied in Holland.[29]

Duties in Holland, at that point, were much heavier compared with those of the generality lands. Yet the Council of State tended to protect the newly acquired territories against being overburdened and preferred lower rates. The councillors seem to have consciously undertaxed the generality lands in order to prevent tax revolts. They also feared outmigration to the Spanish-controlled territories. The continuation of traditional taxes or redemptions was preferred, and duties hardly increased.[30]

As a result of the peace, the Republic lost about 700,000 guilders in contributions, passports and other wartime income. The loss was partly compensated in 1648 by a levy of the Spanish portion of the *beden* and excises which had previously gone to the Spanish Crown as well. Yet a general downward trend was noticed. Kappelhof analysed the tax revenues of several villages (including The Hague taxes, Spanish taxes and local duties); all were tending to decline between 1630 and 1650. Part of the loss must be ascribed to economic stagnation. Population did not increase and war had disturbed agriculture seriously. Yet there is also a general tendency of taxes to decline, if levied at similar rates. The Council of State expressed the expectation, in 1648, that the revenue from the generality lands would not increase much either. Imposition of taxes was not expected to yield more than redemptions or contributions, and the annual revenue from excises tended to decline altogether.[31] Thus even with the conquered areas little opportunity existed for The Hague to increase its independent power *vis-à-vis* local and provincial bureaucracies.

The navy funds: customs

The costs of the navy were officially controlled by the Estates General through the Chamber of Accounts. From the start, it had been decided that the expenses of the admiralties had to be defrayed by the revenue of the customs directly. Originally, no 'provincial' revenue (taxes) was to be used for warfare at sea. The customs were collected by the convoy masters; this constituted the ordinary part of the revenue. In addition, extraordinary customs were imposed, and some extraordinary funds existed, such as prizes, confiscations, and the sale of vessels. Most of the latter extraordinary items were administered by an auction master. Furthermore, extraordinary duties could be levied as well. Centralized tolls were few. A major toll existed in Brabant upon trade routes to the south, and another at Rheinberg, in present-day Germany, which was lost in 1606 but recaptured in 1632.[32]

The customs were levied under the name of *convooyen* and *licenten*. The convoys originated in duties levied by cities, for which, in return, the fishermen and merchants had been protected by special escorting warships. Licences originated in Zeeland. They meant trade with the enemy, and hence with Spain, allies of Spain and regions controlled by the Spanish crown. This was at first not allowed, but as smuggling continued unabated it was found that significant revenue could be had from placing heavy duties upon such trade. Licences often brought in twice as much as convoys. When the province of Holland copied the Zeeland licences in 1573, the yield from this source alone was 850,000 guilders. The cost of a licence came to vary according to the state of hostilities. It could be so burdensome that trade was actually inhibited. The highest licence rates applied to trade with the regions of Breda and Den Bosch (from 1625 till 1637 and 1629 respectively) as the enemy in this area posed the greatest threat to the Union. Second came trade with Spain itself. Third came customs over the Meuse, Rhine, Waal and IJssel; followed by trade to Boulogne and Calais. The lowest licences were for goods to and from Emden, Bremen and Oldenburg in Germany.[33]

Duties, of course, were the cause of disagreements. Zeeland, jealous of Holland ships taking over parts of the trade with the Southern Netherlands, levied the remunerative licence duty upon those ships passing through its waters, whether or not the tax had been paid already in some Holland port. Upon Holland's vigorous protests, a compromise was found in 1590 under the name of the Half Licence Treaty. Henceforth the ships trading with the enemy and passing Zeeland waters but bound for or coming from a non-Zeeland port paid half the duty in Zeeland and half the duty in the home port. The customs duty was called *halve licent*. The admiralty of Rotterdam installed three collectors in Zeeland (in Middelburg, Veere, and Arnemuiden), whereas the Middelburg board had its half-licence custom officers in Rotterdam, Amsterdam, Dordrecht, and Gorinchem (and Den Bosch after 1629). It was a solution which increased the costs of collection, although one might argue that control over illegal shipments increased too.

However, the Treaty of 1590 was violated on a huge scale by both sides. Moreover, Holland started to trade directly with the Flemish ports, trying to avoid Zeeland waters and the Zeeland half-licence officers. Zeeland was furious, and began to impose heavy duties upon 'eastern' goods which were typically Holland articles of trade. The conflict threatened to escalate. Queen Elizabeth of England, who had little interest in a divided Republic, offered mediation. But calm returned when the Treaty of 1590 was renewed in 1597.[34]

Provincial interests clashed again over other customs regulations. Arms, ammunition, horses, salt and grain were generally listed as prohibited exports, but articles like cheese, fish and other edibles might be added. Holland preferred in general freedom to export butter and cheese (which was opposed by Zeeland), whereas Zeeland carried on trade with Flemish ports (to the dismay of Holland). And despite prohibitions, Amsterdam allowed licences (i.e. trade with the enemy) in arms and ammunition. Dutch merchants had not bothered much about wartime regulations, and some had even entered the field of provisioning the Spanish crown with war materials. The Amsterdam merchant Lopo Ramirez sent munitions and grain to Cadiz and Naples. Another ship was detected in Enkhuizen with war supplies, sailing for Portugal but registered for Marseilles. The Bickers themselves, a powerful burgomaster family of Amsterdam, were involved in hiring ships destined for the Spanish viceroy of Naples. Several of these revelations caused a prolonged row in the Estates General in the later 1630s. Even France complained about the attitude of Dutch merchants, yet the city refused access to investigative committees of the central government and nothing really happened.[35]

Much anger was aroused again in July 1648. The admiralty of Middelburg acted prematurely upon the end of the war. Bills were posted in cities such as Antwerp, Ghent, Bruges, and Lille, announcing that, with the prospect of a future decline in the rates, the board was prepared to offer a reduction of one-third in the customs if shipping was directed through the Middelburg ports. However, the admiralty was forced by The Hague to rescind the regulation.[36]

Formally, the Estates General regulated all increases and decreases in customs rates. A general increase in 1584 was opposed by merchant communities in Enkhuizen and Amsterdam. The first major rise dated from 1603 after the admiralties had experienced several mutinies and financial needs were extremely pressing. Henceforth, duties were levied at approximately 5 per cent. These tariffs remained up to 1609, when they were lowered to 3 or 3.5 per cent. In 1621 tariffs returned to the pre-1609 level. These were maintained up to 1651, when a decrease followed in the wake of the peace, although the First Anglo-Dutch War resulted in an increase again.[37]

The yield of the customs showed a general, gradual increase. Figure 4.1 represents these figures, partly estimated, with three-year moving averages. The overall decline in the first years of the seventeenth century coincided with a lower number of registered Dutch ships passing through the Sound. Of major impact was the disruption of trade with Spain and the Southern Netherlands in 1598–1599. Moreover, all licences (i.e. approvals of trade with the enemy) were temporarily abolished, in order to bring about disorder among the enemies' troops.[38]

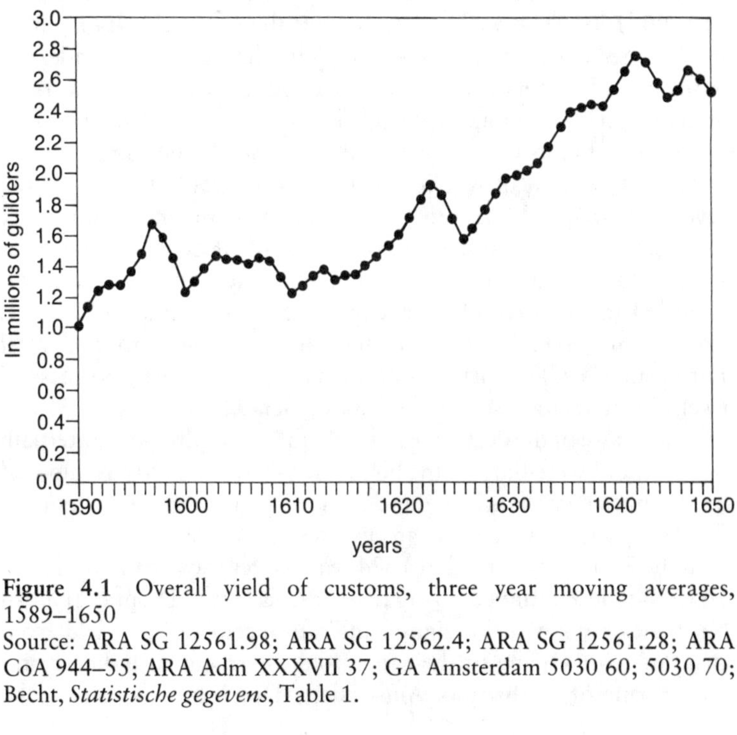

Figure 4.1 Overall yield of customs, three year moving averages, 1589–1650
Source: ARA SG 12561.98; ARA SG 12562.4; ARA SG 12561.28; ARA CoA 944–55; ARA Adm XXXVII 37; GA Amsterdam 5030 60; 5030 70; Becht, *Statistische gegevens*, Table 1.

Yet during the Truce of 1609–1621, the Dutch European carrying trade increased again. The demand for salt, herring and wine in the Baltic was relatively constant, whereas on the other hand the Mediterranean needed Baltic grain, providing the Dutch trade through the Sound with a certain security. Trade routes to England, France, and the Levant were extended. The revenue from the customs was stabilized. As compared with the 1590s, with an average annual revenue of 1.2 million, the 1620s showed yields per year of 1.8 million guilders, increasing to 2.6 million on average in the 1640s.

Amsterdam, more than any other admiralty, gained throughout this period (see Fig. 4.2). Rotterdam and Middelburg did not share in this upward trend to the same degree. Their trade in French wines suffered from the reappearance of Iberian wines in their markets and from the lowering of duties upon German wines. Dordrecht, however, which came under the admiralty of Rotterdam, profited from a revival of traffic on the inland rivers of Rhine and Meuse.[39]

Zeeland, in fact, never recovered its former position after the blow of 1600–1601. The policy of sealing off the river Scheldt may have been a useful temporary expedient, but the decline of trade and industry in Flanders and Antwerp caused an overall downturn of activities in the region. A partial revival was noted in the years 1635–1650 but its revenue was to decline shortly thereafter.[40]

The resumption of war in 1621 was favourable for the overall revenue through the rise in tariffs. But increases in revenue were much lower than might be expected. A sudden decrease of the yield after 1624 coincided with a recession in the Netherlands. A low was recorded in 1629–1630. The war between England and France, starting in 1626, hindered Dutch ships *en route* to the West European coast. Dunkirk privateers made sailing a risky business. A river blockade, imposed by the Estates General in 1625–1629, was another cause of the decline. Above all, the admiralties of Rotterdam and Zeeland were hurt by the blockade. Trade restrictions imposed by Spain, as part of its economic warfare, contributed even more to the disappointing revenue from customs in the later 1620s.[41]

In the Republic the level of 1624 was not reached again until after 1630. Trade continued to increase thenceforth. Despite Spanish blockades, and with no significant rate increases, the yield from customs rose. Owing to their manifold international linkages and the backing of the Bank of Amsterdam, Dutch traders came to be

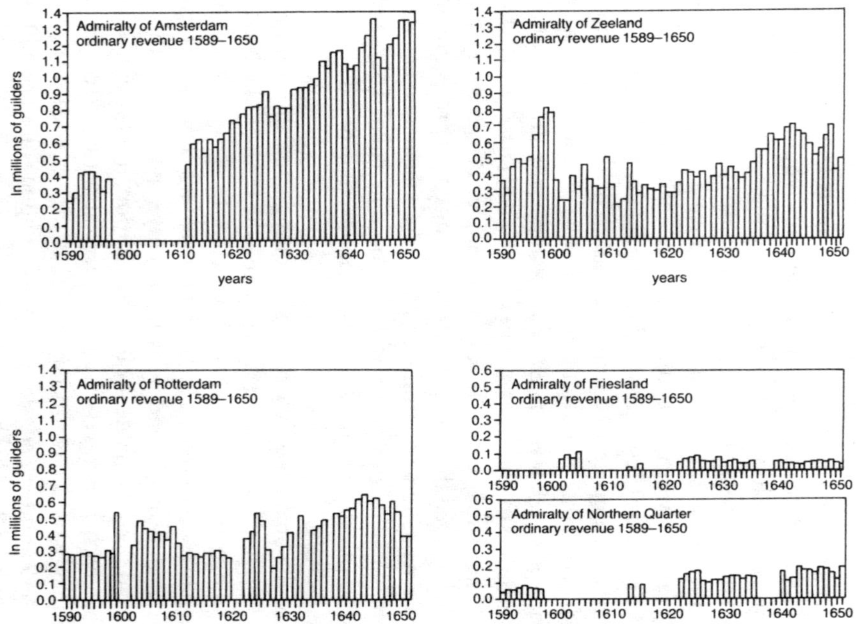

Figure 4.2 Yield of the admiralties of Amsterdam, Zeeland, Rotterdam, Northern Quarter and Friesland, 1589–1650
Source: Graph 4.1

privileged in several parts of the world. Through treaties with Sweden (1640 and 1645) the Dutch paid similar customs rates to Swedish nationals. At times, such agreements were signed with a number of Hanseatic cities too. The Dutch were extremely successful in the East Indies. And at least up to 1642, relations with France were quite cordial. Then, after the death of Cardinal Richelieu, the French started to impose duties on Dutch trade.[42]

The highest yield from customs occurred in 1640–1650. All admiralties gained, except for a short fall in 1644–1645, the time of the Sound crisis. After 1650, only Amsterdam would continue to enjoy rising yields. All other admiralties saw their revenue decline, and stay on that course into the eighteenth century.[43]

Next to the customs, extraordinary duties were levied. A general temporary *lastgeld* was imposed in 1599. In Zeeland, *schipgeld* or *passagegeld* existed. These taxes had to be paid upon the cargo as a whole without taking into account the nature of the goods transported. Most of the extraordinary levies were connected with specific semi-private convoy fleets. For example, the vessels sailing through the Straits of Gibraltar had to pay a *consulaatrecht* in 1615, to pay for the Dutch envoy in Constantinople. Privateers in the Mediterranean urged the Dutch again to organize new protection in the area, for which an additional *lastgeld* of sixteen stuyvers was imposed in 1623. Similar duties were imposed in 1625, 1627 and 1630, and in other years. In addition, ships were ordered to arm themselves heavily.[44]

Owing to the Spanish policy of concentrating upon the northern naval base at Dunkirk, privateers hampered the trade in the North Sea more and more. A duty was imposed in 1631 on the whale fisheries to pay for the escorts. In 1632 a *lastgeld* was imposed at ten stuyvers upon outward-bound ships and twenty stuyvers upon those inward-bound per 100 guilders value. In addition, it was stipulated in 1641 that each Dutch vessel had to carry at least twelve guns, otherwise they would have to pay more, as they needed a strong escort. In 1645 another *veilgeld* was imposed upon ships bound for the North and the Baltic. The revenue was used for the special fleet sent to Denmark to enforce the lowering of the duties. A new temporary duty on the Dutch trade was imposed in 1643, consisting of 0.5 per cent upon outgoing and 1 per cent upon incoming vessels. In return, the North Sea was patrolled by special warships of the semi-private navies.[45]

That these extraordinary duties could amount to a significant source of revenue was shown by some surviving accounts of the *lastgeld* in the 1640s. In 1645, a year of extreme pressure with regard to the Sound crisis, up to 1,211,360 was paid in Amsterdam as *lastgeld* for Mediterranean trade, *veilgeld* (Sound trade), *lastgeld* for the north and *lastgeld* for the west. This was almost the same amount as was paid to the ordinary *convooien* and *licenten*.[46] A positive side effect of such duties was increased security, and thus a lowering of insurance rates, which relieved somewhat the burden upon the skippers.

In all, even excluding the extraordinary duties, the European carrying trade contributed most to the customs. Convoys from the colonial trade were only of marginal importance for the admiralties. The East and West India Companies had separate regulations. Over a period of twenty-two years the VOC would be charged the lower pre-1603 rates. The WIC was exempted from the customs for a period of eight years. The companies did not have to pay several extraordinary levies, such as the *lastgeld*. No province or city was allowed to demand provincial or local customs. Moreover, the companies could pay all their duties in one lump sum, as a kind of redemption, instead of being searched and assessed by the customs officers of the admiralties each time a shipment arrived. The WIC collected certain funds as well, such as a duty of 16 per cent upon the cargo of all private ships trading in the West Indies.[47]

Apart from customs, revenue for the admiralties came from prizes, confiscations, fines, goods sold, and from passports as well as certain market duties, like the horse market in Rotterdam. Prizes were a rich source for the Zeeland admiralty in particular. In 1606, no fewer than 130 privateers sailed from the admiralties. They showed no mercy for anyone in particular: not merely the 'enemy' but French, English, Danish, and German ships were attacked. Their goods were seized, their sailors captured, to be ransomed, or killed. This situation, though, could not continue for long. In the same year, protests from England and France forced the Estates General to curb the privateers' activities. Many of the former *kaapbrieven* were withdrawn, while a caution of 20,000 guilders was required for any new *kaapbrief*. The result was another decline in the official receipts of the admiralties. Moreover, many skippers continued with piracy on their own account. Some moved to the Mediterranean, where they joined the Algerian privateers. Obviously, the Dutch state itself had increased the hazards at sea, about which its merchants would complain so often in later decades.[48]

Yet Dutch privateering remained an official expedient against the enemy. The richest prize in Dutch history was the capture of the Spanish silver convoy in 1628 by Piet Heyn, the admiral of the combined admiralties–WIC fleet. It brought the Dutch state almost 12 million guilders in bullion and was much welcomed in Holland. However, Piet Heyn's was one of the few successful expeditions among a majority of failures. At the same time, many Dutch vessels were lost to privateers of other nations. And prizes caused disappointment among the sailors, who expected some share. In 1629 the sailors of the WIC, disappointed that their position had not improved despite Piet Heyn's prize, rioted in Amsterdam. Nevertheless, the Estates General stimulated privateering through the offer of premiums to the captains. However, the requisite funds were not easy to find, and in 1636 the Zeeland admiralty claimed 313,000 guilders in premiums, of which only one-third was paid.[49]

The WIC, VOC, admiralties and Estates General were not the only ones seeking profits from prizes at sea. Semi-official fleets were built for this purpose too. In Middelburg the Commercie Compagnie coordinating the activities of the city's most prominent merchants set up a *Directie* euphemistically called *ghedestineert tot veylinghe van de zee*, for the security of the seas. It started out with eight ships and sailed the seas in search of booty for a period of three years.[50]

The net result of privateering is hard to calculate. Some booty came in, yet many Republic ships were lost in turn to enemy retaliation. It did increase the risks at sea, and as a result insurance rates tended to rise. Privateering was yet another expedient which increased the power of local elites at the expense of the central state.

The dead weight of the admiralties

All those admiralties and semi-private boards were extremely hard for the central bureaucrats in The Hague to control, especially their superiors in the Estates General. Budgets were rare, as no recurrent *Staat van Oorlog* existed, as it did for the army. The accounts of the admiralties continued to come in years overdue, the admiralty of Zeeland being most delinquent of all.[51] And when they were checked, the fines, prizes, and confiscations were regularly found to be not fully accounted for. Crews were often well below their official complement on paper. Some ships were never fitted out at all. Fraud was also possible by continuing the administration of interest payments on loans that had been repaid years before. As many creditors were ready to accept a smaller sum, such as 10 or 20 per cent or less, instead of waiting two or more years, discounts on admiralty assignments to pay were frequent yet never reported in the books. These irregularities went on unabated.

The most important person within the navy boards, upon whom the trust of the generality rested, was the Advocaat-Fiscaal. Yet he often sided with local interests, as in the scandal that was revealed in 1624–1626 in Rotterdam. The Advocaat-Fiscaal and councillors were found to have embezzled 175,000 guilders of the revenue from fines and compensations. Heavy fines were imposed, and the councillors were imprisoned or barred from office.[52]

But during the lawsuit the generality rulers in The Hague became rather embarrassed by the whole undertaking. The councillors were called thieves by everyone. Even the judges were ridiculed because one councillor fled to Delft. Most alarming of all was the mob that gathered before the town hall and complained about the bad payments by the admiralty. It frightened not only the Rotterdam magistrate but the government in The Hague as well. A contemporary wrote that state authority was 'thrown under the feet of the common man'. Moreover, convictions availed little. One of the new councillors, Johan van der Duyn, was soon accused of embezzling funds again.[53]

After the major suit against the councillors of the Rotterdam admiralty it was proposed to enforce a new oath upon all the sitting councillors. A fierce protest followed, especially in Amsterdam, denouncing the mistrust in their administration, and nothing was done. And another time, in 1635, when the city of Amsterdam thought it useful to increase its control over the admiralty, sailors – allegedly incited by the council – started a violent demonstration before the town hall. The plans were put off.[54]

In the meantime, fraud in the perception of customs was obvious to everyone. However, local authorities were reluctant to impose close supervision, as attracting cargoes through unofficial discounts in rates was extremely profitable for the port, increasing trade in the area. Local socio-economic conditions thus appeared to override central rules. For example, Convoy Master Wiarda in Groningen undercharged customs on butter, cheese, and horses in the 1640s.

The latter duty was contested and problematic, especially in Groningen, where so many farmers were engaged in horse breeding. Upon examination, all other convoy masters of the admiralty in Friesland were found to have allowed evasion of the horse duty too, asking six to nine guilders instead of eighteen. Passports were another highly 'irregular' item: only half or even a quarter of the price was needed in the northernmost provinces.[55]

Frauds continued despite the five to six commissioners general for the customs of the central government. At times, local discontent won over central decisions in this regard. In 1626, Amsterdam did not agree to the appointment of Tapkes as commissioner general. In the middle of the night he was lifted from his bed and told to leave the city within 24 hours.[56]

Tax farming might be one of the possible measures to combat fraud more effectively. In 1596 a plan to farm out one-third of the taxes was proposed. The idea surfaced again, in particular when admiralties needed additional subsidies from the inland provinces. Holland and Zeeland never liked the idea. Nevertheless, it was finally adopted in 1625, and the customs were farmed out for a quart. A tax farmer was to control the collection in return for one quart of the expected revenue, for which he was to receive a quarter of the actual revenue. Three-quarters of the revenue thus remained for the admiralties. The lease was to last a year, starting in September.[57]

The whole experiment was quite wide-ranging: such a large tax farm, over the whole territory of the Republic, had never existed before. The generality salt tax, by comparison, was divided into five or six districts. The revenue from the farms was quite disappointing, though. Instead of rising, the sums actually declined at first, from 478,000 guilders in 1625/1626 to 361,000 in 1627/1628. Thereafter they increased, and ranged between 654,000 and 745,000 in the years 1631 to 1639.[58] The sums corresponded roughly with customs revenue of the preceding year, which constituted the base for the tax farmers' bids.

Yet in the later 1630s the opposition from the Estates of Holland against the tax farm in the customs became more outspoken. The tax farm was dominated by a non-Holland community: a Frisian syndicate. Each year, there was a main farmer, who was backed by participants who provided the capital and stood for caution. Farmers became participants and vice versa. The main farmers were, for example, in 1631/1632 Johan Heerma, in 1633/1634 Ate Trepkes from Bolsward, in 1635/1636 and 1636/1637 Yde Amis Jellema, in 1637/1638 Jan Claesz Vollenhooff, the former burgomaster of Workum, and in 1638/1639 Ulpianus Uytenbroeck.[59] The tax famers were obviously outsiders to the navy board cliques.

Moreover, the tax farmers showed no deference towards the VOC. Johan Heerma reported that in 1634 the East India Company had evaded the customs payment for twelve ships. Enormous sums were involved: the East India Company should have paid 312,193 guilders, instead it had paid only 80,000. In 1638 problems arose once more between the tax farmer and the VOC. This time the accounts of 1625/1626 and 1626/1627 were at stake.[60]

The tax farming of customs was brought to an end because of opposition by Amsterdam. The suits against the VOC were not the only issue at stake. There had been plans to set up a central Chamber of Assurance to organize defence at sea (convoys) instead of the admiralties. There had been plans to transfer the command of the special fleet against the Dunkirk pirates to a central board in Hellevoetsluis, and a temporary management had been set up there already. There had been murmurs in the Estates General about Dutch merchants' hiring of ships to Spain. Even the Amsterdam burgomasters Abraham Boom, Andries Bicker and Jan Cornelisz Geelvinck had had their ships built and sent out to Cadiz or ports in the Mediterranean. The Council of State declared that those who hired ships out to Spain were to be brought to trial.[61] The farming of the customs was just another issue in this field. The combined action of the admiralty of Amsterdam with the city government was aimed at minimizing central control over the navy and trade regulations.

In November 1636 the city council refused to approve the tax farm of customs as demanded by the Provincial Estates. Complaints were voiced about the alleged profits of the tax farmer doing the country more harm than good. But as other Holland cities agreed to the tax farm, Amsterdam was outvoted. Yet the next year the Estates of Holland rallied behind the Amsterdam point of view and declared in August 1637 that they were no longer prepared to approve the farming. This time, Holland was outvoted in the Estates General, and the central authorities continued to farm the tax. The Amsterdam city council denied the right to impose the farm, as there had been no consent, referring to the rule that in taxation none of the constituent members could be outvoted according to the constituency of the generality.[62]

Three councillors of the navy board, who had assisted in the sale of the tax farm, were sued by the city: Mr Cornelis Jongbloed (representative from Gelderland), *Jonkhee*r Ernst van Reede, *Heer* van Vuurse (representing Utrecht) and Johan van der Veer (councillor for Overijssel). They were typically the non-Holland members of the navy board. The next year, the Estates General declared the three admiralty councillors free of the charge by the city of Amsterdam, because they stood on the oath of the generality and not on an oath of the city. The provinces of Holland and Zeeland supported Amsterdam, but all other provinces were against Amsterdam's obstinate behaviour. Yet even a letter from the Stadhouder himself was of no avail.[63]

On 8 February 1639 a weighty delegation of the Estates General arrived in Amsterdam to request moderation and approval for the farming out of the customs. The burgomasters refused to convoke the city council to welcome the delegation. Openly, the central government lost face. A week later Amsterdam declared the delegation an intrusion on the sovereignty of the city and of the Estates of Holland. The central delegates were furious. However, Amsterdam got its way, and tax farming disappeared from the agenda.[64] Thus, admiralty revenue remained in the hands of those who had to spend it and provided the navy councillors with strong leverage on local power.

The limitation of choices at the centre

The shifting of the burden to central sources of revenue was eased by assigning specific revenues to specific expenses. Customs should pay for the navy, the taxes in the generality lands (conquered areas) for the fortifications and government there, and the costs of central government were preferably to be paid by central revenues alone.[65] Yet, in all, the central options of the Dutch state provided little opportunity for autonomous power, as they were difficult to exploit and expand. The salt tax, the only centralized excise levied for any length of time, seemed to be declining in revenue. Neither did the yield from the generality stamp duty increase, nor did passports contribute much to 'The Hague'.

Moreover, the shift of navy costs to the customs entailed a major loss of central control. The seperate establishments of the admiralties enhanced the use of the navy board for local purposes. Also, increases in the rates of customs were limited and mostly temporary, such as the extraordinary *lastgelden*. Dutch rates, apparently, never exceeded 5 per cent and were generally levied at about 3 per cent in the later seventeenth and eighteenth centuries. By comparison, England could increase its rates from 5 even to 25 per cent in the 1690s, yielding significant revenue, almost as much as the excises in the country.[66] What mattered in this respect was the higher degree of centralization in England, and the fact that in England customs were largely shifted onto foreigners (among them Hollanders). In Holland, on the contrary, most shipping remained in Dutch hands, hence customs had to be paid by the Republic's trade itself. As much trade was oriented toward re-exports as well, a double burden was feared. In addition, Amsterdam was anxious to maintain its position as an international staple and the merchants involved had a large say in the Dutch body politic. They preferred low customs rates in order to be able to compete with foreign ports.

Nevertheless, trade seemed to expand. Yet comparing the figures for Dutch trade presented in Chapter One (300 million guilders annually on average), the 2.4 million customs receipts were hopelessly low. It is questionable whether higher rates would have been effective at all, in view of the frauds, when such measures would have encountered considerable opposition from the governing cliques of the five admiralties.

Likewise, the burden in the generality lands remained light. Its yield even tended to decline. Traditional methods such as redemption and contributions were widely used. This was necessitated by the fact that for the greater part of the Eighty Years' War Dutch sovereignty was not recognized in many of the rural districts and no regular taxes could be imposed at all. Adding to the whole was the fragmented structure of 'The Hague' itself, in which – in particular – the Council of State stood against the influential Estates of Holland. The council tried to manage 'its' territories carefully, preventing a political loss through tax revolts or out-migration. Moreover, the end of the war preluded another loss of revenue, owing to the disappearance of contributions and confiscations.

Dutch state makers, then, were less successful than others (for example, Sweden) in having conquered territories to pay for war costs. Neither did they have at their disposal means of exploiting them, as Spain had. Indirectly, some colonial revenue was diverted through customs, but the VOC and WIC had been privileged in respect of convoy rates. No domanial revenue supported centralist policies. Dutch 'central' or 'autonomous' options were, by European standards, highly restricted. Moreover, if there was some germ of centralizing power, of starting a 'monopolization of taxation' process *à la* Elias, it was constrained from all sides. Central revenue (like the salt tax) even declined in proportion to the other means. As a result, the Dutch state became even more dependent upon the provinces, increasing the emphasis on the middle level of government. Several 'core' functions of the state were safely provided for by shifting such items to the quota of Holland. This province not only furnished most of the funds, but also paid almost all the expenses of the central government, the debt charges, and the army provisions. The basis of Holland's position therein was a highly developed taxation system, as will be described in the next chapter.

Notes

1 Aylmer, *Rebellion or revolution*, 6; Jean Meyer, 'Finances, politique et économies dans la seconde moitié du XVIIe siècle', *Annales ESC* 34, 1979, 359; Ralph Davis, 'The rise of protection in England, 1689–1786', *Economic History Review* 19, 1966, 307.

2 Antoni Maczak, 'Executio bonorum and reduktion. Two essays in solutions of the domain–state dilemma', *The Swedish Riksdag in an International Perspective*, ed. N. Stjernquist, Stockholm, 1989; Kersten Krüger, 'Public finance and modernisation: the change from domain state to tax state in Hesse in the sixteenth and seventeenth centuries. A case study', *Wealth and taxation in Central Europe: the history and sociology of public finance*, ed. Peter-Christian Witt, Leamington Spa, 1987, 59; Roberts, *Swedish imperial experience*, 49; E. Ladewig Pedersen, 'War, finance and the growth of absolutism. Some aspects of the European integration of 17th century Denmark', *Europe and Scandinavia: aspects of the process of integration in the 17th century*, ed. G. Rystad, Lund, 1983, 34.

3 Roland Mousnier, *Les institutions de la France sous la monarchie absolue* I, Paris, 1974, 565; Paltiel Katzenelsohn, *Zur Entwicklungsgeschichte des Finanzen Russlands, 1560–1796*, Berlin, 1913, 65; Robert Ashton, *The city and the court 1603–1643*, Cambridge, 1979, 146.

4 Göran Rystad, 'The Estates of the realm, the monarchy, and the empire', *The Riksdag. A history of the Swedish Parliament*, ed. Michael F. Metcalf, Stockholm, 1987, 63, 83, 103; Roberts, *Swedish imperial experience*, 53.

5 Stradling, *Europe and decline of Spain*, 38; Thomas Crump, *The*

phenomenon of money, London, 1981, 139; Dessert, *Argent, pouvoir*, 30; Pierre Petit, *La dette publique de la Russie*, Poitiers, 1912, 6.

6 H. Enno van Gelder, *De Nederlandse munten*, Utrecht, 1965, 90–2, 116–17; Van Dillen, *Rijkdom en regenten*, 355–7.

7 Van Dillen, *Rijkdom en regenten*, 355, 362; on the debates: *Resolutiën* SG 31 January, 26 April, 1 May, 24 July 1619, 18 January, 9 July, 23 May 1622. Another placard of 1645 was to reduce the number of tolerated coins still further. Van Gelder, *De Nederlandse munten*, 112.

8 M. Baelde, 'Financiële politiek en domaniale evolutie in de Nederlanden onder Karel V en Filips II (1530–1560)', *Tijdschrift voor Geschiedenis* 76, 1963, 21, 30.

9 Van Deursen, 'Raad van State onder Republiek', 83.

10 The domains of the Stadhouder, by comparison, yielded about five million in 1645, much more than the revenue of the central government. Yet domains did not become generality revenue. On the figures from Stadhouders' domains: ARA CoS 2109 I.

11 *Groot Placaet Boeck* I, 1825, 1830, 2120, 2188; II, 2163, 2164, 2167, 2169; III, 866.

12 *Groot Placaet Boeck* I, 2189.; Marjolein 't Hart, 'Salt trade and salt tax in the Netherlands', *Le roi, le marchand et le sel*, ed. J.-Cl. Hocquet, Villeneuve d'Ascq, 1987.

13 RAZH FH 826.

14 ARA CoS 2111 I–II.

15 ARA CoA 9: 2 May 1648.

16 See for the region of the Overmaze the map in M. van Dijk, 'Het probleem der verpandingen in de bank Heerlen, 1626–1647', *De Maasgouw. Tijdschrift voor Limburgse Geschiedenis en Oudheidkunde* 107, 1988, 21–2.

17 Those disagreeing with the new rule were allowed two years for proper emigration. B.C.M. Jacobs, 'Eene saecke gehorende tot de domestique huijshoudinge ende politie. Stadsaccijnzen in 's-Hertogenbosch in hertogelijke en staatse tijd', *Fiscaliteit in Nederland*, ed. J.Th. de Smidt *et al.*, Zutphen, 1987, 68; J.J. Roovers, *De plaatselijke belastingen en financiën in den loop der tijden. Een historische schets*, Alphen aan de Rijn, 1932, 31; RAZH Van Slingelandt 251; Van Deursen, 'Raad van State onder Republiek', 86.

18 E.H. Korvezee, 'Belastingen in Noord-Brabant voor 1648', *Varia Historica Brabantica* 4, 1975, 115, 124; A.C.M. Kappelhof, *De belastingheffing in de Meierij van Den Bosch gedurende de Generaliteitsperiode (1648–1730)*, Tilburg, 1986, 79, 381.

19 *Groot Placaet Boeck* I, 1526.

20 Korvezee, 'Belastingen in Noord-Brabant', 103; Kappelhof, *Belastingheffing Meierij*, 85.

21 *Groot Placaet Boeck* I, 1156, 1558; ARA CoA 94: 13 January 1643.

22 *Groot Placaet Boeck* I, 1580.

23 Kappelhof, *Belastingheffing Meierij*, 286.

24 Jacobs, 'Een saecke gehorende', 70; A.C.M. Kappelhof, 'Fiscale bevoordeling van Breda ten tijde van de Republiek', *Jaarboek De*

Oranjeboom 40, 1987, 79.

25 Van Slingelandt, *Geschriften* III, 189, 191, 197; Kappelhof, *Belastingheffing Meierij*, 316. See also Gutmann, *War and rural life*, 41–5.

26 *Groot Placaet Boeck* I, 1526; Van Deursen, *Kopergeld* III, 86; *Resolutiën* SG 15 September 1621, 10 December 1622, 9 May 1623; ARA CoA 94: 6 May 1625.

27 See also analysis by Kappelhof, *Belastingheffing Meierij*, 396 ff.

28 ARA COS 2157, RAZH Van Slingelandt 247, Jacob Cats 77.

29 Quoted by Engels, *Belastingen*, 135.

30 As compared to Spanish-controlled territory, the 'Dutch' areas were taxed much more heavily. Gosses, *Staatkundige Geschiedenis*, 495; Kappelhof, *Belastingheffing Meierij*, 30, 81, 396 ff.; see also Gutmann, *War and rural life*, 15.

31 Kappelhof, *Belastingheffing Meierij*, 287, 381, 497; ARA CoS 2157.

32 ARA CoS 2150.

33 Kernkamp, *Handel op den vijand* II, 11, 30–1; Elias, *Schetsen*, 23; Sickenga, *Bijdrage*, 102; Korvezee, 'Belastingen in Noord-Brabant', 157; for a study of customs in the eighteenth century: J. Hovy, *Het voorstel van 1751 tot instelling van een beperkt vrijhavenstelsel in de Republiek. Propositie tot een gelimiteerd portofranco*, Groningen, 1966.

34 In fact, this constituted a victory for Zeeland over Holland. Kernkamp, *Handel op den vijand* I, 212–14; for the treaty see ARA CoA 91.

35 Israel, 'Strategic regulation', 470.

36 J. van der Poel, 'Het particularisme van Zeeland en de convoyen en licenten', *Archief van het Zeeuwsch Genootschap der Wetenschappen*, 1929, 54.

37 Kernkamp, *Handel op den vijand* I, 145–7; Korvezee, 'Belastingen in Noord-Brabant', 155–6; *Resolutiën* SG 19 April 1621; Israel, *Dutch Republic and Hispanic world*, 121; J.C. Westermann, 'Statistische gegevens over den handel van Amsterdam in de zeventiende eeuw', *Tijdschrift voor Geschiedenis* 61, 1948, 5.

38 Snapper, *Oorlogsinvloeden*, 56.

39 Israel, *Dutch Republic and Hispanic world*, 47–8; Bruijn, 'De vaart', 146.

40 Bruijn, 'De vaart', 210.

41 Israel, *Dutch Republic and Hispanic world*, 152, 209, 212; Noordegraaf, *Hollands welvaren*, 40; Snapper, *Oorlogsinvloeden*, 313.

42 Sickenga, *Bijdrage tot de geschiedenis*, 148; Van Dillen, *Rijkdom en regenten*, 99, 359.

43 Westermann, 'Statistische gegevens', 13.

44 Engels, *Belastingen*, 54; Sickenga, *Bijdrage tot de geschiedenis*, 181; *Groot Placaet Boeck* I, 2574; II, 320.

45 Becht, *Statistische gegevens*, 164, 174; Engels, *Belastingen*, 55; *Groot Placaet Boeck* I, 2572; Oldewelt, 'De scheepvaartstatistiek', 118.

46 Gemeente Archief Amsterdam (GAA) 5030/60.

47 *Groot Placaet Boeck* I, 568; Sickenga, *Bijdrage in de geschiedenis*, 231.

48 Elias, *Schetsen*, 78; Verhees, *Zeeuwse kaapvaart*, 29–30.

49 Prizes constituted about 6 per cent of the Amsterdam admiralty revenue in the 1640s. Based upon from GAA 5030/60. Snapper, *Oorlogsinvloeden*, 301; Elias, *Schetsen*, 122; De Liefde, *Dutch admirals*, 50; on the revolt of WIC sailors see Van der Capellen, *Gedenkschriften* I, 164, 496.

50 Unger, 'Middelburg', 51.

51 In 1641 the last accounts checked by the Chamber of Accounts were: Rotterdam 1637, Amsterdam 1639, Zeeland (September) 1628, Northern Quarter 1636, Friesland 1639. ARA CoA 94: 15 August 1641.

52 ARA SG 12580.3, Resolution SG 15 January 1626; ARA Adm XXXVII Van der Heim, 314; H.C. Hazewinkel, *Geschiedenis van Rotterdam* II, Zaltbommel 1974, 14–15.

53 Van der Capellen, *Gedenkschriften I*, 391.

54 Hartsinck, *Overzigt*, 85; De Boer, 'Een kwarteeuw', 117–18; Elias, *Schetsen*, 94.

55 Checkers were frequently authorized to accept evasions of one-sixth. Oldewelt, 'Scheepvaartstatistiek', 118; Westermann, 'Statistische gegevens', 5; Snapper, *Oorlogsinvloeden*, 297; Johan de Vries, 'De ontduiking der convoyen en licenten in de Republiek tijdens de 18e eeuw', *Tijdschrift voor Geschiedenis* 71, 1958, 349–61. On Friesland: ARA SG 12562.30; CoA 94: 29 March, 20 May, 3 and 17 June 1649.

56 Hartsinck, *Overzigt*, 82; Friesland refused to accept the commissioner Jonghestall: *Resolutiën* SG 30 April 1616.

57 Hartsinck, *Overzigt*, 54; *Resolutiën* SG 24 August 1619, 21 October 1619; Sickenga, *Bijdrage tot de geschiedenis*, 127, states that tax farming started in 1631; Becht argued that it was only applied irregularly between 1625 and 1637: Becht, *Statistische gegevens*, 143–145.

58 According to ARA Adm XLVII 30; ARA SG 12562.23.

59 According to ARA SG 12562.19 and 12562.23.

60 ARA CoA 94: Resolutions SG 19 May 1635 and 29 February 1636; ARA CoA 8: 12, 27 November 1638 and Resolution SG: 7 May 1639.

61 One Amsterdam merchant was reported to have told Frederick Henry to his face that he would continue to trade with enemy Antwerp. Joh.E. Elias, *De vroedschap van Amsterdam 1578–1795. Geschiedenis van het Amsterdamsche regentenpatriciaat*, The Hague, 1923, lxxxvi; RAZH Van Slingelandt 65: 15 August 1637; Boxer, *Dutch seaborne empire*, 113.

62 GAA 5030, 71 II Retroacta vroedschap.

63 RAZH Van Slingelandt 65: 14 August 1637; ARA SG 12562.23 Letters 13 February, 30 April, 14 June, 12 July 1638.

64 Van der Capellen, *Gedenkschriften* II, 22; ARA SG 12562.23; GAA 5030 71 II Retroacta Vroedschap; J. Wagenaar, *Amsterdam in zijne opkomst, aanwas, geschiedenissen, voorregten, koophandel, gebouwen, kerkenstaet, scholen, schutterye, gilden en regeeringe* II, Amsterdam, 1760, 535–7. The farming of the customs was introduced in 1687 again for a period of four years only.

65 RAZH Van Slingelandt 247.

66 Davis, 'Rise of protection', 307, 310.

5

The second shift: provincial taxation

The second major way for states at war to shift their costs was the imposition of taxes upon their territories. In most cases, taxes required the cooperation of the local elites in society as they came to be imposed according to the opportunities that arose of securing majority consent. As a result, taxes did not develop in a unilinear or even way. For example, in England taxation was already an important component of regular Crown finance by the mid-sixteenth century. But during Elizabeth's reign the theory and practice of taxation changed. By the beginning of the seventeenth century, the innovations of the sixteenth century were largely overlooked as attention was focused upon a more traditional, medieval, 'domain' doctrine. Taxes had needed consent by Parliament, and the shift from parliamentary assistance to exploitation of the feudal prerogative did increase the autonomous position of the monarchy again.[1]

In the prevailing political economy of the time, indirect taxes were preferred as being the most equitable distribution. William Petty wrote in his *Treatise of taxes and contributions* in 1662:

> It is generally allowed by all that men should contribute to the public charge debt according to the share and interest they have in the public peace; that is, according to their riches; now there are two sorts of riches, one actual and the other potential. A man is actually and truly rich according to what he eateth, drinketh, weareth, or any other way really and actually enjoyeth; others are but potentially or imaginatively rich, who, though they have power over much, make little use of it; these being rather stewards and exchangers for the other sort, than owners for themselves.[2]

Also, statesmen were conscious of the advantages of excises. They were less dependent upon safe seas, as compared to customs, while direct taxes could count upon serious opposition from the landed elite. In addition, direct taxes required an extensive system of assessment and collection, as any taxpaying household was charged with a specific burden in relation to income or property. However, the assessment of private incomes remained a problem which was far from solved. Indirect taxes, on the other hand, were reflected in price increases, where only a few producers or dealers noticed the shift directly. Bargaining in the latter case might be restricted to those dealers only.

Direct taxation was the harder way of levying funds, but for some states with little urbanization or commercialization it was frequently the only available option.[3] After all, it was commercialization and urbanization that made the levy of excises and customs possible, if only because more goods were transported, sold and resold by comparison with agrarian subsistence economies.

Excises might be imposed in a semi-direct way, though. A notorious example was the *gabelle*, the salt tax in France. It had been imposed since 1331. The yield was significant: in 1641 the revenue of the *gabelle* was twice that of total English revenues. The trade was easily controlled, as virtually every household needed salt, and salt came from a limited number of sources. It was levied as if it was a direct tax: every household had to pay a certain sum, for which a bill was received. With this bill, the family could obtain salt from the state salt dealers. The duty upon salt was heavy and the charge varied according to region, which led to smuggling on a vast scale. The *gabelle* became without doubt a source of much hatred against the state.[4]

In general, however, land taxes provided the bulk of the revenue of most seventeenth-century states. The French *taille* (a direct tax on land) contributed to 60 per cent of France's revenue. In 1634 this tax yielded 26.5 million livres, but it was increased to 39.6 million in 1639. Speaking of Brunswick, Achilles noted that the greater part of the revenues, also in proportion to its inhabitants, came from the rural regions. Cities were undertaxed, as their elites exerted significant influence in government. In Venice too, the city managed to shift a considerable part of the burden on to its *terraferma*. The peasants not only furnished recruits for the army, they also had to pay a disproportionately large sum towards the upkeep of the state.[5]

After central taxation, local and feudal levies influenced the overall picture. In France, it was calculated that the incidence of royal taxation was 11 per cent of the average household income. Yet the feudal burden (including tithes) could constitute significant higher charges. The highest feudal levies were noted in the Auvergne, at as much as 109 per cent of the revenue, although they were much lower elsewhere, the lowest rate being recorded in Basse Bretagne at 3 per cent. With such rates one should not be surprised in finding a low political ceiling of taxation in France. For some communities, evasion was a matter of for survival. Moreover, in France '*contribuer est consideré comme ignoble*', as nobles were exempt from direct taxes, and thus to evade taxes was also a way of retaining social status.[6]

The institutional make-up of a tax constrained the choices of rulers as well. In Poland, the upper and wealthier nobility became the main partners in coalition-building with the state. With their support the danger of revolts was reduced. Yet their very presence in the state offered the opportunity for nobles to gain privileges as to new taxes, which tended to weaken the state apparatus again, as it restricted the fiscal options of the state.[7]

Recurrent taxation upon the peasantry alone, combined with feudal burdens, made revolt much more likely. The fiscal burden rendered them more conscious of political motives. The frequent peasant revolts, due to increased taxation, that spread over France and other parts of Europe in the seventeenth century posed clear limits to the power holders. Troops were needed to enforce taxation, which had its impact upon the character of domination.[8]

However, not all local elites were prepared to assist in the suppression of the revolt, as they could be interested in weakening the central power as well. In the latter case, the relative crisis could well turn into an absolute one. In an analysis of six revolutions in the seventeenth century it was noted that:

> In the first place, we find that the most immediate, though not always the most fundamental, cause of every one of them was finance; in every case it was arbitrary taxation in one form or another, and the complaints that it evoked, that brought matters to a head.[9]

It was another disadvantage of direct taxation that it had to be paid to (local) state officials, whereas indirect taxes could be collected by shopkeepers or publicans. Consequently, direct taxes contributed more towards awareness of a new kind of public domination as compared with indirect ones: accepting direct taxes revealed more about state formation from below. Yet in the more fortunate cases of early modern taxation, institutionalization of taxes within the setting of property rights ensured internal stability and facilitated enduring coalitions between state and domestic elites.[10]

Since few central means of raising revenue were available in the Dutch Republic, most of the war burden was transferred to some sort of central budget. The *Staat van Oorlog* consisted of a proportional allocation of the costs of war to the United Provinces. The provinces were autonomous in the choice and management of their fiscal instruments, on condition that arrears did not accumulate unabated. Generally, most funds were provided by taxes.

Most data survived on the Holland tax system. It was an outstanding set of institutions, taking care of the majority of all Republic funds. As a core province, with the major cities represented in the provincial government, the political ceiling of taxation was likely to be high. The provinces on the inner-periphery (Zeeland and Utrecht) adopted similar taxes. Their socio-economic and political structure resembled that of Holland. More difficulties were encountered with the shift towards the more peripheral provinces in the north (Groningen and Friesland, maritime and clay-soil agricultural) and in the east (the inland, mostly sandy soil provinces of Gelderland, Overijssel and Drenthe). In all, taxation in the core provinces was revealed as quite exceptional, not only in a European perspective, but also *vis-à-vis* the inland provinces of the Union.

The exceptional structure of taxation in Holland

The history of the Holland taxes was based in the city. For two or three centuries already, cities had burdened their subjects with excises and property taxes. The basic characteristics resembled the public finances of the Italian city-states and those of the Hanseatic cities such as Hamburg and Gdansk. Urban centres of Flanders and Brabant had provided the Holland magistrates directly with institutional and financial models. But the novelty of the Holland fiscal system was that it encompassed a region larger than a city alone: the whole province experienced more or less the same tax burden. In 1543 the first provincial excises were introduced on a permanent basis. The advantage for the Holland region was the existence of an urban population upon which was deployed a great variety of taxes. By the time of the revolt, the public finances had outgrown their teething problems, including initial revolts.[11]

At the same time, the burden of church tithes and feudal duties was relatively light. Few exemptions existed. Only the Stadhouder with his family and foreign envoys did not have to pay taxes. Central colleges at The Hague enjoyed specific exemptions. Now and then, in particular with regard to extraordinary taxes, the college of nobles might be exempted, or a city was allowed to redeem a tax. A few territories were excluded altogether because of seignorial rights. The barony of IJsselstein paid annually 4,000 guilders to the province, and no taxes. The county of Buren likewise contributed 7,300 per year. Culemborg had only taxes on food and drink, as well as the *verponding*, but no other taxes. But these seignories were small and limited.[12] Consequently, Holland could dispose of a fairly broad tax base when warfare expenses soared during the Eighty Years' War.

The ordinary direct tax for Holland was a property tax: the *verponding*, which affected land and house owners. The land taxes were levied after deduction of the polder and dike duties at a rate of 20 per cent of the rental value. Houses paid 12.5 per cent, less than land because the costs of maintenance of the buildings were not deducted beforehand. The *verponding*, originally established to provide the taxes (*beden*) for the sovereign overlord, was collected (and not farmed out) by local tax officers for the separate tax districts. Registers were extended to other kinds of property, such as bonds and obligations. The sum was decided upon centrally, the burden divided over a proportional allocation in quotas to tax districts, which became an annual fixed charge in the seventeenth century. The last revision of the allocation dated from 1585.[13]

In addition to the *verponding*, extraordinary property taxes might be imposed, such as a second or third *verponding*, a capitation tax, a hearth tax, or in the way of extraordinary property assessments (called *1000e*, *500e*, *200e penningen*) at 0.1, 0.2 or 0.5 per cent of the value. This kind of taxation had a long tradition as well. Assessments could reach exceptionally high rates, more than 10 per cent in times of emergency. The extraordinary property taxes were levied upon land, houses, obligations, manors, tithes and offices. Special registers distinguished the taxpayers in two categories: those owning more than 2,000 guilders were called 'capitalists' (from 1621), and those owning 1,000 to 2,000 guilders were the so-called 'half capitalists' (from 1625). People owning less than 1,000 guilders were fully exempt from extraordinary property taxes. A proposal from

1641 to introduce another level, from 20,000 or 30,000 upwards, was not accepted.[14] The word 'capitalist', here used in its earliest meaning, clearly designated someone owning property.

The valuation was based upon estimates by the magistrates. Individual households might protest against a valuation, but only seldom did 'capitalists' request to be assessed lower. Holland burghers preferred to belong to the upper class of property holders. The *Politijck Hant-Boecxken* of 1650 argued that paying towards the highest qualification had several advantages: a burgher would not readily acknowledge the inferiority of his riches, and a 'capitalist' had more opportunities of obtaining credit.[15] Quite a difference from France, where tax evasion was a distinction of the upper classes!

In addition, there were the Holland stamp duties, levied upon documents of sale and deeds. Taxes on collateral succession (death duties), goods sold by auction, and sales of fixed assets were included under this item. Flat rates predominated, which resulted in a relatively higher burden for the small owner: a regressive effect but not uncommon for the time. In fiscal sociology, stamp duties are alternatively regarded as direct taxes because they bear on signs of property, or as indirect taxes because they relate to the service of the registration and safeguarding of property.

Exceptional for Holland were the manifold excises. They were called *gemeene middelen* and they provided the bulk of provincial revenue. All excises were farmed out. Major towns became the centres of tax districts, to which the surrounding regions were subordinated. The Northern Quarter of Holland (with seven constituent cities) was put on a general quota for *verponding* and excises of 18 per cent *vis-à-vis* the Southern Quarter (with eleven constituent cities). At first, the division coincided reasonably well with population estimates. However, as the Northern Quarter economy stagnated and population declined, the distribution became highly inequitable.[16]

The first Act for excises dated from 1583, and was renewed in 1586. It applied to both Holland and Zeeland. The majority of duties were levied upon necessities: beer, grain, salt, and cloth. Beer, after all, was not a luxury, but the common beverage of the time. Salt, equally, was of daily importance, above all in the storage of perishables (meat and fish) and the raising of cattle. Another major tax was introduced in this province in 1605: on peat. Excises upon luxury items such as wine or silk were not absent, but the yield was so much smaller as compared with the excises on necessities that it could never support a state during a prolonged war. The weighage (*waag*) burdened spices, butter, cheese, grain, seeds, iron, candles, yarn and other goods frequently sold at markets. In 1600 this market duty was extended to include a duty on goods sold by measure (*ronde maat*). It affected a lot of necessities of the common people, such as grain, coal, beans, seeds, salt; building materials such as chalk, tarass; and tan for the leather industry. All these duties, the core of Holland's fiscal system, weighed primarily upon the necessities of ordinary people, apart from taxes on wine and the weighage for spices.[17]

Cities had the right to grant special exemptions from taxes, such as for the poor, for students, and hospitals. The area within two miles of the city walls was subject to city taxation. Often, the sale of beer and wine there was prohibited. Trade in grain and beer between cities was taxed separately, and beer coming from the countryside paid a heavy imposition. Furthermore, provincial customs and local duties persisted. The drainage boards demanded taxes for the maintenance of dikes. These were mainly a land tax or duties upon sown lands. As for the finances of the cities themselves, most of the revenue came from the wine and beer excises. These levies were subject to provincial approval because they affected the 'central' tax revenues. The fortieth penny (the stamp duty on sales of property) was accompanied in general by an eightieth penny for the cities.[18]

The regressive burden of some excises was reduced as they came to be levied as a semi-direct tax, according to the property-tax registers of capitalists and half-capitalists. An early example was the salt duty. The wealtiest ('capitalists', households with more than eight persons, farmers with four cows or more, and innkeepers) had to pay for a bill from the tax farmer, after which they could obtain a certain amount of salt free of tax. Those who were less well-off, the 'half-capitalists', paid half the duty for the tax bill. Small households and the poorest could buy their salt from the salt dealers, who were charged a reduced duty by the tax farmer again.[19]

The salt duty was an excise that burdened towns and rural districts alike. Specific agricultural duties were the taxes on cattle and sown lands. They were actually semi-direct levies, based upon the ownership of animals and the acreage under crops. Different rates were applied, according to the soil, the produce and the composition of the cattle. Other taxes which extracted much from the villages were those on milling and horses. The latter was levied upon the sale of the beast.[20] In the 1680s, the taxes upon wine and soap came to be levied semi-directly as well.

In the first decades following the Acts of 1583 and 1586 additions to the Holland excises were minor. The tax on cloth was even abolished, because of the complications of collecting it, due to the manifold varieties. The addition to the weighage (*ronde maat*) and the reform of the salt tax into a semi-direct one has been noted, but most other taxes in the 1590s were either extraordinary property taxes or stamp duties. One was a tax on obligations and bonds, lowered shortly thereafter as it was thought to hurt the credit of the province. Another tax was the duty on unfounded lawsuits, which was also thought up as a device to reduce litigation in the Republic. A major stamp duty was introduced, too, in 1598: the fortieth penny upon property sold at auction, upon the sale of all fixed property and upon collateral succession (death duties, at 2.5 per cent of the value). It was to become one of the major stamp duties in the Republic. The next year, in 1599, the death duties (including gifts) were increased to a thirtieth penny. Temporary, extraordinary measures in these initial decades had been forced loans (*capitale impositie*, reintroduced in 1600–1602), additional *verpondingen* or the extraordinary hearth tax of 1600 (at one guilder per hearth).[21]

However, the burden of war caused a major change in 1604–1605. The provincial authorities started by reintroducing the tax on woollens. New duties came to burden luxury textiles (such as damask, velvet, silken cloths), candles, peat and peat cutting, coal, firewood, fruit and fish (sturgeon and salmon). The duties on candles and on fuel affected industries in particular, but also common households. Existing taxes were increased as well. Additional levies in 1605 were imposed on vinegar, cloth (in particular textiles from Utrecht, Munster and Limburg – a measure to protect Leiden's industry), weighage, milling, beer, soap, and meat. This policy made the whole taxation system more regressive than before. The tax on slaughtered meat was increased. The soap duty was raised threefold and was followed by another impost upon its production. Additional measures were enacted in 1606 and 1607, partly upon luxury items such as spirits and wines. Woollens (the more common textiles) paid increases of 43 to 76 per cent. A new tax was introduced which would hurt the Holland building trade henceforth: on bricks, tiles, chalk, and tarass.[22]

Worst of all for the poorer classes were additions to duties for grinding corn. The duties, levied according to weight, were increased fourfold. Only buckwheat, a staple diet for the poor, rose less: 200 per cent. Through weighage, grain was affected too. The weighage for grains, wax and rice was doubled; duties on sugar, copper, gunpowder and starch increased 150 per cent, and the weighage on spices rose five to fifteenfold. The beer duties increased 21–100 per cent, depending on the kind of beer. The *dunne bieren* remained exempt. They were very light, cheap, and fresh beers, consumed mainly in the countryside, and control over consumption would have been very hard indeed. But taxes on the more common city beers increased 50 per cent. Another duty was imposed on beer to help pay off Holland's debts.[23]

In these three years (1605–1607), then, the indirect tax burden increased significantly. It was the first major increase since the 1580s. Moreover, a tax was levied in 1606 of 1.50 guilders per hearth, upon a proposal of the Estates General. Local magistrates were allowed to exempt the poorer dwellings by imposing heavier charges on the wealthier households, in order to avoid disturbances. Fortunately, expectations of the Truce resulted in some relaxation. No new taxes were raised, and the burdensome semi-direct taxes on agriculture were decreased in 1608. Duties on cattle were lowered, and the tax on sown land was abolished altogether. In general, it had proved more difficult to extract funds from the countryside than from the cities.[24]

Thus, when the Republic entered the Truce, the province levied manifold indirect taxes, very regressively through the heavy duties upon corn milling and beer in particular, with few duties burdening 'luxuries' such as wine and expensive textiles. No new taxes were imposed in these years, but neither were existing taxes abolished. Only the duty on coal was removed in 1612. Of all the taxes on fuel, it had been the least important. The duty on the sale of horses was changed into a semi-direct tax of 1.20 guilders per year, to be paid annually by the horse owner.[25]

Yet the resumption of the war with Spain in 1621 witnessed major new increases. The tax burden was legitimated as follows:

> to prevent the violent invasion planned by the Spanish and their allies upon these territories, for which they have gathered enormous armies, pressing upon the frontiers to bring these lands under their slavery and their force . . .[26]

Table 5.1 lists tax policies in the last three decades of the war. These pointed to continual increases. In the meantime, only some minor decreases occurred: in 1623 and 1624 the duty on spirits, in 1624 the duty on tobacco, in 1625 the duty on cloth, in 1628 the duty on peat cutting, in 1642 the duty on buckwheat, in 1644 the duty on tobacco again, and finally in 1649 the duty on wagons.

The basis for Holland's tax policy remained indirect through the imposition of permanent excises. Throughout the period 1620–1650 extraordinary property taxes were imposed too, based on the valuation lists of the cities, but they were always temporary. The 0.5 per cent rate came to be applied commonly and replaced the 0.1 and 0.2 duties. The capitation tax of 1622 was an exception and was not repeated, and there were three hearth taxes during our thirty years' period.

The years in which funds were needed urgently were always characterized by the levy of extraordinary taxes, as in 1621–1623 (the resumption of the war, siege of Bergen op Zoom), 1625–1628 (the threats at sea and the land campaigns, the loss of Breda and the start of the siege of Den Bosch), 1631, 1635, 1637–1638, 1643–1644 (the Sound crisis) and 1646.

As for ordinary taxation, however, Holland persisted in the years 1621–1627 by raising the levels of the existing excises. Land tax increases were opposed by Leiden, Enkhuizen and the nobility. An easier measure was the increase of weighage for sugar and spices. More burdensome was the increase by 50 per cent in the duty upon common cloth, which was much resented by Leiden's textile industry, but it was enforced for only four years. Duties on luxury textiles were increased and a new tax on oils was introduced.[27]

In the years to follow many more taxes were increased and voted for. As for popular consumption, new taxes were imposed on herring and salted fish, which were part of the popular diet. Vinegar, candles, salt, weighage for cheese, and butter carried new duties. Beer and grain were taxed significantly more heavily. Breweries had to pay a new tax on their production. Compared to 1583, when the public had paid 20 per cent on the low-priced, popular beers and 90 per cent on the more expensive and foreign ones, the duties in 1624 were respectively 70 and 170 per cent of the price. *Dunne bieren* remained exempt. Grinding corn in general became more expensive, for wheat, maslin and buckwheat alike, somewhat less so for rye. Grains were affected too by an increase of 50 to 55 per cent on the market duties

Table 5.1 *Taxation increases in Holland, 1620–1649: extraordinary duties, land taxes, stamp duties and excises (temporary measures in brackets)*

year	*extraord.*	*property*	*stamp duty*	*excises and semi-direct taxes*
1620	—	—	—	—
1621	0.1%	land tax	—	weighage, cloth, oils
1622	2 × 0.2% capitation	—	ships	herring, beer, coal
1623	0.5%	—	—	coal, peat, peat cutting vinegar, salt, soap bricks, tobacco
1624	—	—	paper s.	wine, salt, butter, weighage, beer
1625	0.5%	—	lawsuits	[brewers], grinding corn cattle, weighage
1626	0.1%	—	—	spirits, candles
1627	0.2% hearths	land tax	paper s.	grinding, arable land peat cutting, coal, bricks
1628	0.5%	—	—	[soap, wine, cloth]
1629	—	—	—	[distilling]
1630	—	—	—	—
1631	0.5%	—	—	—
1632	—	land tax	—	—
1633	—	—	—	—
1634	—	—	—	—
1635	0.5%	—	—	—
1636	—	—	death d.	servants, grinding corn
1637	hearths	—	—	[pitch], beer
1638	0.5%	—	—	—
1639	—	—	—	pitch
1640	—	—	—	—
1641	—	—	—	wagons, weighage, salt
1642	—	—	—	salt
1643	0.5%	—	—	—
1644	0.5% hearths	—	—	[spices]
1645	—	—	—	[spices], meat
1646	0.5%	—	—	—
1647	—	—	—	—
1648	—	—	—	—
1649	—	—	—	—

Source: RAZH FH 802; Jacobs Cats 12; *Groots Placaet Boeck vervattende de placaten, ordonnantiën ende edicten van de Staten-Generaal der Vereenigde Nederlanden*, ed. C. Cau, The Hague, 1644; P. H. Engels, *De belastingen en de geldmiddelen van den aanvang der Republiek tot op heden*, Utrecht, 1862, 57–143; R. J. C. van Maanen, 'Hollandse vermogingsheffingen in de 17e en 18e eeuw', *Nederlands Archievenblad* 88, 1984, 71.

of the *ronde maat*.[28]

Excises, by their nature, had tended to burden the cities more than the countryside. In 1625 and 1627, relatively late, the countryside was to get its share. The produce of the land was charged by reintroducing the tax on sown land, which had been abolished in 1608. The duty was double the former rate. Farmers had to pay more for their cattle too: a 50 per cent increase in the duty on keeping horned beasts.[29]

It was not only farmers and the city populace who were hit by the excise strategy. Industry was to notice the burden of war through several increases in the tax upon fuel. First, the tax on coal was reintroduced. Peat became much more expensive, hurting industry and individual households alike. The tax on peat cutting was increased, bearing initially upon agriculture, but passed on to the consumers in the cities. Trade got its share as well. Customs had risen to the pre-Truce level again. Weighage for copper, iron and other metals became more expensive. The building trade noticed the war burden in a new duty on bricks and tiles (*grove waren*).[30]

In their turn the lower classes in the city (beer, grinding corn, cloth, butter), industry (peat, coal, bricks), trade (weighage) and agriculture (sown lands, cattle, cutting of peat) were all affected. Alternatives to the burdening of the lower classes were taxes on luxuries, the stamp duties and the property taxes. As for luxuries, some items were increased as well, wine in particular. At first, this tax was opposed by Dordrecht as regards German wines, by Rotterdam as regards French, and by Amsterdam as regards both. Nevertheless, the next years witnessed wine duty increases. A new tax was put on tobacco, mainly a duty on imports, but the yield was altogether insignificant.[31] The tax on spirits was reduced, probably a measure to combat illegal distilleries, as it coincided with a reform in the nearby province of Utrecht as to the same tax. Weighage for spices and sugar was increased, but on the whole the record indicates that taxation of luxuries remained relatively low.

Stamp duties were increased as well. The year 1624 was of major importance because of the introduction of the paper stamp (*klein zegel*). It was the invention of a clerk of the Estates of Holland, Johannes van den Broecke. This new tax was imposed on all documents with a certain legal status, and, beside being a revenue-raising expedient, it was also a help to individuals in protecting the legal status of requests, legacies, passports, safeguards, etc. In the following years, the stamp duty was extended continually. The duty on groundless lawsuits was raised by 20 per cent. An extension of the fortieth penny duties was the inclusion of the sale of ships in the category of 'fixed property'.[32] Stamp duties affected capital owners through a tax on obligations and bonds too.

Property taxes were increased slightly. The land tax was extended to newly reclaimed lands and a hearth tax was imposed at one guilder. The siege of Bergen op Zoom provided the excuse to introduce a capitation tax at one guilder in 1622, but it was extremely unpopular. Leiden, a city with a high percentage of poor within its city walls, argued that it was actually dangerous to count and write down the names of so many poor. Subsequently the Provincial Estates allowed cities to use part of the tax to be spent on the poor, in particular during 1623 and 1624, when grain was short, in order to avoid food rioting.[33]

Yet the policy of excise increases could not be continued the whole war period throughout. The years 1628 to 1635 were characterized by little additional taxation and several attempts at reforms. Instead of increases, Holland was looking for improvements in collection. Several taxes were farmed out that had been collected before – such as the fortieth and thirtieth pennies and the general stamp duty – a measure thought to reduce the amount of fraud in the collection by the secretaries of the cities.[34] The tax on cutting peat was reduced.

The land tax became more equitable, as a *verponding* revision was introduced in 1632. Obviously, the disadvantage was the quota system, through which traditionalism prevailed. In a region with such rapid economic growth and such a fast-expanding population as Holland, revisions would be necessary on a regular basis. However, a revision of the 1585 distribution had been opposed by the cities of Alkmaar, Leiden and Amsterdam. After all, those experiencing the largest population increases profited most from the existing distribution. Amsterdam, for example, which housed 15 per cent of the population of Holland in 1622, contributed only 5.5 per cent of the *verponding*. The political crisis of 1618, however, paved the way for fiscal changes. Amsterdam bowed to the inevitable and finally, in 1623, a commission was installed to bring about a new apportionment.[35]

The revision of the *verponding* quotas was concluded in 1631. It was expected to yield 3 million guilders instead of the former returns of 1.5 million to 1.6 million. The estimate was too optimistic: the revenue was only 2.4 million. One-third came from houses, two-thirds from land. The new distribution remained in force throughout the rest of the seventeenth century. It was soon unrepresentative again, as population growth was concentrated in the Amsterdam, Leiden, Rotterdam and The Hague areas, whereas the whole Northern Quarter and the other Southern Quarter districts experienced a decline in population and economic activity.[36]

Another overall reform was put forward, in the collection of the beer, wine, cloth, soap and salt taxes. The idea was to concentrate on taxing the articles upon arrival in port or at the place of manufacture, instead of at the wholesale or retail stage. This project of the *Vijf Speciën* together with the revised land tax went under the heading of equalization of the taxes, to be extended to the other provinces. Although the Estates General accepted the proposal, it was never introduced. In Holland, the refusal of Amsterdam blocked the favourable decision of all other constituent cities.[37]

Nevertheless, the policy of heavy excises of 1605–1607 and 1621–1627 was not resumed in the former fashion. Two new taxes imposed after 1635 had a semi-direct character. The keeping of servants (*heeregeld*) became taxable at one guilder per servant. The other new semi-direct tax was imposed on wagons and ships. Amsterdam in particular was reluctant to levy this duty, probably on account of the fact that so many common people were taxed directly and because of its enormous impact on this thriving commercial centre. It was the only tax to be abolished when peace was concluded. Another semi-direct tax, the salt duty, was increased twice, first by extension to some previously exempt regions of The Hague and Enkhuizen, second by imposing an additional burden upon 'capitalist' households only. Milling duties were raised once more in 1636, after the four preceding years had witnessed a decline in the price of rye. In that year, 13.5 per cent of the price of wheat and 11.5 per cent of the price of rye went in taxation. Other taxes introduced in 1636–1645 were only minor. A tax on pitch and tar, tried out shortly in 1637, was introduced permanently in 1639. Duties on beer were extended to shipboard. Weighage was increased slightly. Spices carried a special temporary burden in 1644 and 1645, the duty on meat saw an increase, and in 1644 rates for tobacco were decreased. From 1646 to 1650, no new taxes were introduced. Yet no taxes were abolished either, apart from that on wagons.[38]

Taxation in the semi-periphery: Utrecht and Zeeland

The provinces of Zeeland and Utrecht were close to Holland, geographically and in institutional make-up. They shared the history of patrimonial Habsburg territories, and had regularly been used to approve *beden* to their overlord. Both provinces introduced a wide range of excises at an early stage too. Utrecht's provincial consent to taxation was promulgated in 1577, with imposts levied on wine, beer, spirits, vinegar, grain, cloth, salt, weighage, sown land, cattle, peat, and meat among other things. The land tax was levied on a traditional system called *oldschiltgeld*, and was apportioned according to a registry of 1539. Zeeland implemented the same Acts as Holland in 1583, and the land tax was called *verponding* too.[39]

The rates of the excises were at first similar to those in Holland. Yet Utrecht stepped up its taxation well before 1600, and several taxes were implemented even prior to Holland, such as those on peat and bricks, the duties on the sale of fixed assets and the death duties. Beer, weighage, salt, and milling grain carried new duties too. As compared to Holland, quite a number of luxuries were taxed, such as the wearing of golden chains, duties on mortgages, rents and obligations, taxes on finished cloths, gold thread and other expensive textiles. Zeeland, on the other hand, was more reluctant to impose additional taxes, although the *ronde maat* (the addition to weighage) was enacted, the salt duty was made a semi-direct tax too, and the duties on horses and cattle were increased.[40]

In Utrecht, it turned out that the excises functioned well in the larger cities, but encountered difficulties in the countryside. Therefore, the Estates decided to increase the *oldschiltgeld* by 50 per cent, while cities experienced excise increases. Duties therefore differed in this province. Of all excises, the tax on grinding corn was increased recurrently, with the effect that the rates were double Holland's. In the wake of the Truce, neither in Utrecht nor in Zeeland were taxes reduced, apart from the Utrecht house tax, which was abolished in 1610.[41]

Yet in the years prior to the resumption of war, Utrecht prepared itself financially for the military effort to come. In this respect, the province was unequalled within the Republic. Duties on wine, beer and spirits were stepped up considerably in the last year of the Truce. As a result, Utrecht had the advantage of having to increase only one excise (salt) in the early 1620s, together with the reintroduction of the house tax. But by 1625 Utrecht was having to resort to tax increases again, first the duties on meat and soap, then Utrecht copied Holland's stamp duty. In the five years from 1627 to 1632 increases on beer, grinding corn, wine and butter followed. Stamp duties and direct taxes were stepped up as well. The house tax was tripled in 1629 (to be reduced only in 1653). Land was to bear an extraordinary burden which lasted four years (1631–1635) and the semi-direct tax on cattle was increased too.[42]

The years 1636 and 1637 witnessed more tax increases: on beer and wine. A new tax on tobacco was imposed. In 1640 the excise on milled grain was raised and a new duty was imposed on sheepskin (to be abolished after 1653), another on luxury coaches, and a duty on the retaining of servants, although the latter was levied apparently only once. In 1647, despite the prospect of an immediate conclusion of the peace, the duty on milled grain for the city dwellers was increased again.[43]

In Zeeland, fewer additions were enacted as compared with Holland and Utrecht. When Jacob Cats, the well-known statesman and poet from Holland, completed a comparative study of the excises in Holland and Zeeland in 1635, he found almost all Zeeland rates were lower. The only exceptions were spirits, paying double the Holland rate, and the duties on agriculture: on horses, on cattle and on sown land.[44] Yet in 1637 a major reform was put through too. Excises were increased and some new taxes introduced. Wine, beer, grinding corn, sown land, soap had to pay more towards the provincial coffers. New taxes were imposed on carriages and horses, on oils and on fish. This policy was continued in 1641, when the tax on retaining servants was introduced, and in 1644 there was a major addition to the salt tax.[45]

Provincial customs were a moot point. Zeeland protested against Holland's duties upon the transporting and export of peat, as its industries lacked fuel since the provincial peat production had declined. Another issue was the inland grain trade. Zeeland had a vital interest in the production of grain crops. Amsterdam had strong links with the international grain trade, and wished to keep grain customs as low as possible. Zeeland, on the other hand, preferred higher duties on incoming grain.[46] As a result, the political ceiling for Union taxation was quite low in this province, which strove so openly, against Holland's policies.

Problematic taxation in the periphery

The extraction process in the more peripheral territories differed widely from that in the core provinces. Excises were hard to introduce in those rural regions, which were less differentiated and less commercialized as compared with the maritime west. Socio-economic conditions, in other words, looked much like those in the rest of Europe. The poorer sandy-soil regions were characterized by a kind of subsistence economy, such as large parts of the county of Graafschap and Veluwe (both in Gelderland), Twente (in Overijssel), Zevenwouden (Friesland), and the *landschap* of Drenthe. On the other hand, the maritime clay-soil region in the north, in Friesland and Groningen, and the river districts such as along the IJssel in Salland (Overijssel) and the Betuwe (Gelderland) were more commercialized. The cities of Overijssel and Gelderland, together with the city of Groningen, enjoyed a long tradition of prosperity and had accumulated strong institutions and privileges.[47] Yet their economic base contracted, like that of Europe generally in the seventeenth century.

When the provinces joined the Union, most of them introduced some new provincial excises. Yet in general, the imposition was restricted. The rates were invariably lower as compared with those levied in the core provinces. Of the semi-direct duties, those upon agriculture such as paying for the keeping of cattle and for tilled land were exploited to the full. Furthermore, former taxes persisted, mainly upon land.[48] Mostly, the sums were allocated among districts on a quota system. In Gelderland, the proportion was 47 per cent, 31 per cent and 22 per cent respectively for Betuwe (Nijmegen), Veluwe (Arnhem), and Graafschap (Zutphen), the three autonomous quarters of this province.

Up to the Truce, few additions were made to the existing duties. Also, hardly any tax was abolished during that twelve year interlude. Yet the resumption of war in 1621 found all the provinces in trouble. Arrears in the payment of the quota were recurrent, and some companies failed to pay. The Estates General sent delegations to Overijssel and Gelderland, to discuss the imposition of new taxes. They encountered, above all, opposition from the powerful cities, as the latter refused to comply with centralized provincial taxation and demanded part of the revenue for their own administration.

Less problematic were the land taxes. After all, they were not a novelty. Thus existing direct taxes increased, but as the burden varied from city to city and district to district, with different taxes in each of the quarters, the incidence was unequal. For example, in Gelderland, the cities in the Quarter of Betuwe (Nijmegen) kept one-third of the excises for themselves, in the Quarter of Graafschap (Zutphen) one-fifth. Local city taxes added to the inequality of the burden.[49]

The success of taxation policies varied. In the north, the Groningen finances were barely organized when war started again in 1621. The burden of taxation was low, with few excises and an unrevised old land tax. Not surprisingly, the province got into difficulty in paying its quota to the *Staat van Oorlog*. An extraordinary hearth and property tax, together with a transformation of the salt excise into a capitation tax, were the first measures. By 1623, further excises could no longer be avoided on corn milling and tobacco. A semi-direct tax upon the keeping of horses was introduced, with a tax upon the revenue from offices, industry, and from the wages of servants. The latter had the appearance of an income tax and as such was a novelty in the Republic. A major reform was put through in 1628 with new duties on wine, beer, milling grain, soap, vinegar, cloth, meat, tobacco, weighage, and on keeping cattle, and horses. Grinding corn came under strict control by the demolition of 'unauthorized' mills in the countryside. The capitation tax was doubled. A new tax on peat and the *ronde maat*, as additions to the weighage, were introduced too. The *verponding* arrived, and yielded more than the traditional land tax, although it never replaced the hearth taxes in the city itself.[50]

To the west of Groningen, efficient policies were slower to make their appearance. In Friesland, an extraordinary five-hundredth of a penny property tax was levied in 1623. Yet excises had to be voted for too, under the condition, however, that the cities were allowed to keep one-third, and that they could buy out the land tax of the province. These policies were still insufficient for the rising costs of war, and the payment of the quotas slipped further into arrears. In 1632 a reform was proposed by the Estates, yet it was not introduced because the economy was 'exhausted'. Another project dated from 1633, under which most of the Groningen 1628 taxes were to be copied, but only a meagre version of the capitation, hearth and income taxes was actually introduced. By 1635 and 1636 the payment problems of Friesland came to a head. The office of the provincial receiver was in great disorder too. Only through direct intervention of the Council of State were some new taxes introduced, and the cities gave up their right to one-third of the excises.[51]

Drenthe was situated near the southern border of Groningen and Friesland. Some excises that had been introduced in the first decade of the century were increased in 1621: those on foreign beer and on grinding corn. Yet arrears soon accumulated. In 1622, the company of horsemen under Beaumont needed payment of 20,000 guilders directly. Some minor new taxes were introduced in subsequent years: on sheep, an export duty on oxen and pigs, and peat tolls. Of more immediate impact were the changes in 1629–1630. Brewing suffered an increased burden. The duty on grinding corn was replaced by a capitation tax: 0.80 guilder upon every Drenth who was over one year of age. In 1630, extraordinary duties were imposed upon cattle, capitation, and land. The latter was rendered permanent in 1644.[52]

In Overijssel, the province imposed new excises in 1622 too, but only on the condition that the cities retained one-third of the yield. The nobility could buy out their part of the excises.[53] Yet these measures proved inadequate, and a new duty was introduced upon publicans, called the *verkleining der kannen*. Beermugs were made smaller while taxes remained as of old, hence taxation rose in proportion but the consumer did not notice the increase. In addition, the province established customs at its borders: on peat, cattle, beer, soap, salt, flour, and groats, despite the prohibition under the Union of Utrecht.[54] A new Act imposed a capitation duty, which was calculated according to the property owned, at 0.1 per cent. The duty on sown land was increased in 1626 to 5.70 guilders for a *morgen* and a hearth tax was imposed permanently in 1628. Land taxes were revised in 1630, but then still excluded cities, feudal duties, tithes, and mills. From 1635 stamp duties were imposed on sales of fixed assets and on death duties.[55]

So far the results of taxation had varied, yet in the province of Gelderland no major changes occurred at all during the last three decades of the war. When Gelderland joined the Union, a couple of excises had been introduced, but the rates were low. Now taxes had been proposed constantly since the 1620s, yet the fiscal autonomy of the quarters proved imperative. In fact, only the land tax was revised in 1643. Financial problems were solved by extraordinary charges upon the existing direct taxes, or by introducing a minor new excise, such as a duty on tobacco in the Veluwe.[56]

Yield and distribution of the burden

It was obvious that the fiscal conditions of the inland provinces resembled those in much of the rest of Europe. Their provisions did not attract international attention. By contrast, the core of the Republic, in particular the Hollanders, stood out, and they acquired the reputation of being the most heavily taxed nation in Europe. Excises came to be thought of as a typically Dutch measure. Even Flanders, in so many ways similar in structure to Holland, did not indulge in such a plethora of excises. 'Dutch' also was the principle of equality in taxation, resulting in a broad tax base, which was a major point of difference from Europe as a whole.[57]

In Holland, increases in taxation had been major, in particular during 1605–1607 and during the 1620s. The yield of the excises and semi-direct duties increased from 4 million guilders in 1608 to almost 6 million guilders in 1624 and to over 9 million guilders in 1645.[58] Figure 5.1 represents this development. The trend was interrupted by relatively low years, like 1627, 1632 and 1638–1639.

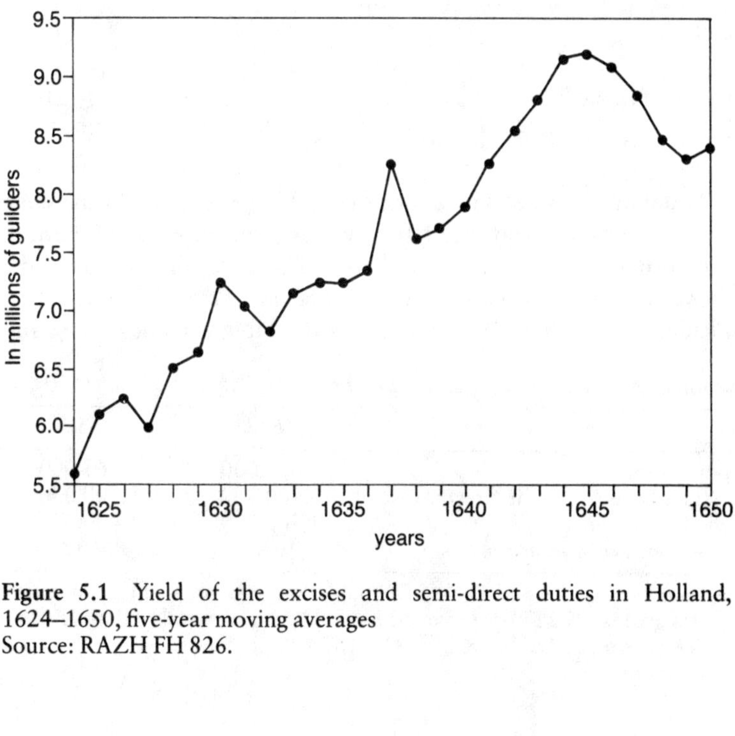

Figure 5.1 Yield of the excises and semi-direct duties in Holland, 1624–1650, five-year moving averages
Source: RAZH FH 826.

These changes could not be accounted for by policy measures to decrease in taxation, but could have been due to the expectations of the tax farmers, who lowered their bids after a year of poor trade. After 1645, the yield declined altogether. This might have been a sign of a stagnant economy becoming evident in the decades thereafter.[59]

Owing to the continuous shift towards excises in Holland, the direct taxes came to constitute a smaller proportion of the province's revenue. Table 5.2 presents two surviving budgets that were drafted in a similar fashion, which may be used for the purpose of comparison. A relative decrease in direct taxes is evident, despite a reorganization in 1632. Indirect taxes, on the other hand, increased. The yield of the stamp duties remained largely the same, but they declined in relative importance.

Table 5.2 *Distribution of Holland's revenue, 1600 and 1640, in percentages*

type of revenue	*1600*	*1640*
direct (*verponding*)	30.6	22.3
indirect (excises and semi-direct taxes)	63.9	70.9
stamp duties (*zegel, 20/30/40th penny*)	5.6	3.0
other	—	3.7
total	100.0	100.0
[in million guilders	3.6	10.8]

Source: RAZH FH 797 *Memorie*; Jacob Cats 23.

Population figures, in the meantime, did not increase at the same rate as tax yields. And as inflation was neglegible during this period, the burden of taxation per head rose. This is commonly called the incidence of taxation and is reconstructed in Table 5.3. The actual incidence must have been higher, as the table excludes the stamp

Table 5.3 *Incidence of ordinary taxation in Holland, 1622 and 1650*

	1622	*1650*
population	671,000	765,000
yield, excises and semi-direct taxes	5,500,000	8,400,000
yield, *verponding*	1,500,000	2,400,000
incidence per head in guilders	10.43	14.12

Source: see Fig. 5.1 and Table 5.2; population: J. G. van Dillen, 'Summiere staat van de in 1622 in de provincie Holland gehouden volkstelling', *Economisch Historisch Jaarboek*, 21, 1940, 167–89.

duties, the customs, all extraordinary duties and all local taxation. Also, the tax farmers' extraction was higher compared with their tax leases.[60] Even without the exact knowledge of such additional charges, Table 5.3 indicates a considerable increase.

Looking at the distribution of excises and semi-direct duties themselves, those on necessities constituted the majority, as is shown in Table 5.4. Most revenue from these duties on necessities came from the taxes on beer, corn grinding, peat and coal, and butcher's meat, which constituted also the main expense of the common people. Property, assessed only as an extraordinary expedient apart from the *verponding*, did not carry a continuously greater burden, whereas milling grain, beer and peat were taxed more heavily on a permanent basis. The weighage actually increased many of these taxes still further. The taxes on luxuries constituted a minority of the charges: almost 9 per cent in the Southern Quarter and 4 per cent in the Northern Quarter. In the latter district, which was less urbanized, the semi-direct duties on agriculture and salt weighed relatively heavier.[61]

Table 5.4 *Distribution of the farmed taxes in the Southern and Northern Quarter of Holland in 1650, percentages*

taxes	*Southern*	*Northern*
semi-direct taxes, mainly agricultural taxes and salt	10.5	17.7
taxes on necessities, mainly beer, milling, peat and meat	74.6	71.6
taxes on luxuries, mainly wine	8.8	4.0
weighage	6.2	6.7
total	100.0	100.0
[in guilders:	6,870,904	1,539,629]

Source: RAZH FH 829.

The obvious advantage for Holland was a broad and varied tax base. The Hague, which housed on average the wealthiest households of the Republic, contributed out of proportion to the property taxes. Gouda, Alkmaar and some smaller Northern Quarter cities paid more than their populations warranted in salt tax, probably owing to the extensive dairying and the herring fisheries. The tax on beer burdened the urbanized tax districts, such as Amsterdam and Rotterdam, in particular. The impact of trade was noticeable as over two-thirds of the weighage duty came from Amsterdam alone. Also, Amsterdam paid relatively more for the tax on keeping servants by comparison with the other cities. The duty on wine came mostly from The Hague again. Apparently, in this 'little Paris of the north' more wine was consumed than in any other city of Holland.[62]

A major difference between Holland on the one hand and Zeeland and Utrecht on the other was the burden upon the countryside. Despite the fact that both semi-peripheral provinces had introduced a wide range of excises, the burden of direct taxation weighed heavier. In 1627 a deputy from Zeeland, Knuyt, made a comparison between the land taxes in Zeeland and Holland. According to his calculations, a *morgen* (about two acres) in Zeeland paid 4.6 guilders, but in Holland only 1.8 guilders. After the Holland revision in 1632, the latter still paid just 2.9 guilders. In Utrecht, the direct duties were more burdensome too, partly through the recurrent imposition of house and hearth taxes. Due to the old allocation system, the land tax varied greatly according to district, from 1.05 guilders to 8.50 guilders per *morgen*.[63]

An emphasis on taxation of land was even more apparent in the peripheral provinces of the Republic. The proportion of direct taxation versus indirect taxation in provincial revenue was roughly three to two. Yet by contrast to the semi-periphery, the rates of land taxes seemed more restricted. In Gelderland, even after the reform of the land tax in the 1640s, land paid 16.7 per cent of the rental value after deduction of local duties, whereas houses paid 11.1 per cent. This was still lower as compared to the Holland *verponding*, which was respectively 20 and 12.5 per cent.[64] Yet such figures were subject to change as the rural population were recurrently faced with extraordinary measures. A complaint by the nobleman Alexander van der Capellen is illustrative. After the cities of the Quarter of Zutphen had refused to impose a hearth tax in 1628, the lands were burdened with an additional duty, and Van der Capellen sighed:

> It is a hard and inequitable means, to give the countryside one blow after the other despite ruin and destruction; and to have the cities pay only the ordinary means with exemption of all extraordinary burdens [. . .]. Common expenses must be born evenly.[65]

As a result of privileges in taxation enjoyed by the cities, the tax burden was inequitably shifted towards the 'common' lands and the smaller communities, who did not command such advantageous regulations.[66]

Among the actual excises of the peripheral provinces, those on corn grinding and beer were by far the most important. Hardly any revenue was derived from the duties upon luxuries or weighage, if such were imposed at all. Among all the provinces, the duty on milling grain was highest in Utrecht, whereas some of its other duties were more burdensome as compared to Holland. And whereas the incidence of taxation in this latter province must have been comparable to Holland, the burden was probably much lower in the other provinces of the Union, with perhaps Gelderland having the lowest *per capita* burden.

The barriers to taxation

Although most obstacles to an effective taxation policy were apparently to be found in the inland provinces, some were not totally absent at the heart of the Republic either. These barriers to taxation could be listed as follows: inter-city rivalry, administrative obstacles, urban–rural dichotomies, disputes over quotas, a decline in trade and wealth, destruction due to warfare, existing privileges and redemptions, low political ceilings of taxation, and outright tax revolts.

As for the impact of inter-city rivalries, the advantage of having one major urban centre was demonstrated by the province of Utrecht, which prepared itself financially before war was resumed in 1621, and which imposed many new taxes even prior to Holland. Groningen too, where the city hardly encountered opposition from other urban centres, stood out in reforming its financial system, mainly by reducing the powers of the tax farmers, by introducing the first income tax, and by imposing firm control over its milling.[67] By contrast, in Holland tax policies had been hampered by the competition of cities in preventing revisions of quotas and the imposition of specific taxes.

In Friesland, it was the administrative regulation of representation that held up fiscal reforms. The bulk of the revenue came from the land tax, which was raised according to a valuation list dating from 1511, called the *floreen*. The tax was related to voting rights and as such firmly entrenched in the whole socio-political structure of the province.[68] But the most notorious example of administrative failure was Gelderland, in which the three quarters remained financially autonomous. The Receiver General of the Union had to deal with three separate accounts from this province. Attempts at unifying Gelderland's administration, particularly in 1643–1644, had no lasting results.[69]

One insurmountable barrier within Gelderland was the allocation as between the three quarters. Graafschap contested its quota, and demanded that Betuwe and Veluwe should increase their tax rates to the Graafschap level before new taxes were approved. Yet the latter two quarters were unwilling to meet this condition. And when finally some agreement was reached upon in 1622, it was undone again by a careless move on the part of the nobility of Nijmegen, who had the list of taxes printed secretly in advance. This infuriated the cities, with the result that the latter withdrew their consent. Moreover, a controversy arose about taxation on beer brewed in the countryside. The cities demanded a ban on all rural breweries. As the nobility defended the rights of their rural districts, this held up all further decisions.[70]

The provincial administration was further hampered by the privileges of the cities. In the eastern provinces, voting was frequently deadlocked between urban and rural delegates. Above all the cities clung to their fiscal independence, and demanded part of the provincial excises for their own use. At times, cities refused to implement provincial decisions. Even in Drenthe, which was predominantly rural, this constituted a problem with Coevorden. In 1629 that garrison town had rejected the new capitation tax which was to replace the milling duty. Then the reform of the land tax in 1644 was thwarted. Coevorden was forced to acquiesce in 1647, on the condition, however, that Coevorden would get one-third of the revenue and that existing arrears were remitted. In the meantime, milling was continued as a separate duty there.[71]

For long, excises could not be introduced within the province of Friesland at all because of the eleven cities' compounded negative vote. Finally, they agreed, but on the condition that one-third of the revenue was theirs and that they were allowed to redeem the provincial land tax. Similar opposition affected all Overijssel policies up to the 1620s.

But most notorious of all were the urban–rural dichotomies in Groningen. Both the city and the countryside had their own provincial administration. In 1615 a dispute arose about the costs of administration of the country district. The *Ommelanden* wished to increase the amount reserved from the land tax for their own administration from one-eighth to one-sixth. This measure was disputed by the city. After intervention, the Estates General agreed with the latter. Another issue concerned the tax on horses. Instead of the duty, the countryside levied a 10 per cent land tax to raise an equivalent sum. The city wished to increase its direct control, assuming that in this region, where horse-breeding was one of the main sources of income, the tax on horses should yield more. But this time the Estates General approved the alternative.[72]

The animosity between city and countryside remained. Disputes over actual fiscal policies centred around the imposition of a land tax the Holland model on which would be disadvantageous to the countryside, or the impositions which were disadvantageous to the city such as the excises, a hearth tax, or a house tax. Such discontent arose over the capitation tax that in 1648 the district *Oldambt* revolted because of repeated grievances and declared itself independent. But the revolt was put down by the city soldiers, being backed up by the Estates General again.[73]

As compared with the other provinces, rural dwellers in Holland were less confronted with the growing needs of the state than their urban counterparts. The emphasis on excises tended to burden the cities, whereas only a small proportion was made up of the duties on horses, cattle and sown land. Even the land tax derived a significant portion (one-third) of revenue from houses. In most other states, and in the inland provinces of the Republic, direct taxes on land constituted the major revenue item, and added as such to the urban–rural controversies.

One might ask why the Holland cities did not shift the burden on to the countryside more. Yet such a shift was not always in the interest of city dwellers. Many burghers had acquired land, and landowners were responsible for the burden of the *verponding*. By comparison, in France, bourgeois landowners managed to shift the burden on to the village dwellers, because their lands were often exempt, either because of city privileges or because of non-taxation of absentee ownership. Therefore, increased taxes on land would not burden themselves.[74] Secondly, feudal structures in many other states facilitated the extraction of revenue from the peasantry – first in the guise of tithes and feudal rents, later as land taxes. In Holland, though, even the owners of seigneuries could not dispose of forceful extraction measures by tradition. The feudal burden had been extremely low, and with the reclamation of land difficult to impose.

Moreover, most polders were drained by city dwellers. Thirdly, the high costs of polder and dike maintenance limited the capacity to pay for warfare; newly reclaimed lands always remained exempt from the land tax for a period of fourteen years. Also, the process of land reclamation had established drainage boards (*waterschappen*) that gave the landowning farmers a voice in local administration and a means of preventing an unequal shift of the burden.[75]

By comparison, in Zeeland for example, the rural population was caught in a much firmer grip than in Holland. The drainage board that might have constituted a defence of the rural community was under the firm control of the urban magistrate, at least in Walcheren.[76] And even the excises showed a dominant pattern of semi-direct taxation upon on horses, carriages, arable land, cattle, and salt.

Such policies could be explained by the fact that the tax base was not as broad as in Holland. The cities were smaller, and the economy of the region contracted after Antwerp's fall in 1585. Options were reduced in other provinces too, by allowing the switching of some taxes, such as in Utrecht and Gelderland. This offered ready sums to the provincial receiver but limited future extensions of taxation. In addition, cities and nobility claiming ancient rights as to taxation narrowed the tax base even more. In Drenthe, church goods and gentry manors were exempt up to 1663. In Friesland, Zeeland, and Overijssel the lands in use by the nobility did not have to pay land taxes either.[77]

The decline of trade was, obviously, a factor that contributed to tax difficulties in much of the Republic outside the core. Population contracted and the economy stagnated, which linked these regions with the general European pattern. Yet an additional argument counted too: the presence of enemy troops. The inland provinces, above all Overijssel and Gelderland, suffered most directly from war in the shape of passing armies and nearby battlefields. Even in Groningen, as late as 1624, seven villages and a convent were burnt and people ransomed. Whereas the cities could benefit from the installation of a garrison, the countryside, being outside the republican redoubt, was open to military threat. Furthermore, enemy troops could demand significant money contributions. Up to the 1630s, regular sums were paid to the Spanish by Drenthe, Overijssel, and Gelderland. That ceased after the victories of Frederick Henry had significantly reduced the Spanish influence in the area.[78]

The arguments of enforced contributions to the enemy and wartime destruction were exploited to the full in disputes over the quotas at the Estates General at the Hague. And in fact, both Overijssel and Gelderland managed to have their quotas temporarily lowered in the 1620s, despite fierce protests by (mainly) Friesland and Groningen, two provinces which found it almost as hard to raise funds for warfare. Yet Gelderland was allowed in the 1620s to lower its quota from 5.5 per cent to 4.25, because of the hardships of war, the loss of the Upper Quarter (the region of Venlo), and the payment of contribution to the enemy. This regulation persisted up to 1634. Overijssel, which regarded its quota of 3.5 per cent as too high, even refused to send deputies to the Chamber of Accounts of the generality in The Hague up to 1623. In the 1620s, owing to the hostilities, the quota was reduced to 2.25 per cent. At first, the new regulation lasted only a couple of months, but it was extended. Finally, in 1636, it was raised to 3.5 per cent again. Additional remittances for wartime losses were granted incidentally too.[79]

Inland, consent was particularly reluctant with regard to navy subsidies. Drenthe, in fact, never paid the extraordinary navy quotas of 1629 and 1630 of 20,000 guilders each, because as a landlocked province it had little to gain from the admiralties.[80] Yet despite existing arrears in the quotas in the case of Gelderland, voting for petitions in The Hague nevertheless continued. As it was the province to vote first, a tradition stemming from its status as a duchy, Gelderland felt it should keep up the spirit of the Union.[81]

Disputes over quotas lowered any political ceiling of taxation. Furthermore, failure to pay the voted sum, for whatever reason, could eventually result in intervention by the Estates General. In particular since the resumption of war in 1621, delegates from The Hague visited the individual Provincial Estates and tried to persuade them to introduce new taxes.[82] Yet such intervention had been necessary prior to the Truce too. Peasant disturbances were endemic in the outer districts of Overijssel and Gelderland in the later sixteenth century. And the first impositions of new taxes in Drenthe necessitated outright repression. Troops were sent in 1604–1605, first because the province was unwilling to pay its arrears, and the second time because the Estates of the province themselves requested help to restore order. Posters announcing the tax farming had been torn down. When fees on grinding corn were increased by 50 per cent in 1603, rioting occurred in the garrison city of Coevorden in 1604 too. In 1610 the magistrates again requested military support, from the same Coevorden troops, to enforce the farming out of the taxes in the countryside.[83]

But with the resumption of war, Drenthe soon got into fresh trouble. The secretary of the province Weijnichmans noted that means to extract resources failed:

> The money does not fall like snow to us, we cannot shake it from the trees, we cannot cut it from the bogs, neither do we have golden mountains [. . .]. I am curious what will happen and whether they [The Hague] will treat the poor inhabitants with more hostility and with less indulgence as ever happened from the side of the enemy.[84]

The Council of State indeed took six Drenthen as hostages to induce them to pay for the troops. By comparison, the Spanish had never resorted to such brutal measures. Gelderland delegates too were made hostage after arrears had accumulated on behalf of their quarter, as in 1625, when the burgomaster of Nijmegen, Gerhardt Vervoort, and the secretary of the city, Lambert Goris, came to The Hague to take part in a session of the Estates General. Again, in 1640 some inhabitants of the same city were put in jail in Crèvecour in order to force their quarter to pay.[85]

In Groningen, the Estates General intervened at regular intervals. The first occasion was after the province had failed to provide its quota to the generality in 1604–1605. An army under Captain Olivier van Tempel arrived in the city and a list of Holland excises was enforced, to be farmed out by the Estates General. Then, since the urban–rural differences remained so sharp, The Hague recurrently had to settle the disputes, above all in the 1620s. The tax reform of 1628 was only brought about through central intermediation.[86] However, the central delegates were less succesfull in neighbouring Friesland, where they were confronted with unwillingness at all levels.

By the time war had resumed in 1621, nothing had been done in the field of taxation to put matters on a better footing in Friesland. In 1626, the Council of State, fearing a delay of another year, decided to enforce taxation in April. The hostility of the local population, however, prevented their plans, as a violent demonstration followed in Leeuwarden. A mob attacked the house in which the delegates of the Estates General were staying. In June the Frisian Stadhouder had to report that the citizens had disarmed the soldiers and seized the keys of the city gates, to prevent the entry of troops from Groningen.

The house of a burgomaster was pillaged, the windows of the Stadhouder's house and others were smashed, *grietmannen* (local justices) were attacked, and the Court of Friesland was occupied. The Estates General sent more troops. The cities once more asked for a delay in the introduction of the excises. The Stadhouder, too, recommended delaying tactics. In the end, no reforms took place. Some of the rebels were arrested, but in spite of pressure from the Estates General no one was convicted.[87]

In the 1630s new tax proposals were put forward. Matters, however, seemed to be decided by popular unrest again. In 1634 students in the university town of Franeker revolted against the tax farmers, as their privilege of exemption had been removed. In Harlingen a mob pillaged the house of the burgomaster, Bonnema. The latter was a deputy in the Chamber of Accounts in the generality and the people thought that he was responsible for the voting of the new taxes. The office of Receiver Rosema fared the same fate. Troops had to restore order.[88]

A provincial committee was installed, but proved unable to untie the financial knot. Instead, it provided a history of the recent disturbances, and pointed to the obstacles to the province's acceptance of Holland-centred taxation. In the meantime, the office of the receiver of the province, Jan van Bootsma, was in great disorder, and he was unable to service debt charges or pay troops. Furthermore, the province unilaterally disbanded some of the troops in its allocation, in obvious breach of the Union of Utrecht.[89]

In January 1637, another delegation of the Council of State arrived in Leeuwarden. The reasoning of the council is worth quoting, as warfare and taxation were regarded as positive for the Dutch economy:

> [. . .] war is ruinous for other countries, but it did strengthen the United Provinces in its trade, riches, and power, it did improve its territories and cities, and those funds extracted from the common people seemed to return by other ways again, like the waters which are transported by the rivers into the sea and which are returned by nature to its resources in a way unknown to us [. . .][90]

The council's cure for Friesland's failure to pay – how could it be otherwise? – was new taxes. It decided to take immediate steps, as it wanted to have the new taxes farmed out by April of that year. It had some provincial domains sold in order to obtain 400,000 to 500,000 guilders for the most pressing needs. In the end, some new taxes were introduced, the receiver was convicted, and the troops received their pay. The cities gave up their right to a third of the excises, but continued to enjoy lower rates for the *floreen*.[91]

At first, it seemed that the council could get away with this. But in the cities, the legitimacy of the Council of State's action in introducing taxes in a sovereign province was being seriously questioned. To appease opposition, the delegation from The Hague visited each of the eleven Frisian cities with troops and had reluctant magistrates removed. It was successful in all but one, Dokkum, the seat of the Frisian admiralty. There the magistrate worded an official protest against the authoritarian attitude of the council, that Friesland's liberty had been violated. Other cities and quarters rallied behind Dokkum. No winner emerged. Unrest remained, partly because troops were not paid, and in June 1637 another revolt started in Leeuwarden among the guard of the Frisian Stadhouder.[92] Yet at least the main fiscal barrier had been removed through The Hague's actions in the preceding year.

By contrast, few revolts occurred in the heart of the Republic. During the last three decades of the war, one major disturbance broke out following the impost on butter in 1624. It was also a year of harvest failure. In Geertruidenberg the tax farmer was chased out of town. In Amsterdam the tax farmer's office was stoned, and troops occupied the streets to defend the weighage and to restore order. Smaller disorders were noted in Delft, The Hague, Leiden, Hoorn, and Enkhuizen. In Haarlem the situation got seriously out of hand. It had started with a market woman from nearby Spaarndam, who refused to pay the new duty to the tax farmer. Bystanders formed a mob and stoned the officer's windows. The next day, the woman could not be arrested as she was defended by other townspeople. The violent demonstration that followed was put down by the local militia, at the cost of five killed and eight arrested. The Provincial Estates even sent 150 soldiers. The tax itself was maintained, but the duty was collected before the wares entered the market.[93]

Such civil disorders were concentrated in the cities, related to the fiscal structure, as the shift of the burden of war was first palpable through new excises. But most tax protests remained isolated and were easily controlled by the city militias, the *schutterijen*. In addition, troops could be called in under city command. In all, the populace was well used to these kinds of taxes, and regarded them as part of the common round.[94]

Also, by contrast with the more peripheral provinces, the local elites did not side with the lower classes' protests against taxation. This was due to the high political ceiling of taxation, related to the fact that Holland commanded a large part of the Union's political goals. Ousiders marvelled at the willingness to consent to taxation. The English ambassador Sir George Downing (1623–1684) reported:

> . . . its strange to see with what readyness this people doe consent to extrordinary taxes, although their ordinary taxes be yett as great as they were dureinge the warr with Spaine . . .[95]

Furthermore, the fact that most taxes were indirect contributed to the social peace: discontent was aimed at shopkeepers or tax farmers, perhaps at local magistrates, but not against the government in The Hague.

The great advantage for Holland was not only a high political ceiling of taxation, but also the great variety of taxes that made its strength, in turn by the differentiation in the socio-economic structure itself. All economic sectors were affected by taxation. What Amsterdam contributed in weighage, Dordrecht equalled in the duty on horses, whereas The Hague contributed more in luxury and property taxes. The whole system was based on Holland's ability to adapt traditional taxes, in particular the city excises, to the modern era. The tax burden had never been so great and amazed many foreign visitors.

Illustrative of contemporary admiration for the Holland tax system was the comparison of the English civil servant Samuel Pepys. He wrote in his diary in 1664 that Sir Philip Warwick, the Secretary to the Treasury, had showed him:

> . . . a discourse of his concerning the Revenues of this and foreign States. How that of Spayne was great, but divided with his kingdoms and so came to little. How that of France did and doth much exceed ours before quantity, and that it is at the will of the Prince to tax what he will upon his people; which is not here. That the Hollanders have the best manner of tax, which is only upon the expense of provisions, by an excise.[96]

But these taxes were high. In Holland, the tax burden per head increased by 21 per cent during 1620–1650. In Leiden 60 per cent of the price of beer, 25 per cent of the price of bread and 14 per cent of the price of meat went in tax. Moreover, despite the peace settlement of 1648, hardly any taxes went down. Above all the expense of the debt charges upon the loans contracted during war had to be met. Therefore, the funds appropriated by the provincial government remained undiminished and were even extended in the subsequent decades. Charles Wilson has reconstructed the incidence of tax with the help of King's estimates at the end of the seventeenth century. He found a burden of £1 4*s* 0*d* pound sterling for England, £1 5*s* 0*d* for France, whereas in the Netherlands each inhabitant paid £3 1*s* 7*d* in taxes.[97]

These high taxes persisted in Holland because local elites never supported such lower-class revolts as occurred. The political ceiling of taxation was too high. First, because Holland cities were able to put their stamp upon the Union's policies. Second, because part of the revenue was used for the payment of interest on the public debt.[98] In that regard, major urban elites profited from the excises and extraordinary property taxes, in particular through the investments in obligations of the Union and of Holland, which will be discussed in Chapter Six.

Notes

1 J.D. Alsop, 'The theory and practice of Tudor taxation', *English Historical Review* 382, 1982, 26–30. For a reaction, see G.L. Harriss, 'Theory and practice in royal taxation: some observations', *English Historical Review* 383, 1982, 819.

2 Quoted by William Kennedy, *English taxation 1640–1799: an essay on policy and opinion*, New York, 1913, 65.

3 Krüger, 'Public finance and modernization', 56; Gabriel Ardant noted the difficulty of states operating in agrarian subsistence economies: 'Financial policy and economic infrastructure of modern states and nations', *The formation of national states in Western Europe*, ed. C. Tilly, Princeton, 1975, 164.

4 Meuvret, 'Comment les Français voyaient l'impôt', 308; also François Hincker, *Les Français devant l'impôt sous l'ancien régime*, Paris, 1971, 120; Charles Tilly, *The contentious French. Four centuries of popular struggle*, Cambridge, Mass., 1986, 105. England also imposed monopolies instead of excises in the late 1630s, constituting a much more overt intervention in domestic order. See for example the pamphlet *Een t'samenspraeck ofte voorghevallene discours tusschen Mr. Alderman Abel ende Richard Kilvert, de twee voorname Projecteurs ofte Practicijns van de wijn-pacht*, 1641 (KB Pamphlet 4758).

5 Dessert, *Argent, pouvoir*, 17; W. Achilles, *Die steuerliche Belastung der Braunschweigischen Landwirtschaft und ihr Beitrag zu den Staatseinnahmen im 17. und 18. Jahrhundert*, Hildesheim, 1972, 228–9;

For Hesse: Krüger, 'Public finance and modernization', 59; J.-Cl. Hocquet, 'Venise, les villes et les campagnes de la Terreferme (XVe XVIe siècles). Elements d'une problématique', *La ville, la bourgeoisie et la genèse de l'état moderne*, Bielefeld/Paris, 1988, 218.

6 Hincker, *Les Français devant l'impôt*, 41, 53; Mousnier, *Les institutions*, 565.

7 Antoni Maczak, 'The conclusive years: the end of the sixteenth century as the turning point of Polish history', *Politics and Society in Reformation Europe*, ed. E.I. Kouri and Tom Scott, London, 1986, 518–20.

8 Tilly, *The contentious French*, 139; Roland Mousnier, *Peasant uprisings in seventeenth century France, Russia and China*, London, 1971, 306; Yves-Marie Bercé, *Croquants et Nu-Pieds. Les soulèvements paysans en France du XVIe au XIXe siècle*, Paris, 1974.

9 R.B. Merriman, *Six contemporaneous revolutions*, Glasgow, 1937, 15–16.

10 Cf. Schumpeter, 'Crisis of the tax state'; Pocock, *Machiavellian moment*, II; Colin Brooks, 'Public finance and political stability: the administration of the land tax, 1688–1720', *Historical Journal* 17, 1974, 281–300; Douglass North, *Structure and change in economic history*, New York, 1981, 22; Mark Gould, *Revolution in the development of capitalism. The coming of the English revolution*, Berkeley, 1987, 362–3.

11 P. Blok, 'Het budget eener Hollansche stad omstreeks 1400', *Bijdragen voor de Vaderlandsche Geschiedenis en Oudheidkunde* III-1, 1882, 308; J.W. Marsilje, *Het financiële beleid van Leiden in de laat-Beierse en Bourgondische periode 1390–1477*, Hilversum, 1985, 267; R.M. Dekker, 'Wij willen al den duyvel aff hebben! Protesten tegen belastingen in het verleden', *Fiscaliteit in Nederland*, ed. J.Th. de Smidt *et al.*, Zutphen, 1987, 40.

12 Cf. J.C. Naber, *Een terugblik. Statistische bewerking van de resultaten van de informatie van 1514*, Haarlem, 1970, bijlage XVII. Within the Republic, Vianen, Leerdam and Ameland enjoyed similar privileges. Engels, *Belastingen*, 135.

13 See also J.A.M.Y. Bos-Rops, 'Van incidentele gunst tot jaarlijkse belasting: de bede in het vijftiende eeuwse Holland', *Fiscaliteit in Nederland*, ed. J.Th. de Smidt *et al.*, Zutphen, 1987, 21; H. Terdenge, 'Zur Geschichte der holländischen Steuern im 15. und 16. Jahrhundert', *Vierteljahrschrift für Sozial – und Wirtschaftsgeschichte* 18, 1925, 98.

14 Craeybeckx, 'Aperçu sur l'histoire des impôts', 10; Van Deursen, *Kopergeld*, 25. RAZH Jacob Cats 10; R.J.C. van Maanen, 'Hollandse vermogingsheffingen in de 17e en 18e eeuw', *Nederlands Archievenblad* 88, 1984, 63; P.W. Klein, 'De heffing van de 100e en 200e penning van het vermogen te Gouda, 1599–1722', *Economisch en Sociaal-Historisch Jaarboek* 31, 1967, 43: in 1625 the limit of exempion was lowered from 2,000 to 1,000, whereas at the beginning of the seventeenth century the limit had been 3,000 guilders.

15 *Politijck Hantboecxken van de Staet van 't Nederlandt, vertoonende den florissanten Staet ende veelvoudighen Middelen, tot onderhoudinghe van de wijdt-beroemde Republijck*, The Hague, 1650, 169.

16 On the development of the Northern Quarter: A.M. van der Woude, *Het Noorderkwartier. Een regionaal historisch onderzoek in de demografische en economische geschiedenis van westelijk Nederland van de late middeleeuwen tot het begin van de negentiende eeuw*, Utrecht, 1972.

17 See *Groot Placaet Boeck* I, 1491, 1599, 1637, 1683, 1694, 1790, 1802, 1837, 1882; *Politijck Hant-Boecxken*, 1650, 170–2.

18 For example, see accounts of Rotterdam in Gemeente Archief Rotterdam (GAR) 3088. RAZH FH 829; T.S. Jansma, *Tekst en uitleg*, The Hague, 1974, 43; J.C. van Dalen, *Geschiedenis van Dordrecht*, Dordrecht, 1931, 294, 450; P. Blok, 'Stadsfinanciën onder de Republiek', *Verslagen en Mededelingen van de Koninklijke Academie van Wetenschappen Letteren* V-2, 1917, 229–30; *Groot Placaet Boeck* I, 1694, 1768, 1782, 1874, 1886; Roovers, *Plaatselijke belastingen*, 25.

19 *Groot Placaet Boeck* I, 1803; on a salt tax farmer: A.C. Kersberger, 'Adriana van Oringen. Pachteresse en collectrice van imposten', *Rotterdams Jaarboekje* 4e reeks II, 1934, 90; GAA 5052 notebooks tax collectors.

20 *Groot Placaet Boeck* I, 1934, 1941.

21 *Groot Placaet Boeck* I, 1929, 1952, 1962, 1970, 1985. Van Maanen, 'Hollandse vermogensheffingen', 62.

22 *Groot Placaet Boeck* I, 1866, 1873, 1874, 1878, 1901, 1914, 1925.

23 Beers consumed onboard ship, which had previously been exempted, were included in taxation henceforth as well. *Groot Placaet Boeck* I, 1694 ff.

24 Van Dalen, *Geschiedenis van Dordrecht*, 468; *Groot Placaet Boeck* I, 1941.

25 *Groot Placaet Boeck* I, 1878, 1937.

26 Act to introduce the provincial stamp duty in 1624. Quoted by Engels, *Belastingen*, 93. In this case, the tax was double-sided: all documents for lawsuits, requests, sale of property, mortgages, obligations and others obtained legality against the payment of a minor duty. Other taxes were mere revenue raising.

27 *Groot Placaet Boeck* I, 1901, 1914. Israel, *Dutch republic and Hispanic world*, 150; Van Deursen, *Kopergeld* III, 60.

28 *Groot Placaet Boeck* I, 1694 ff., 1724, 1772. Another duty upon breweries for their corn grinding did not last longer than six months, its collection being probably too complicated.

29 *Groot Placaet Boeck* I, 1945, 1949.

30 *Groot Placaet Boeck* I, 1881, 1921, 1925; Israel, *Dutch Republic and Hispanic world*, 150.

31 *Groot Placaet Boeck* I, 1862.

32 *Groot Placaet Boeck* I, 1977, 1985, 1994, 2001, 2006, 2050. Van den Broecke never got a reward for his invention despite the promises of the Estates. It was copied by other provinces and many other states. See on this subject: J. van der Poel, *De geschiedenis van het Nederlands fiscaal zegel 1624–1954*, Deventer, 1951.

33 Van Deursen, *Kopergeld* III, 61.

34 Jacob Cats was one of the persons behind several proposals: W.E. de Boer, *Het Archief van Jacob Cats, 1634–1651*, The Hague, 1977, ix. *Groot Placaet Boeck* I, 1970, 2001.

35 Jan den Tex, *Oldenbarnevelt* IV, Haarlem, 1960, 181; Van der Capellen, *Gedenkschriften* I, 612; Engels, *Belastingen*, 117.

36 According to a list of new houses built in 1632–1654, population growth was concentrated in Amsterdam, Leiden, The Hague and Rotterdam. RAZH Jacob Cats 10; GAA, 5030/137.

37 ARA SG 12548.205; Van der Capellen, *Gedenkschriften* I, 459.

38 *Groot Placaet Boeck* I, 1599, 1772, 1941, 1988–89, 1992–3; Van Deursen, *Kopergeld*, 38; Clé Lesger, *Huur en conjunctuur. De woningmarkt in Amsterdam, 1550–1850*, Amsterdam, 1986, 47; Lamens, 'Landelijke heffingen', 474.

39 *Groot Utrechts Placcaat Boek* II, 570; III, 949; Engels, *Belastingen*, 59 ff.; Sickenga, *Bijdrage*, 69.

40 *Groot Utrechts Placcaat Boek II*, ed. Johan vande Water, Utrecht, 1729, 579, 599, 604, 661, 682, 712, 725, 777, 832, 854, 861; J.Th. de Smidt, 'Vier eeuwen overdrachtsbelasting?', *Fiscaliteit in Nederland*, Zutphen, 1987, 56; Engels, *Belastingen*, 59 ff; RAZH Jacob Cats 12; *Groot Placaet Boeck* I, 1637–94, 2030–58.

41 *Groot Utrechts Placcaat Boek* III, 950.

42 *Groot Utrechts Placcaat Boek* II, 548, 564, 609, 653, 726, 748, 767, 780, 781, 817; III 950; Engels, *Belastingen*, 75.

43 *Groot Utrechts Placcaat Boek* II, 585, 609, 656, 661, 732, 751, 858, 879, 887; III, 547. Grain and wine were generally much higher as compared to Holland. In addition, the city of Utrecht levied many separate duties in addition to the provincial excises. Also, the smaller cities had their imposts. Wine and beer especially were taxed. In addition, customs duties existed on wine, beer, grain, oil, soap, peat, etc. According to an overview in the late eighteenth century, the Utrecht revenue came from direct taxes in the proportions: 34.1 per cent, stamp duties: 15.4 per cent, tolls: 2.5 per cent, excises: 48.1 per cent. Sickenga, *Bijdrage*, 325.

44 RAZH Jacob Cats 12.

45 *Groot Placaet Boeck* I, 2016, 2034, 2046, 2048, 2058. Sickenga, *Bijdrage*, 390; Engels, *Belastingen*, 63, 64, 104.

46 On Zeeland's peat: L. van Wallenburg, 'Darinkdelven in Zeeland', *Nederlandsche Historiën* 5, 1971, 52–4. Only at the end of the century did Zeeland manage to introduce higher grain customs. Van der Bijl, *Idee en interest*, 6.

47 As compared to Holland, the city's autonomy was larger *vis-à-vis* its former overlord *and* the provincial government. Fockema Andreae, *Nederlandse staat*, 12; P.H.J. van der Laan, 'Die städtische Autonomie in den nördlichen Niederlanden bis zum 17. Jahrhundert', *Autonomie, Wirtschaft und Kultur der Hansestädte*, Weimar, 1984, 101–10.

48 Reitsma, *Centrifugal and centripetal forces*, 209, 274: the author is more positive on the 1600 introduction of excises in Overijssel. Most revenue continued to come from land or cattle. See his table on p. 270 for the low contribution by the cities. Cf. the evaluation of the introduction by the *Tegenwoordige Staat der Vereenigde Nederlanden* XXVIII (Overijssel), Amsterdam, 1739, 182. Nevertheless, we can agree with Reitsma that the overall tax yield had increased significantly as compared to the 1570s.

49 For example, in Arnhem in 1622, a publican had to pay the following per barrel: 0.70 guilder for the magistrates (traditional city excise), 1.25 guilders for redemption of the house tax, 1.25 guilders for the garrison and lodgings, generality expenses, 0.60 guilder for the service of the city's debt, 1.20 guilders for the generality, 0.20 guilder hop excises and 1.00 guilder as an additional duty. Van der Capellen, *Gedenkschriften* I, 33; Engels, *Belastingen*, 63.

50 Matthey, 'Fiskaal compas', 229–30, 280, 307; L.S. Meihuizen, 'Sociaal-economische geschiedenis van Groningerland', *Historie van Groningen*, ed. W.J. Formsma, Groningen, 1981, 327; Rijksarchief in Groningen (RAG) Res GS 24 June 1622, 27 September 1622; Engels, *Belastingen*, 59 ff. Stamp duties did not exist until later in the century. The *ronde maat* was abolished in 1629. The capitation duty was abolished in the 1650s, together with the tax on income from industry, on offices and on servants. The hearth tax was reduced as well. M.G. de Boer, *De woelingen in Stad en Lande in het midden van de zeventiende eeuw*, Groningen, 1893, 40, 53.

51 The Frisian *Vijf Speciën* did not burden salt, soap, cloth, beer and wine, as their title suggested, but hearths, horses, cattle, arable lands and capitation. Lieuwe van Aitzema, *Historie of verhael van saken van staet en oorlogh in, ende omtrent de Vereenigde Nederlanden* II, The Hague, 1667, 9, 159; on this author, see Gees van der Plaat, 'Lieuwe van Aitzema's kijk op het stadhouderschap in de Republiek (1652–1669) en de crisis van 1650', *Bijdragen en Mededelingen betreffende de Geschiedenis der Nederlanden* 103, 1988, 341–72; *Groot Placaat en Charterboek van Vriesland* V, ed. G.F. Baron thoe Schwartzenberg, Leeuwarden, 1768, 334, 433; Sickenga, *Overzicht belastingen Friesland*, 15, 25; S.J. van der Molen, 'Sociaal palet', *Geschiedenis van Friesland*, ed. J.J. Kalma *et al.*, Leeuwarden, 1973, 376.

52 Stamp duties and weighage did not exist. Paul Brood, *Grondschatting, omslagen en haardstedengeld. Een handleiding voor het gebruik van de archivalia*, Assen, 1980, 11; Zijlstra, *Des lieven geldes*, 39, 76; Sickenga, *Bijdrage tot de geschiedenis*, 347; Jan Bieleman, *Boeren op het Drentse Zand 1600–1920. Een nieuwe visie op de 'oude' landbouw*, Wageningen, 1987, 173.

53 RAZH Van Slingelandt 251.

54 The Union of Utrecht (article 18) forbade provincial customs, but by then other provinces had introduced them as well. *Tegenwoordige staat*, 218.

55 Sickenga, *Bijdrage tot de geschiedenis*, 317, 353, 365, 450; Slicher van Bath, *Een samenleving onder spanning*, 32; *Tegenwoordige Staat*, 218, 222–3; see for a re-evaluation of Slicher van Bath: Jan Luiten van Zanden, 'De opkomst van een eigenerfde boerenklasse in Overijssel, 1750–1830', *AAG Bijdragen* 24, 1984, 105.

56 Van der Capellen, *Gedenkschriften* II, 56; Sickenga, *Bijdrage tot de geschiedenis*, 332, 354.

57 Jan Dhondt, *Estates or powers. Essays in the parliamentary history of the southern Netherlands from the XIIth to the XVIIIth century*, Kortrijk-Heule, 1977, 155–7; R. Murris, *La Hollande et les Hollandais au*

XVIIe et au XVIIIe siècles vus par les Francais, Paris, 1925, 232. See also Marjolein 't Hart, 'The Devil or the Dutch? Holland's impact on the financial revolution in England, 1643–1694', *Parliaments, estates and representation* 11, 1991, 39–52.

58 Van Deursen, *Kopergeld*, 31; RAZH FH 826.

59 The study by Noordegraaf of living standards in Holland reported harvest failures in the years 1621, 1647–1648 and 1650. Grain shortages and high prices were noted in 1624 and 1631. Noordegraaf, *Hollands welvaren*, 34, 41. The latter might account for the low period of 1631, whereas the harvest failure of 1648 may have had its effect upon the trade in that year. It signifies that Noordegraaf's 1624 concided with the only major tax revolt of the period. For the years 1626, 1637–1638 and 1645–1647 no explanation is to hand, although the latter may point to the start of the stagnation of the Dutch economy of the later seventeenth century. Also, tax yields tend to decline when there are no major additions.

60 The actual burden of excises might have been approximately 10 per cent higher. For the beginning of the eighteenth century, B.E. de Muinck, *Een regentenhuishouding omstreeks 1700. gegevens uit de privéboekhouding van Mr Cornelis de Jonge van Ellemeet, ontvanger-generaal der Verenigde Nederlanden, 1646–1721*, The Hague, 1965, 316–20, calculated the incidence of taxation for a minister (including local duties) at 13 per cent; for a labourer it was 15 to 16 per cent. A study by Fritschy estimated the burden of farmed taxes per head of household to have been more than 5.4 per cent in 1600, about 9.5 in 1608 and 10 per cent in 1648. Wantje Fritschy, *De patriotten en de financiën van de Bataafse Republiek. Hollands krediet en de smalle marges voor een nieuw beleid (1795–1801)*, The Hague, 1988, 51.

61 Lamens, 'Landelijke heffingen', 471.

62 GAA 5030/137; RAZH FH 826 and 829. H. Enno van Gelder, 'Haagsche cohieren', *Die Haghe Jaarboek*, 1913–14, 14. The duties on wine from this town brought in 45,000 guilders, more than the yield of Leiden, Delft, Rotterdam, and Dordrecht taken together. It must be said, however, that collection of taxes was probably more reliable there as well, as The Hague did not have financial autonomy: Van der Capellen, *Gedenkschriften* I, 447. See for the semi-direct taxes in the eighteenth century: H.A. Diederiks, 'De collecteurs van de gemene landsmiddelen in Amsterdam en omstreken in de tweede helft van de 18e eeuw', *Tijdschrift voor Geschiedenis* 90, 1977, 484–502.

63 Van der Capellen, *Gedenkschriften* I, 442.

64 Matthey, 'Fiskaal compas', 215; Van der Capellen, *Gedenkschriften* II, 56; Sickenga, *Bijdrage tot de geschiedenis*, 332, 354; Bieleman, *Boeren op het zand*, 177–8; *Tegenwoordige Staat der Vereenigde Nederlanden* XXVI (Friesland), Amsterdam, 1739, 181, 394–6.

65 Van der Capellen, *Gedenkschriften* I, 470.

66 *Resolutiën* SG 2 July 1622, 1 July 1623; Sickenga, *Bijdragen tot de geschiedenis*, 293; ARA SG 12548.173.

67 See also Chapter Seven.

68 Grever, 'Politics and society during the 1660s', 1; Guibal, *Demo-*

cratie en oligarchie, 105. The *floreen* was an old coin, valued at twenty-eight stuyvers.

69 A.L.M. de Wolf, 'Fiscale reschtspraak in Gelderland', *Fiscaliteit in Nederland*, ed. J.Th. de Smidt, Zutphen, 1987, 46; Poelhekke, '1609–1672', 133.

70 Van der Capellen, *Gedenkschriften* I, 128, 132–3, 137, 163.

71 Brood, *Grondschatting*, 24; Zijlstra, *Des lieven geldes*, 41.

72 Matthey, 'Fiskaal compas', 254; Sickenga, *Bijdrage*, 85; Formsma, 'Jonkers en boeren', 67; Hidde Feenstra, *De bloeitijd en verval van de Ommelander adel 1600–1800*, Groningen, 1981, 104.

73 ARA SG 12548.254 and 278 'Groningen tegen Ommelanden'; C.E. Dijkstra, 'De Oldambten tegen de stad ... Een vruchteloze strijd', *Groningse Volksalmanak. Historisch Jaarboek voor Groningen 1974–1975*, 1975, 49, 52.

74 Philip T. Hoffman, 'Taxes and agrarian life in early modern France: land sales, 1550–1730', *Journal of Economic History* 46, 1986, 43; Jansma, *Tekst en uitleg*, 45; J.W. Marsilje, 'Les modes d'imposition en Hollande 1477–1515', *Publications du Centre Européen d'Etudes Bourguignonnes* 28, 1988, 159–72; Terdenge, 'Holländische Steuern', 107.

75 From the thirteenth century to the fifteenth, drainage boards may have provided the landowning farmers with an institutional outlet which prevented overburdening by the cities. Hendrik van der Linden, 'Een nieuwe overheidsinstelling: het waterschap circa 1100–1400', *Algemene Geschiedenis der Nederlanden* III, Haarlem, 1982, 60–77.

76 M. van Empel and H. Pieters, *Zeeland door de eeuwen heen*, Middelburg, 1959, 534.

77 Attempts in Overijssel in 1627, 1633 and 1637 to have them pay the land tax failed. Sickenga, *Bijdrage in de geschiedenis*, 297, 336, 343; Reitsma, *Centrifugal and centripetal forces*, 9; Dircksen, 'Enige opmerkingen over belastingheffing', 248; Bieleman, *Boeren op het zand*, 173; Feenstra, *Bloeitijd en verval*, 103.

78 Zijlstra, *Des lieven geldes*, 70–5; Dijkstra, 'De Oldambten tegen de stad', 46; Feenstra, *Bloeitijd en verval*, 105; *Resolutiën* SG 29 July 1614, 17 April 1624; RAG Res GS 233, 28 July 1624; ARA CoA 94: 30 April 1631 and 9 September 1632, 8: 14 April 1638 on remissions as a result of warfare burdens.

79 Van der Capellen, *Gedenkschriften* I, 452, 480; II, 53–4; *Resolutiën* SG 31 January, 29 June 1622; *Tegenwoordige staat Overijssel*, 229, 231, 235.

80 According to Zijlstra, the *f*790,481 were never paid either. Zijlstra, *Des lieven geldes*, 82, 85, 101.

81 Van der Capellen, *Gedenkschriften* I, 396.

82 ARA SG 12548.173 'Stukken betreffende bezending 1622'; *Resolutiën* SG 1 July 1623.

83 Zijlstra, *Des lieven geldes*, 79; *Resolutiën* SG, 22 March 1610.

84 Zijlstra, *Des lieven geldes*, 76, May 1622.

85 Poelhekke, '1609–1672', 153; Aitzema, *Historie of verhael* II, 9.

86 De Boer, *De woelingen in Stad en Lande*, 4–5; RAG 701 'Register'

1595/1612/1622; ARA SG 12548.298 'Groningen tegen Ommelanden'.

87 Van der Molen, 'Sociaal palet', 376; Aitzema, *Historie of verhael* II, 116–17; ARA SG 12548.176 and 179: 'Geschil gemene middelen Friesland 1625'.

88 Aitzema, *Historie of verhael* II, 159.

89 *Ibidem* II, 428; *Groot Placaat en Charterboek* V, 352, 393; Guibal, *Democratie en oligarchie*, 58, 108.

90 Quoted by Aitzema, *Historie of verhael* II, 427.

91 *Ibidem* II, 431–7; H. Terpstra, *Jacob van Neck, Amsterdams admiraal en regent*, Amsterdam, 1950, 168–9; F.N. Sickenga, *Overzicht van de geschiedenis der belastingen in Friesland, voor en tijdens de Republiek der Verenigde Nederlanden*, Leeuwarden, 1868, 15; *Groot Placaat en Charterboek* V, 433.

92 The matter coincided with an overall reform in appointments of city magistrates (1635–1636). Guibal, *Democratie en oligarchie*, 46; Aitzema, *Historie of verhael* II, 432–7; Terpstra, *Van Neck*, 168–9; Sickenga, *Overzicht belastingen Friesland*, 15; *Groot Placaat en Charterboek* V, 433.

93 See Van der Capellen, *Gedenkschriften* I, 276; R.M. Dekker, *Holland in beroering. Oproeren in de 17e en 18e eeuw*, Baarn, 1982, 30.

94 On tax revolts in Holland: Dekker, *Holland in beroering*, 28; cf. W.Ph. TeBrake, 'Violence in the Dutch Patriot Revolution', *Comparative Studies in Society and History* 30, 1988, 148; Ton Zwaan, 'Politiek geweld, maatschappelijke structuur en burgerlijke civilisatie. Een verkenning van de binnenstatelijke geweldpleging in de ontwikkeling van de Nederlandse samenleving 1648–1960', *Sociologisch Tijdschrift* 9, 1982, 433–75.

95 Quoted by Wilson, 'Taxation and decline', 118.

96 *The Diary of Samuel Pepys* V, London, 1972, 68.

97 Wilson, 'Taxation and decline', 120, 122; J.A.F. de Jongste, *Onrust aan het Spaarne. Haarlem in de jaren 1747–1751*, Dieren, 1984, 46–7, noted payments in Haarlem towards taxes (including city excises) upon butter of 7.3 per cent, upon peat 56 per cent (!), upon firewood of 30 per cent and upon grinding corn of 15.7 per cent. Ruud Liesker, 'Tot zinkens toe bezwaard. De schuldenlast van het Zuiderkwartier van Holland 1672–1794', *Bestuurders en Geleerden*, ed. S. Groenveld *et al.*, Amsterdam, 1985, 158, for figures for the eighteenth century.

98 See for an eighteenth century account of consciousness of that relationship between taxation and public debt: Wantje Fritschy, 'De patriottenbeweging in Nederland. Een verzetsbeweging tegen een financiële oligarchie?', *1787: De Nederlandse revolutie?*, Amsterdam, 1988, 61; see for a general treatment Pocock, *Machiavellian moment*, 426 ff.

6

The third shift: public loans

Before the sixteenth century few European states contracted substantial long-term debts at all. By the eighteenth century almost all were permanently indebted. With the increases in the scale of warfare, due to the military revolution, taxes could bring no immediate solution. Until the new revenues were collected, the troops for whom the money was intended would be ready to mutiny for their pay. Wars impelled states to find other solutions. Some were able to find a temporary way out, such as confiscations or forced contributions. However, a move towards the future by way of contracting voluntary loans became one of the best options. It was a step into the next few years or even into the next generation, as future funds had to be found either for the amortization of the debt or for payment of the interest. When such state obligations were handled with care a public debt emerged, now so characteristic of present-day national states.[1]

Many states found themselves borrowing from foreigners. To discover funds at home was a rare luxury, reserved in the main for a few city states such as Genoa and Venice. In the sixteenth century Spain raised many loans in Antwerp or in Genoa, and in 1626–1627, Olivares contracted funds from the Portuguese Jewish community. In 1619 the first Romanoff, Michael Féodorovitch, borrowed 20,000 roubles from James I of England. In the 1620s the Habsburg emperor borrowed 6 million guilders from Hans Witte, a Dutch Calvinist financier.[2] Such loans tended to increase the dependence of the state's rulers upon such wealthy fundholders. On the other hand, they could act more independently *vis-à-vis* their own financial elites, which fact might have certain political advantages.

The revenues to fund interest payments on loans might entail a shift towards the home community again, as, in the main, taxes had to provide the resources for debt charges. Some states, however, were (temporarily) in a position to circumvent this confrontation with the home community. Sweden could draw upon its regular revenue from copper mines, and Spain could sustain its precarious loan policy for several decades because of the flow of silver from its American colonies. Although these funds were always a mere fraction of the whole revenue needed, they did secure the necessary interest payments on loans. Eric Wolf argued:

> The silver of the new world also enhanced the revenues of the crown. [. . .] American silver underwrote large-scale military operations in Europe and the growth of a bureaucracy far beyond the ultimate capacities of the Spanish economy. Deficit spending was made up by loans from foreign financiers only too happy to lend against future imports of silver [. . .]. Spain thus never developed a coherent economic policy; the imperial bureaucracy acted simply as a conduit of wealth into Italian, south German, and Dutch coffers.[3]

Such regular and secure funds enabled a state to play one foreign investor against another. But then, for Spain, the decline of colonial revenues mattered: in 1616–1621 they were a mere 40 per cent of what they were in 1596–1600. And even Sweden had become too dependent upon Dutch loans, which proved fatal when the United Provinces themselves were absorbed by a sudden and expensive war in 1672.[4]

Secure management of the public debt was one of the major challenges for early modern states. Many failed to construct a trustworthy and enduring relationship with financial elites. As a result, sixteenth and seventeenth-century Europe witnessed recurrently defaulting governments. 'Bankruptcies' occurred when the state was unable to continue the payment of interest. Among others, Spain fell financially in 1607, 1627 and 1647; France defaulted in 1648. Recurrently, European princes invoked absolute powers to stay solvent. They repudiated debts, lowered interest rates, debased currencies, and lengthened the periods of loans. With such breaches of trust, interest rates were likely to be high. Rates of 10 to 20 per cent were no exception. For decades the English state sustained its borrowing by selling Crown property and confiscated goods, so as to secure payments for interest. In France the lending business even involved personal danger. The recurrent *lits de justice* (royal juridical sessions) were apt to condemn major officers-lenders for 'mismanagement', and some financiers even paid with their lives.[5]

In addition, forced loans were still used extensively. Foreigners within the home community were the first to experience these exactions, but such loans could burden the officers of the state themselves or entire city populations, as in Venice and Lübeck. They decreased the willingness of individuals to invest in the state. After all, one could never be sure what future demands of the state's coffers might be.[6]

The sale of offices could be a kind of disguised loan policy as well. The newcoming officer paid a certain sum stipulated in the contract to the state, and the state paid interest on the sum. Moreover, these officers provided most short-term loans to the French king. The advantage was that the cooperation of the domestic elite was acquired. But it was an expensive asset which was likely to burden the country in the future. It rendered the king utterly dependent upon his accountants. They provided the funds, which they derived from royal taxation, depriving the state of tax revenue again. The highest noblemen were involved: even Richelieu and Mazarin received interest upon their loans to the king. Reforms and retrenchment seemed unlikely in such a setting.[7]

Likewise, the English king became dependent upon his tax farmers in the 1630s and 1640s. London goldsmiths replaced them as major government lenders in the 1660s. A more regular and stable system of long-term borrowing was made possible by intermediaries such as provincial estates and municipal governments, like the Hôtel de Ville of Paris or the Estates of the Pays d'Etats in the case of France. In all, mismanagement of loan policies might be another cause of civil disturbances. Julian Dent wrote: 'Whatever the Fronde afterwards became, it began partly as a revolt of the rentiers seeking payment of their rents.'[8]

Yet public debt was not always a merely negative burden for the domestic elites, if it was issued at home. Russia contracted loans in exchange for privileges with landed owners and convents. In Brabant and Flanders the local elites managed to enrich themselves through the governmental floatation of loans. Overall, Venetian patriciates were paying less to the state in direct taxes than they were receiving in interest and repayment of capital sums.[9]

Obviously, not only a political ceiling of taxation was at play: one could speak of a political ceiling for domestic public loans as well. The national public debt system that emerged in eighteenth-century England was exceptional. Interest payments were secured by way of regular, mainly indirect taxation. Loans were voluntary and contracted over the long term, at relatively low rates of interest. The Bank of England came to supervise the government's financial policies. It was called the 'financial revolution in the state'.[10]

Shifting the burden of war to a secured system of public debt was quite difficult for most European states in the seventeenth century, although the effort was worth while. This chapter follows the Dutch loan policy and the emergence of a public debt. Holland's credit was outstanding and supported the credit policies of the generality. Subsequently, the public debt of the generality and the admiralties are analysed. Dutch credit was supported by a wide range of domestic investors, as is shown in a study of the creditors of the state.

A provincial financial revolution

At the time of the outbreak of the Dutch Revolt, the public debt of the province of Holland was sustained by the strong trust of its domestic investors. The administration of credit within the province of Holland was facilitated by long-term contracts at low rates with a high degree of stability. The cities, of course, had a long tradition of long-term financing, yet in the sixteenth century the system was raised at provincial level in three consecutive steps. First, since 1515, the Estates of the province had coordinated control and sale of the *renten* (loans). Second, from 1542 onwards the Estates shifted the funding of *renten* from the uncertain method of subsidy to new and permanent taxes, in particular excises, administered by the provincial Estates themselves. And third, in 1553 the Estates gave up compelling their wealthy subjects to purchase *renten* and thus allowed a 'free market' in government bonds to emerge.[11] From then on voluntary loans dominated, which raised the political ceiling of the public debt, although forced loans reappeared incidentally.

In those first decades, the Provincial Estates developed great solvency and were extremely careful in managing their loans. Nevertheless, the beginning of the Revolt was full of hardships, and in 1581 suspension of payments was ordered. In 1586–1587 a forced loan was issued in Delft, Leiden, Rotterdam and The Hague. These measures were supplemented in 1584 by an extension of the *verponding* (land and property tax) to the revenue from annuities and obligations. A duty of 15 per cent was imposed. A decrease followed in 1590, resulting in a charge of 12.5 per cent. Six years later another reduction took place: the duty was halved to 6.25 per cent.[12]

Even these taxes were highly contested. In 1599 it was resolved to do away with the tax upon obligations, as money was badly needed. Fear was expressed that the moneylenders would become reluctant to invest their funds in government bonds. However, the province could not manage without a tax of this kind and it was reimposed in 1601 at the rate of 12.5 per cent. Forced loans were issued again in 1600–1602, and in 1604 a temporary tax was once more imposed on the provincial obligations.[13] Thereafter, the tax on obligations stabilized and forced loans disappeared until the 1670s.

Three kinds of long term bonds existed: obligations, *lijfrenten* (or life annuities) and *losrenten*. In the strict sense of the term, all three could be called obligations, but this name was reserved for the loans issued by the receivers themselves, for which they charged a commission or brokerage (*makelaardijgeld*). Originally, obligations had been contracted as an emergency measure, when city finances fell short, to secure credit. As funds did not become available for amortization, obligations were renewed every six months, and became long-term assets. For the debt charges, the receivers' private credit stood as a guarantee.[14]

The *lijf*- and *losrenten* were the traditional way of raising revenue for the province, based upon funding by city excises. No brokerage was paid here. The *lijfrente* was an annuity upon the life of a person. The payment ceased after his or her death. The buyer of a *lijfrente* did not necessarily have to be the person nominated in the loan: often, his or her child was named. Also, it was possible to have the annuity made in favour of two or more nominees. Then the payment of interest ceased only after all nominees had died, but rates of interest were lower, naturally. As for the ordinary one-person annuities, the interest was almost always double that of the obligations or *losrenten*. No distinctions were made as to the age of the nominee. Such annuities were much sought after, and at regular intervals it was stipulated that one could buy a *lijfrente* only in combination with a *losrente*.[15] The *losrente* was a permanent loan, mostly contracted with a named person, and could be amortized upon request. They were easier to transfer than *lijfrenten*.[16]

For any provincial long-term loan, be it in the form of obligations, life annuities or *losrenten*, consent was needed in the Provincial Estates. The total burden was divided among the major tax receivers on a quota basis: the provincial receiver at The Hague for the province, the local receivers in the six large traditional cities (Dordrecht, Haarlem, Delft, Leiden, Amsterdam, Gouda) plus the local receivers in Rotterdam, Gorinchem, and Brielle. The quota roughly reflected the relative proportion in tax yields. In a minority of cases the distribution was different, as in 1642 with a loan to the admiralty of Rotterdam for which bonds were sold in Haarlem, Leiden and Rotterdam, and another loan in 1646 for the *Groote Visserij* (herring fisheries), when sums came only from the provincial receiver and the receivers of Delft, Rotterdam and Brielle.[17]

By comparison with its neighbours, Holland had the advantage of relatively low rates of interest. In 1606, all loans contracted at rates higher than 8.3 per cent were reduced by the Estates of Holland. At the same time, a duty was imposed on beer with the specific purpose of paying off the debt of the province, and all new loans were negotiated at a rate of 7.1 per cent. Life annuities paid 11 to 14 per cent, depending upon the number of nominees. In 1611 an overall reduction to 6.25 per cent was promulgated, which was reduced again in 1640 to 5 per cent, and in 1655 to 4 per cent. By then the English king was still being forced to pay 10 per cent and the French monarch even 15 per cent. Despite these conversions, confidence in Dutch finance remained as steady as ever. It pointed up the great flexibility of public debt management.[18]

Such a smooth-running public debt was characteristic of the core of the Republic, and was shared by both Utrecht and Zeeland. Now and then a special tax was imposed for the payments of interest: a duty upon beer in Holland, duties on wine and beer in Zeeland, new customs, or a tax upon peat in Utrecht. But in the north and east it proved more difficult to establish credit at the provincial level, as a crucial prerequisite was the central coordination of taxation. There, the debts contracted were mostly short-term and paid back as soon as possible. Many loans were only issued through the intermediation of Holland or Union receivers. After all, some provinces were not regarded as creditworthy because of their forced contributions to the enemy, such as Drenthe during 1621–1632. The servicing of debt was less stabilized, because of the limited range of excises available as an instrument. Recurrently, extraordinary property taxes were imposed to pay off old debts, or provincial domains were sold. By 1640, Friesland's debt stood at 5.4 million guilders, whereas by the end of the war Gelderland owed about 1 million guilders.[19]

The advantage of the core over the other provinces was the wealthy city dwellers who were ready to invest in these kinds of securities. In addition, despite the fact that it was a municipal institution, the Bank of Amsterdam which was established in 1609 was a major backbone of the financial policies of the province. Although it was not allowed to lend money, the bank occasionally provided the city of Amsterdam and the VOC with funds, and with its accumulated wealth it could be regarded as the place of last resort for the Dutch Republic. The highest financial officers held their accounts with the bank. Though not officially connected with the Dutch state, the bank added significantly to general public trust in government finances.[20]

Of all the provinces, the public debt of Holland rose the most. A look at the provincial budgets shows that loans were indispensable in view of the annual deficits in the provincial budget. In 1629 plans were put forward to build up a reserve of funds with loans, but the treasury did not hold the money long. It soon had to be spent on all kinds of emergency payments.[21] As Table 6.1 shows, the revenue continued to fall short of the expenses.

Table 6.1 *Expenditure and ordinary revenue of Holland, 1630–1640 (guilders)*

year	*expenditure*	*revenue*
1630	13,482,090	9,149,240
1634	16,423,916	10,192,580
1640	16,527,948	10,847,690

Source: RAZH Jacob Cats 22 and 84.

The debt of the province had fluctuated between 1 million and 5 million before 1620. With the resumption of war, it increased rapidly, as new borrowing in the first five war years, 1621 to 1625, averaged 1.8 million annually. A sharp rise in 1626 showed a total of 5.3 million guilders of new loans contracted. Over the next five years, from 1627 to 1631, the annual amount of loans contracted was almost 3 million, and a new peak was reached in 1632 with 5.7 million guilders. This borrowing policy coincided with the rapid build-up of forces during the Dutch counter-offensive against the Spanish Habsburgs. By the end of the Eighty Years' War, estimates of the total amount of the debt ranged between 125 million and 147 million guilders – at least, more than a thirtyfold increase. Debt charges came to constitute an ever increasing part of the province's expenses, rising over 53 per cent in the 1650s.[22]

The Union's debt

Such sky-rocketing increases were an imponderable for the generality of the United Provinces, since no financial revolution materialized as in Holland. In fact, the first and the third steps of such a revolution were taken, respectively the centralizing of the sale of loans and the stimulation of a free domestic market by renouncing forced loans. But the second step, the imposition of regular and permanent taxation to pay for the debt charges, was never enacted, apart from some minor duties as upon salt and temporarily upon soap and beer.

The financial situation was not favourable at the start. The United Provinces had been forced to proclaim the suspension of payments upon their interest charges in 1581. Such a situation, a moratorium on payments, was usually called a 'bankruptcy' of the state. Interest rates were still quite high: 8 to 12 per cent. But as trade developed and war prospects improved in the 1590s, credit was re-established. This was mainly due to the intermediary role of the province of Holland. Much of the debt was first floated temporarily (short-term or floating debt), but soon transferred to long-term arrangements. By the seventeenth century, major arrears in interest payments were a thing of the past. The number of foreign creditors had been reduced as a deliberate policy, because of the tendency for Dutch citizens to be ransomed by the claimant in the event of non-payment of interest.[23]

The long-term debt of the generality dated from 1596. Up to that time, loans had been repaid in the short or medium term, supported by powerful Holland intermediaries. To pay off a long term loan from England, taxes on soap and beer had been imposed and Flushing, Brielle and Rammekens were pawned. They were redeemed in 1616. The generality debt was not easily changed to a 'funded' basis, as the only tax lasting longer and used for interest payments to the Receiver General was the one on salt.[24] In the main, revenue used for interest payments was variable, such as the income from passports and safeguards, confiscations, contributions from enemy territories, and foreign subsidies.

Often, additional credit was necessary, and powerful merchants were asked to stand surety in the contract for a generality loan. Johan van der Veeken from Rotterdam, for example, provided security for loans contracted by the Receiver General. Guarantees could be provided by high officials in the central state machinery as well, such as the Treasurer General, Brasser. At other times, support was sought from the Estates of Holland as a body, the city of Amsterdam, the admiralty of Amsterdam, or the East India Company. When they refused to cooperate, the central government found itself in great difficulty. In 1621 and 1623, when the Estates of Holland were prepared to guarantee only their quota for a loan, the Receiver General could scarcely get his loans subscribed. These years assumed a crisis character for the Dutch state.[25]

The Doubleth family furnished the first Receivers General of the Union. Such a state banker had to be a wealthy, trustworthy man, with good connections in political as well as financial circles. He was the most important civil servant apart from the more political bureaucrats like the First Clerk of the Estates General, the Treasurer General, and the Secretary of the Council of State. The Receiver General was expected to receive all funds destined for the central government, that is, from the provinces (quotas), generality lands, passports, public loans and some smaller funds. His administration was enormous, and he had to employ his own clerks. Almost every day debt holders, claiming their interest, were received at his house at the stately Voorhout in The Hague, near the Binnenhof where the Estates General convened.[26]

This semi-private banking house of the Doubleths managed to secure the credit of the Dutch generality during most of the Eighty Years' War. Their obligations constituted the bulk of the public debt of the Union, which increased steadily after 1596. Figure 6.1 represents the debt contracted and still extant in 1649. The actual number of loans must have been considerably higher, but they could not all be traced, as they were repaid before the end of the war. Even during the Truce of 1609–1621 new loans were issued. War expenses on the whole slowed down, but Dutch involvement in several central European crises, such as in the Palts and Bohemia, necessitated immediate funds. At sea, privateers forced Dutch vessels to arm themselves. In addition, Flushing, Brielle and Rammekens were redeemed from pawn with the British.

In all, the generality debt stood in 1618 at 4,893,960 guilders,

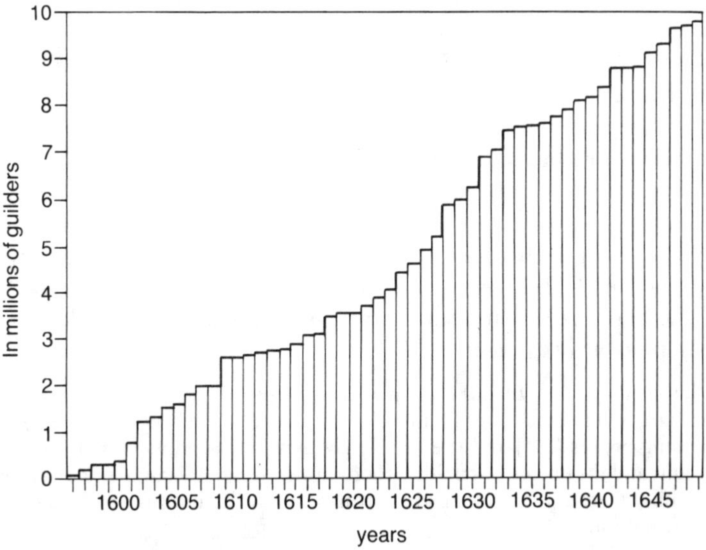

Figure 6.1 Long-term loans contracted by the generality (accumulated and still extant in 1649)
Source: ARA CoS 2103 IV and RAZH SH 1291 a.

with the debt service amounting to 318,113 annually.[27] As war was likely to be resumed, the Council of State tried to rid itself of the long-term generality debt incurred up to 1618. Fears of restricted credit because of the heavy burden were not imaginary. Never before had the Dutch state been faced with such a large, continuous burden. Even the debt of the province of Holland, up to that time, had never exceeded 5 million guilders. Holland and Zeeland welcomed the proposal to reduce the debt. They preferred increased taxation, or new taxes, especially in the generality lands, but also in the other provinces, to redeem the loans. Other provinces were less willing. Utrecht and Friesland reacted stubbornly, stating that they did not want to pay for debts incurred through the arrears and defaulting of others. Groningen proposed to find a solution in the customs: they should pay for the old debts. Customs were one of the more autonomous measures of the state, circumventing bargaining at the center. But the Council of State described this idea as an illusion: the customs were not even sufficient to pay for the navy.[28]

It was decided to bring the debt service under the allocation of the quota for Holland, despite Utrecht's protests as Holland would have to pay less in military expenses in return. Holland's credit was rightly regarded as the strongest and such a solution undoubtedly had positive effects upon future loans of the Union.[29]

In subsequent years the Estates General tried to contain the debt as much as possible, and to reduce the burden of the debt charges. The 1620s, however, the years of continuous war pressure, saw a mushrooming of the debt. A steep rise occurred in the years 1627 and 1628. In the 1630s the pressure diminished, although a peak was reached in 1632. At times, the manifold loans prevented the Receiver General of the Union from contracting new ones. Nevertheless, in a pamphlet it was stated:

> I know very well, that the country is in urgent need of funds, and that warfare is very costly, but I know also, that costs as such are not opposed to making profits [. . .] and even if the country has no money, it still has its credit, and the enemy has neither funds nor credit, that I could not deny that we might wear out the enemy through this war, because this land has sufficient funds.[30]

Quite so: after all, Spain had gone bankrupt in 1627, and its soldiers were waiting to be paid, whereas the Dutch army's pay continued in a reasonable fashion. To improve control, it was decided in 1628 that all generality loans needed the formal approval of both the Council of State and the Estates General, whereas before that date the consent of either of the two had been sufficient.[31]

One of the possible ways to reduce the debt charges was abolition of the 0.5 per cent brokerage fee (*makelaardijgeld*) on the semi-private obligations of the receivers. A proposal to do away with the brokerage fee was voiced in the early 1620s. But the measure was not easy to enact. Some feared that creditors would withdraw their funds, because the financial contract was to become more public, and public credit was still lower as compared with the private receiver's credit. In addition, receivers voiced complaints about the reduction in their earnings (see Chapter Seven).[32]

But of superordinate significance was to have the payment of the interest secured, which had been guaranteed by the semi-private bankers of the state before. Holland managed to abolish the commission in 1640 without any major difficulty for its own tax district receivers. For the generality, with no significant revenue of its own, dependent upon the will of the provinces, this step was problematic indeed. A solution was found by allocating the whole payment of the interest on the generality loans to the quota of the province of Holland again, as had been done before in 1618. In 1644 the brokerage on the interest payments was done away with for the generality officers, although they were allowed to continue the commission when new loans were contracted.[33]

As failure to pay soldiers and sailors always constituted a danger for a state at war, most of the Union's debt was incurred on account of the military. The Dutch system of quotas was not watertight because of delayed decision-making by the provinces and recurrent *defecten* upon the petitions. A safety valve was necessary, a function which was performed locally by the captain or *solliciteur-militair*, who provided the pay in anticipation of government funds. At central level, the Receiver General of the Union procured the funds, at times even to pay off the debts of the local intermediairies. The latter accounted for 10 per cent of the Union loans, as is shown in Table 6.2 which shows the breakdown of the debt into the following items.

Table 6.2 *Origin of the generality debt as of 1649*

item	*guilders*	*%*
soldiers' pay	2,507,945	32.2
army supplies	489,730	6.3
fortifications	2,039,651	26.2
foreign policy	1,019,758	13.1
admiralties	785,762	10.1
debt conversion	787,208	10.1
miscellaneous	158,800	2.0
total	7,788,854	100.0

Source: ARA CoS 2103 IV.

Almost one-third of the debt consisted of soldiers' pay. Much of it arose in the period of the Dutch counter-offensive, during 1626 up to 1633. Yet the resumption of war itself had seen a bold initiative: in 1620 it was decided to pay all soldiers one month in advance and to get rid of all arrears before hostilities began. After all, 'the wealth of the country could well afford this' and it was thought a major boost to the morale of the troops.[34] But as funds did not come in as quickly as expected because new taxation did not materialize in the provinces, a large part of the burden was passed on to the Receiver General.

Arrears in the pay of certain companies were another cause of that debt. In the early 1620s troops in the pay of Groningen, Drenthe, and Friesland had reason to complain. Soldiers were reported to have deserted. As the provinces' credit failed, the receivers asked the Receiver General of the Union to contract loans against the future revenue from the province. The problem recurred constantly because of default on payments, in particular for Friesland up to the 1630s, whereas difficulties with Groningen and Drenthe subsided.[35]

Grave shortcomings were noted in Zeeland's payments in 1626 and 1627, when the province bluntly refused to pay some companies on its allocation. Non-payment by Overijssel seemed to have occurred particularly in the years 1622 to 1634. But above all, Gelderland seemed a lax provider of soldier's funds. Analysing the debt as a result of default on payments to troops alone during 1621–1649 totalling 297,285 guilders, Gelderland alone was responsible for 49 per cent of the failed funds. Zeeland and Overijssel shared second place with 22 per cent each, while Friesland was fourth and last on this list with 8 per cent. Apparently, companies on the allocation of Holland, Utrecht and Groningen were better paid, which corresponds well with major tax increases in those provinces (Chapter Five).

Next in Table 6.2 come payments for fortifications, at 26 per cent. Often, the labourers at these works were soldiers as well, and non-payment was almost as dangerous as non-payment to troops. Moreover, fortifications frequently turned out more costly than budgeted, while the responsibility was shared by cities, provinces, and the Council of State, which complicated accounting. In particular, when the Truce had ended, Dutch cities had to strengthen themselves. In 1621 mention was made of strikes of workmen at the fortifications of Ravesteijn and Gennep. A contractor was even stabbed so seriously that the latter feared for his life, but the Council of State urged the provinces in vain to furnish the funds approved for fortifications quickly.[36]

For the navy the Receiver General had to raise emergency funds as well. The fact is no surprise in view of the tardy provision of means by the inland provinces. A major liability was the admiralty of Rotterdam, whose inland vessels were regularly threatened by mutinies. Another drain was the unfortunate West India Company, which absorbed half of the loans for the admiralties.[37]

Most of these loans were actually contracted for the provinces in anticipation payment upon consents in ordinary or extraordinary petitions. But getting the provinces to pay proved very hard indeed. Some provinces might dispute the loan itself, accusing the Estates General or Council of State of acting high-handedly, as some companies might not have been accepted officially on their allocation. In the meantime, not only the original sum but also the interest started to mount up.

In the *Staat van Oorlog* budget of 1620 6.0 per cent was devoted to interest payments. Sums needed for debt charges increased thereafter. At first, the funds were voted by extraordinary budgets. In 1630, 100,000 guilders were voted for the payment of the new debts of the generality. From 1632 to 1638 this amount was 200,000 guilders per year. After 1639 it was necessary to vote 420,000 guilders for the purpose, which gradually increased to 480,000 in 1643.

In the revision of the budget for 1643, the sums necessary for interest payments upon the generality loans were incorporated into the ordinary *Staat van Oorlog*. Once more they were apportioned mainly to Holland. Between 1643 and 1648 more new loans were contracted, due to the Sound crisis and the West India Company among other things. Extraordinary subsidies for the interest amounted to 510,000 guilders in 1646, 520,000 in 1647 and 530,000 in 1648. The generality followed Holland's decision to reduce interest rates from 6.25 per cent to 5 per cent in 1649. Holland took over the greater part of the generality debt in 1650, with the result that a debt of approximately 6 million was left over on the *Staat van Oorlog*, entailing annual interest of 302,206 guilders or 5.1 per cent of the total budget.[38] Holland's credit obviously backed up the republican state machinery in the end.

Next to the central state's debt, loans had been contracted in the generality lands too. The interest was paid on a capital sum of 652,020 guilders in 1642 and of 961,435 in 1648, an increase of almost 50 per cent in those six years only. As revenues were insecure because of the war, interest rates were higher as compared with Holland. On average, they commanded 6.75 per cent in 1642. In the years following, they were reduced to 6.25 per cent, and in 1649 another general reduction in interest followed. The rate became 5 per cent, which applied to all loans of the generality offices.[39]

A special category were the *renten* on the *beden* of Brabant, the provincial loans that had been contracted in the sixteenth century.

After the capitulation of 1629, Den Bosch refused to make further interest payments to the creditors. But the Council of State was eager to retain credit facilities in the area and ordered the city to reserve 4,000 guilders annually. Agreement on the partition of these *renten* was finally reached between Spain and the Republic in 1650.[40]

Admiralties' arrears and debts

Since their establishment in the late sixteenth century, the admiralties were almost constantly in need of additional funds. Loans had been contracted by the earliest equipage masters 12 per cent. They had to speculate in herring, grain and other goods to pay the seamen. By the 1590s the navy finances had been stabilized, and interest rates declined. But the Rotterdam admiralty was still contracting loans at 12 per cent in 1604, despite the fact that money could be had at 9 per cent, which reflected the precarious financial position of this central admiralty. In 1610 Rotterdam was still paying an interest rate of 8 per cent on its new loans, which was on the high side as compared with other generality officers. By then, 6.25 was the prevailing rate for all government loans. The admiralty of Amsterdam's credit was stronger, as it did occasionally have a surplus. During the Truce it even provided the generality with funds to pay off some of the generality debts and mediated a loan to the VOC. Its credit showed in its interest rates: in 1601 9 to 10 per cent was paid, in 1604 7 or 8 and in 1607 6 to 6.5 per cent.[41]

But in 1626 the admiralty boards were all in such difficulty, even Amsterdam, that the plans voted in the Estates General, however modest in themselves, could not be realized. As the payment of interest was insecure, no new loans could be contracted either. A special commission investigated the arrears as well as the extent and nature of the long-term debt. For that year, the arrears in payment to the sailors, equipage masters and others amounted to almost 6 million guilders (see Table 6.3).

All admiralties had more arrears than their annual expenses, let alone their annual revenue, which fell short of the expenditure anyway. The position of Amsterdam was actually the least unfavourable, its arrears being only 2.5 the size of its annual revenue. For Rotterdam and the Northern Quarter the figure was eight times, and for Zeeland six. Moreover, old and expensive debts lingered on. By 1628 Rotterdam was still paying 9.7 per cent interest on average.

Table 6.3 *Arrears in 1628, annual expenses and annual ordinary revenues (1626–1628) of navy boards, in guilders*

navy board	*arrears*	*ann. exp.*	*ann. rev.*
Rotterdam	1,640,252	1,100,000	200,000
Amsterdam	1,947,975	1,592,402	800,000
Zeeland	1,308,076	588,248	242,132
Northern Quarter	841,818	796,201	110,100
Friesland	33,522	n.a.	n.a.
total	5,771,643	n.a.	n.a.

Source: GAA 5030/60. Friesland was not included in the research of the commission but its arrears were 33,522 according to ARA SG 12561.54.2: 'Schulden admiraliteiten'.

Amsterdam, the Northern Quarter and Zeeland paid interest ranging from 6.2 to 6.3, which was similar to the official generality rate of 6.25 per cent. Friesland paid on average 7 per cent.[42]

Five years later, it appeared that Rotterdam's debt had slightly increased, but at least most of it had been converted to a 6.8 per cent interest rate on average. However, owing to the continuous pressure of the Dunkirk privateers, the navy debts had accumulated. According to the budgets for 1633, they totalled 2,871,835 guilders, of which both Amsterdam and Rotterdam took a share of over a million guilders. Yet a tremendous increase in debt charges for the admiralties was still to come in the last decade of the Eighty Years' War and in the first Anglo-Dutch War of 1652–1654. According to an analysis of navy budgets, between 1641 and 1654 payments in respect of debt charges had trebled from roughly 5.5 per cent to 16 per cent of all navy costs.[43]

Investors in the public debt

The enormous rise in public debt, from the generality, from the admiralties, and above all from the province of Holland, provided ample opportunities for investment by the burghers. It should be recalled that the Dutch Republic's debts were largely domestic and voluntary. Between 1620 and 1650 no forced loans were issued at all. The majority of loans were floated in small tranches, with the result that many small and large capital-owners saw their finances connected with the well-being of the state. The body of *renteniers* grew. An estimate by William Temple mentioned a total of 65,000 in the 1660s. Even during the hard pressed times of 1628–1630 the credit of the provinces remained strong.[44]

The structure of credit centred around the receivers. As semi-private state bankers, their local contacts ensured new loans for the generality, the province or the admiralty. For example, the receiver Pieter van Loon who collected the *lastgeld* for western trade in Amsterdam issued 62,100 guilders in obligations in the years 1644 and 1645. Of the twenty-four subscribers, at least seven investors stood in a close family relation to Pieter van Loon: sisters, brothers, and in-laws, providing up to 42 per cent of the sum.[45]

The receivers of the provinces and of the Union naturally had to depend upon a wider circle of investors. In the books of the Receiver General of the Union that survive, dating from 1649 and 1650 and listing subscriptions to his semi-private obligations, 3,501 entries were found. A large number, up to 56 per cent, had bought the obligations anonymously. The smallest amount subscribed was fifty guilders, the highest single subscription 39,750 guilders. The total amount was 6,037,004 guilders, hence the obligations were 1,700 guilders on average.

Of the 1,700 named buyers, only 15 per cent could be traced back in registers of the Dutch elite, owing to the fact that occupation or place of origin is rarely mentioned. Yet even this fact is relevant in itself, as it points to the spread of obligation holders. They were not just from the most important political circles, not just the magistrates in the main cities, not just the most important merchants, although these groups may have provided the largest investors.[46]

There were, in fact, an amazing number of people who brought their funds to the coffers of the state, who obviously trusted the state, and among them were quite ordinary persons. Of those 1,700 known buyers, 1,178 names were left after double subscriptions were combined. Table 6.4 shows the amounts subscribed by category. It is remarkable that the proportion of females subscribing to these loans was quite large: 41 per cent. Apparently, women had a significant say in the management of their funds. Yet, in general, their investments were somewhat smaller as compared with those of male subscribers. Looking at their percentage distribution over six categories in Table 6.4, they were clustered in the two smallest categories, whereas most males bought obligations in the group of 1,001 up to 2,000 guilders.

Those having the title of *heer* or *vrouwe*, owners of a manor,

Table 6.4 *Percentage distribution of the amount subscribed to the Receiver General of the Union, 1649–1650*

amount	*males*	*females*	*all*
0– 500	14.3	28.5	20.6
501– 1,000	26.0	27.4	26.7
1,001– 2,000	28.2	21.0	24.4
2,001– 5,000	21.9	16.0	19.3
5,001–10,000	6.9	4.9	6.5
10,001 and over	2.6	2.1	2.5
total	100.0	100.0	100.0

Source: Marjolein 't Hart, 'Public loans and lenders in the seventeenth century Netherlands', *Economic and Social History in the Netherlands* 1, 1989, 124.

invested most, 6,000 to 6,100 guilders on average. They even surpassed the group of collective investors, whose mean subscription amounted to 4,500 guilders. These institutions – church boards, guilds, orphanages, poor houses, and collective inheritors – comprised 7 per cent of all known subscriptions.

The largest single subscriber was *Heer* Mr Davidt le Reu de Wilhelm (1588–1658), who invested 54,000 guilders in eleven parts. His wife's sister was married to the Receiver General of the Union. He was a man of considerable political influence in central politics: he became Councillor of the Stadhouder Frederick Henry and Councillor and Superintendent for Brabant as well.[47] He was followed by the four church boards of Enkhuizen, who invested 47,750 guilders. Other major subscribers were to be found in the highest circles of The Hague: the councillors in the High Court of Appeal, *Heer* Nicolaes de Bije and Jacob Schotte, the councillor in the Court of Holland, *Jonkheer* Willem van Lier, and the goldsmith and future burgomaster Johan van der Maa. Among the smaller subscriptions, lower-level civil servants were noted, like Barent Langenes who was an usher to the Chamber of Accounts, or Willem Schade who was a clerk in the Council of State. Maritje Cornelis was the wife of a shoemaker in The Hague. The smallest loan was fifty guilders from a woman named Weijntje Jans.[48]

As for the loans of the province of Holland, far more books listing the names of debt holders have survived. Looking at an analysis based on samples, the number of collective subscriptions was higher as compared to the Receiver General of the Union: 20 per cent against 7 for the latter. A majority came from the University of Leiden underwriting *losrenten* of the Leiden tax receiver. After deducting the collective loans from the whole, the proportion of females subscribing proved approximately the same: 40 per cent. The lowest subscription came from Neeltje Cornelis in Dordrecht: only fourteen guilders in 1650 with an annual interest of fourteen stuyvers (only 0.70 guilder). Obviously, the local receivers could count upon persons in their proximity willing to help make up their loan quotas.[49]

Loan instruments differed widely from one receiver to another. The Amsterdam, Delft and Brielle tax district receivers mainly issued obligations, the annuities and *losrenten* being additional measures only. Others did not use the instrument of obligations at all: the tax district receivers of Rotterdam and Gorinchem, for instance, concentrated on annuities and *losrenten* only, the traditional means of public finance.[50] The receivers of the admiralties and the Receiver General of the Union predominantly issued obligations. The latter were easier to transfer as compared with *losrenten* and annuities, while they involved higher subscriptions too. The analysis also shows that the cities attracted capital from other areas. In Haarlem and Leiden, 47 per cent of the investors were not based in the city itself, a figure which proved much lower in Amsterdam, where it was only 16 per cent. Inhabitants of the Northern Quarter in particular invested in such bonds, although Amsterdam residents invested in Haarlem bonds and vice versa too.

As with the loans of the Receiver General of the Union, those of Holland showed a similarly wide spread of investors. Again, The Hague bureaucrats were major creditors, such as the president of the Court of Holland, Mr Johan Dedel, and the president of the High Court, *Heer* Mr Cornelis Haga, but also Amsterdam merchants, such as the famous banker William Bartolotti or Pieter Trip. The latter was the largest investor, with 78,000 guilders in Amsterdam alone. Maria van Berckel bought an obligation of 11,200 guilders from her brother, the provincial receiver. She was married to the local receiver in Rotterdam. The latter's father and sister Joost Verschuyren de Oude and Anna Verschuyren were among the subscribers as well. In the lists also were famous burgomasters, like Cornelis Bicker, *Heer* van Swieten. He was a director of the VOC and deputy to the Estates of Holland. His fellow burgomaster Cornelis de Graeff was on the list too. The future *raadpensionaris*

Johan de Witt invested in obligations in Amsterdam, although the receiver of his city of Dordrecht must have offered the opportunity for investments as well.[51]

Smaller investors, though, figured as well. Lijsbet Jans and Elisabeth Claesdr were both *dienstmaecht* (servants). An orphan of the sailor Steven Cornelisz bought a *losrente* of 124 guilders, while compass makers, peat dealers, shippers, and coopers were among the subscribers too. Some sums did not even add up to the 100 guilders, but they must have been welcome to make up the loan quotas of the receivers.[52]

But there were differences as to the sums subscribed. As compared with subscriptions to the loans of the Receiver General of the Union, those of the provincial receiver of Holland listed higher average amounts, about 2,400 guilders in the last three decades of the Eighty Years' War. Such figures were different again for the separate tax district receivers: in Amsterdam the sums averaged 3,200 guilders, but in Rotterdam only 1,500. Analysed over time, however, the trend showed even more decentralization of the funds. Amsterdam's mean had been 2,300 guilders in 1,628 and 3,600 guilders in 1650, whereas Rotterdam's mean jumped from 1,000 to 1,900 in the same period. By comparison, the subscriptions of the receiver general of Holland increased only from 2,300 to 2,500 on average from 1628 to 1650. The central (Union) receiver attracted less as compared to the regional receiver, and the latter again less as compared to local units (the city receivers). The Hague was of importance, and remained so, but power and resources seem to have increased at other centres in Holland at a much faster rate, at least in Amsterdam and in Rotterdam. This pattern coincided with the development of political decision-making in Holland towards increased local oligarchization. Looking at the amounts invested, there was greater confidence in the finances of Holland *vis-à-vis* those of the Republic, and again greater confidence in the city finances *vis-à-vis* those of the province. Apparently, in the last decades of the Eighty Years' War, the financial position of the bureaucratic centre was relatively weakened.

The excellence of Dutch credit

Despite minor hitches, Dutch public credit was exceptional for seventeenth-century Europe. No other state, except maybe Genoa, could borrow more cheaply than the Dutch. Although inland provinces and individual admiralties experienced difficulties in contracting long-term loans, the overall excellence of Dutch state credit was underwritten by Holland. It was one of the major causes of its military success and facilitated the spreading of the financial burden of war. The great elasticity of its money market, the access to the world's financial centre and international commercial capital flows, sound financial institutions (in particular the Bourse and the Bank of Amsterdam), a large body of *renteniers*, and above all the success of the financial revolution in Holland must be mentioned as major contributors to this phenomenon. That the generality debt was only partially secured through funding and that the extent of indebtedness remained concealed from the public did not seem to do any harm.

In part, the Dutch success must be explained by the fact that the chief investors were magistrates and politicians themselves. They were close enough to their local receiver with whom they had contracted loans. At times, they were urged to invest by their political leaders so as to stimulate other buyers. The federal structure implied also a large degree of local political control. Other secure investments were found in land and houses, but already by 1700 the capital invested in government bonds exceeded all other.[53]

By comparison with most other European states, the Dutch money market was well prepared for a large public debt. The Republic had the advantage over other states in commanding a commercialized and thriving economy. Public credit, public taxation and commercialization interacted well with each other. As Jan de Vries has noted, the high level of taxation compelled the Dutch rural community to commercialize, in order to find cash for the tax payments.[54] In turn, loans furnished the urban elites with a regular income, for which they were well prepared to vote in new provincial taxes, which resulted in a high political ceiling for taxation.

Some contemporaries thought the financial success had to do with the land registry, which allowed mortgages, a safe kind of investment. Probably, the tradition of shipping companies (*rederijen*), in which vessels were financed collectively by a group of small investors, often including the skipper himself, contributed to the habit of investment in financial shares. In city-states such as Venice and Gdansk, similar traditions existed in trade and shipping, involving many small investors. Not only shipping but agriculture too formed a base for the money market: typically Dutch was collective investment in land reclamation or peat fields. Occasionally, the market was affected by conjunctures, like the tulip mania of 1637. These crises, however, had no long-range effect on Dutch credit as a whole. Only in the course of the eighteenth century was Amsterdam surpassed by another powerful financial centre: London.[55]

The long-term debt of the Republic dated from 1596, although Holland's debt was much older. In all, the public debt was heterogeneous, reflecting the federal structure of the government. There were obligations of the Dutch Republic issued by the Receiver General of the Union. There were obligations of the individual provinces – mostly from Holland, some from Zeeland and Utrecht, and a few from the other provinces. The Holland provincial bonds were sold either by the provincial receiver at The Hague or by the receivers of the separate tax districts. The admiralties issued loans, and there were annuities and obligations from the individual cities. As for colonial trade policy, the East and West India Companies issued shares in their original capital. These securities were exchanged at the Bourse which was established in 1611. There, government bonds were in demand, despite the fact that most of them were not interchangeable. Even the forms of the generality loans were not uniformly worded. But when they were sold they commanded a good price on the market. The credit of the Republic was underlined by the fact that the old bonds of the sixteenth century were sold at 112 and 113 per cent of their value.[56]

In the management of the debt, the difference from Europe as a whole concentrated on three key points. First, Dutch loans were domestic. The strong support of the inhabitants in the core province was noticeable, where a decentralized system of loans secured the control of local elites over the issuing institution. Second, they were largely voluntary. Although the public finances of the Dutch Republic resembled those of city-states in several respects, the latter continued to resort to forced loans. Hamburg was perhaps another exception in this regard. And third, they were funded by regular taxation. As for funding, Sweden and Spain had also been succesful in funding their debts through copper and silver mining. But Holland was an exceptional example of funding through taxation. Together with the extent of excises and the limited range of central sources of revenue, the advanced management of public credit in the Dutch case was one of the major reasons why little bureaucratization occurred, as will be seen in Chapter Seven.

Notes

1 Parker, 'Emergence of modern finance', 561; Charles P. Kindleberger, *A financial history of Western Europe*, London, 1984, 158, 296; for an eighteenth-century opinion: Ida Nijenhuis, 'Isaac de Pinto en de lof der staatsschuld', *Groniek* 10, 1984, 18–28.

2 Stradling, *Europe and decline of Spain*, 68; Elliott, *Richelieu and Olivares*, 69; Petit, *Dette publique*, 5; Maland, *Europe at war*, 65, 91.

3 Eric R. Wolf, *Europe and the people without history*, Berkeley, 1982, 113.

4 Roberts, *Swedish imperial experience*, 48–51; Thompson, *War and government*, 68.

5 Aylmer, *Rebellion or revolution*, 72; Richard Bonney, *The King's debts. Finance and politics in France 1589–1661*, Oxford, 1981, 20, 279; Julian Dent, *Crisis in finance. Crown, financiers and society in seventeenth century France*, Newton Abbot, 1973, 239.

6 Michael Knapton, 'City wealth and state wealth in northeast Italy, 14th–17th centuries', *La ville, la bourgeoisie et la genèse de l'état moderne*, Bielefeld/Paris, 1988, 200; Marie-Louise Pelus, 'A Lübeck et Hambourg au XVIIe siècle: crise financière, conjoncture économique, potentiel économique, progrès économique. Une série des questions', *ibidem*, 246, 248, 255; Hocquet, 'Venise, les villes', 217–18.

7 Bosher, *From business*, 13; Bonney, *King's debts*, 277; Dessert, *Argent, pouvoir*, 87; Dent, *Crisis in finance*, 45.

8 Dent, *Crisis in finance*, 51.

9 Knapton, 'City wealth', 200; Petit, *Dette publique*, 6.

10 Dickson, *Financial revolution*, 23.

11 Tracy, *Financial revolution*, 1–3, 57, 60, 111, 217–18.

12 J. Smit, *Inventaris van het archief van de Financie van Holland*, The Hague, 1947, 40.

13 D. Houtzager, *Holland's lijf- en losrenteleningen voor 1672*, Schiedam, 1950, 53.

14 *Ibidem*, 127.

15 After 1652 an *attestatie de vita* was required for each payment of interest. Smit, *Inventaris*, 20.

16 Blok, 'Stadsfinanciën onder Republiek', 234 – gradually the proportion of *lijf-* and *losrenten* declined, that of obligations (easier to transfer) increased.

17 RAZH FH 249; RAZH Jacob Cats 18.

18 Houtzager, *Holland's lijf- en losrenten*, 54–5, 63, 79, 91. See also Violet Barbour, *Capitalism in Amsterdam in the seventeenth century*, Ann Arbor, 1963, 82; for the development of interest in the later seventeenth century: E.H.M. Dormans, *Het tekort. Staatsschuld in de tijd der republiek*, Amsterdam, 1991, 67–77.

19 RAG Res GS 24 June 1622; Feenstra, *Bloeitijd en verval*, 105; Van der Capellen, *Gedenkschriften* I, 117; II, 76; Aitzema, *Historie of verhael* II,

734; Zijlstra, *Des lieven geldes*, 47–9, 102–3.

20 Van Dillen, 'Amsterdam's role', 382.

21 Houtzager, *Holland's lijf- en losrenten*, 55.

22 Engels, *Belastingen*, 23–4; based on RAZH Jacob Cats; Dormans, *Het tekort*, 66.

23 Houtzager, *Holland's lijf- en losrenten*, 45; Van Dijk, 'Geldelijke druk', 185.

24 *Resolutiën* SG 2 November 1621.

25 *Resolutiën* SG 2 and 3 February 1607, 28 June and 7 July 1621, 15 September 1622, 5 August and 26 October 1623, 24 January 1624; ARA CoA 94: 17 February 1627 and 28 January 1628. On Johan van der Veeken: J.H. Kernkamp, *Johan van der Veeken en zijn tijd*, The Hague, 1952.

26 ARA CoA Resolutions 9 October 1630. On the Receiver General see also De Muinck, *Een regentenhuishouding*; Isaac Capadose, *De Algemeene Rekenkamer en de Rekenpligtigheid in Nederland*, The Hague, 1856, 41; Marjolein 't Hart, 'Staatsfinanciën als familiezaak tijdens de Republiek: de ontvangers-generaal Doubleth', *Fiscaliteit in Nederland*, ed. J.Th. de Smidt, Zutphen, 1987, 57–66.

27 This amount excluded the sums contracted for foreign states and princes: the Palts, Brandenburg, East Frisia, Emden and Sweden, totalling 1,286,127 guilders. ARA SG 12548–194: Register loans generality until 1619.

28 *Resolutiën* SG 9 February, 27 August, 21 October 1619, 29 July 1620, 27 October 1621; ARA SG 12548.194.

29 ARA CoA *Staat van Oorlog* 1621.

30 *Treves-Krack. Door een gesprek van twee slechte gesellen, alle Patriotten tot opmerkinghe voor-gestelt*, The Hague, 1630; see for the difficulties of Doubleth: Van der Capellen, *Gedenkschriften* I, 573.

31 ARA CoA 94 Instruction Receiver General.

32 ARA CoA 94: 22 January 1621. For specific difficulties arising out of calculation of the makelaardijgeld: CoA 8: 22, 26, 31 March 1638; 94: 17 June 1634, 10 February and 12 March 1635. An estimate of the yield for the generality if the interest was reduced from 6.25 per cent to 5 per cent and the brokerage abolished: 190,000 guilders annually, CoA 9: 29 September 1640.

33 ARA SG 12548.252 Makelaardijgelden; RAZH Jacob Cats 79 'Makelaardijgelden'; ARA CoA 94: 27 and 18 August 1642, 10 January, 28 March, 11–17 April, 5 May 1643. For new instructions: see art. 30: no brokerage money and art. 42: loans were to be issued in name of the state: ARA SG 12561.105, 19 March 1644.

34 *Resolutiën* SG 31 August 1620.

35 *Resolutiën* SG 17 August 1621 (Frl), 11 and 13 May 1622 (Dr), 5 August, 2, 26 September, 19 October 1622, 20 November 1623 (Frl); ARA CoA 94: 23 February 1624 (Frl).

36 *Resolutiën* SG 12 July, 2, 3 and 20 August, 15 November 1621. See also 17 and 22 October 1622; ARA CoA 8: 9 February 1630, 28 September 1634; 9: 13 and 22 November 1641.

37 Based upon calculations of ARA CoS 2103.IV.

38 Houtzager, *Holland's lijf- en losrenten*, 154; ARA *Staten van Oorlog*; ARA CoA *Staat van petitiën.*

39 RAZH Slingelandt 247; Jacob Cats 77; *Groot Placaet Boeck* I, 1502.

40 Korvezee, 'Belastingen in Noord-Brabant', 115; Kappelhof, *Belastingheffing Meierij*, 86.

41 Oldewelt, 'De Hoeffijserse schuld (1616–1681)'; ARA SG 12561.100: 'Schulden Hoeffijsser'; Terpstra, *Van Neck*, 155; Elias, *Schetsen*, 24, 94.

42 ARA Adm 3399; for the work of the commission see ARA CoA 8: 14 and 15 November 1628 and CoA 94: 7 November 1628.

43 Amsterdam's debt excluded the debt for Brandenburg; ARA SG 12561.98; Adm 3399.

44 Van der Capellen, *Gedenkschriften* I, 553; Barbour, *Capitalism in Amsterdam*, 81.

45 RAZH FH 249, register of obligations; E.A. Engelbrecht, *De vroedschap van Rotterdam 1572–1795*, Rotterdam, 1973, 227; Elias, *Vroedschap*, 443.

46 Cf. the following registers: Elias, *Vroedschap*; Engelbrecht, *Vroedschap*; H.P. Fölting, *De Vroedschap van 's-Gravenhage 1572–1795*, Pijnacker, 1985; A.J. van der Aa, *Biographisch Woordenboek der Nederlanden*, Amsterdam, 1964; *Biografisch Woordenboek van Nederland*, ed. J. Charité, The Hague, 1979; F. Nagtglas, *Levensberichten van Zeeuwen*, Middelburg, 1893; *Nederland's Patriciaat*, The Hague, 1910; *Nederland's Adelsboek*, The Hague, 1925.

47 His family was known later as Leu de Willem. See on the Huygens' connection also P.J.A.N. Rietbergen, 'Den Haag, 20 april 1660: de bruiloft van Susanna Huygens', *De Zeventiende Eeuw. Cultuur in de Nederlanden in Interdisciplinair Perspectief* 3, 1987, 181. On the Doubleth family see Robert Fruin, 'Uit het dagboek van een oud-Hollander', *De Gids* 33, 1869, 372; also 't Hart, 'Staatsfinanciën als familiezaak'.

48 Van Gelder, 'Haagsche Cohieren', 23; ARA CoS 2103 IV; Fölting, *Vroedschap*, 137–8; Nagtglas, *Levensberichten Zeeuwen*, 607.

49 See Marjolein 't Hart, 'Public loans and lenders in the seventeenth century Netherlands', *Economic and Social History in the Netherlands* I, 1989, 119–40; based upon RAZH FH 246, 249, 251, 252, 278, 279, 281, 283, 289, 296–316.

50 Cf. also RAZH Van Hoornbeek 66 for 1684.

51 Van Gelder, 'Haagsche Cohieren', 23; Elias, *Vroedschap*, 175, 266; Klein, *De Trippen*, 35, 184; Engelbrecht, *Vroedschap*, 137.

52 RAZH FH 248.

53 Parker, 'Emergence of modern finance', 572; Houtzager, *Holland's lijf- en losrenten*, 47, 162; Peter Burke, *Venice and Amsterdam. A study of seventeenth century elites*, London, 1974, 56–7. Studies of budgets of eighteenth-century city elites show percentages of 50 to 70 per cent deriving from state, provincial and city *rentes*. M. Prak, *Gezeten burgers. De elite in een Hollandse stad, Leiden 1700–1780*, Amsterdam, 1985, 117; J.J. de Jong, *Met goed fatsoen. De elite in Gouda 1700–1780*, Amsterdam, 1985, 109; L. Kooijmans, *Onder regenten. De elite in een Hollandse stad: Hoorn*

1700–1780, Amsterdam, 1985, 100.

54 De Vries, *Dutch rural economy*, 210; on investments abroad see James Riley, *International government finance and the Amsterdam capital market 1740–1850*, New York, 1980.

55 Andrew Yarranton, *England's improvement by sea and land to out-do the Dutch without fighting, to pay debts without moneys*, London, 1677, 3; De Vries, *Economy of Europe*, 226; Frederick C. Lane, *Venice, a maritime republic*, Baltimore, 1973, 46; Maria Bogucka, 'Die Beziehungen zwischen dem Handelskapital und der Städtischen Produktion in Danzig im 16. und 17. Jahrhundert', *Bürgertum, Handelskapital, Städtebünde*, ed. K. Fritze, Weimar, 1975, 69; cf. discussion in Klein, 'Wereldhandel edele metalen', 185.

56 J.J. Weeveringh, *Handleiding tot de geschiedenis der staatsschulden* I, Haarlem, 1852, 4. Property holders obtained additional security when, in 1651, a law was promulgated which confirmed the negotiability of bonds. De Vries, *Economy of Europe*, 227.

Part III

Consequences of the shift

7

Civil servants in a fragmented state

War and the ensuing process of change necessitated the establishment of new offices of state. In early modern Europe, such a development typically led to two interlocking bureaucracies: one for the direct management of military affairs, another for the acquisition of the resources needed for warfare.[1]

Although these bureaucracies differed from what obtains nowadays, they did constitute the beginnings of present-day massive states. Strictly speaking, a bureaucracy is a type of formal organization, defined by sets of rules and instructions, characterized by a hierarchy, fixed salaries, and a strict separation of private and public. As such, few civil services of the seventeenth century were really modern-style bureaucracies.[2] But bureaucratization moved on, albeit gradually. The civil service grew in terms of budget and personnel in relation to the area and population. Frequently, bureaucratization entailed the extension of power beyond initial purpose. For example, civil servants may have been service-oriented at first, but in the end they became actual state rulers. Bureaucratization also meant growing internal formalization and regimentation within organizations.[3]

States differed as to the size and scope of their bureaucracies. Some appeared more autonomous and more centralized than others. However, centralization is not equivalent to bureaucratization, although they often join hands. Centralization is the concentration of power into one hierarchical system with a geographical centre. It does permit standardization and control and hence stimulates bureaucratization. Centralization is likely to win over centrifugal forces, as a centre attracts the best talent: the pay will probably be better and it can offer more opportunities for advancement in status.

The concept of state strength need more clarification here as well. In my definition, a state is strong if it has developed a bureaucratic administrative apparatus that has coherent boundaries, rules, and capacity. Such a state establishes a rational field of administration for resource mobilization (taxes and manpower), creates some sort of a public order, and coordinates collective efforts (such as infrastructure development and defence). Also, that a state is weak does not mean that it cannot be brutally repressive.[4]

It was expected that the extent of the process of shifting war costs on to society would explain differences in state strength. The case of England, for example, seemed to deviate significantly from the general European pattern of state making. A lesser burden of war – because of its insular position – meant that only a weakly bureaucratized state was created. Hence, political scientists constructed a typology in which 'strong' states such as France, Prussia, and Spain opposed 'weak' states (or 'non-states') such as Great Britain and the United States.[5]

High war costs, then, were generally held responsible for the construction of cumbersome bureaucratic structures. In such states, deference to the central power always mattered, even for the powerful Spanish Minister Olivares, who declared, 'I have no father, children or friend, except for him who serves the king well.'[6] State institutions, once established under the stamp of an authoritarian monarch, proved hard to change. In France, the creation of offices proceeded headlong in the 1630s, but Cardinal Richelieu stated in his *Testament Politique*:

> Les financiers et les partisans sont une classe séparée, préjudiciable à l'Etat, mais pourtant nécessaire. Ce genre d'officiers est un mal dont on ne saurait se passer mais qu'il faut réduire à des termes supportables.[7]

After all, the creation of offices had been a way to provide the state with urgently needed funds. In 1638, 38 per cent of the revenue came from the sale of venal offices. In 1642, however, the figure was only 10.5 per cent, and in 1661 a mere 0.8 per cent: obviously, the market had been swamped. In the meantime, the financiers had come to dominate the state. Their offices could not simply be abolished, as that would have meant the repayment of the contracts, and no funds were ever available for such a great expense.[8]

This kind of bureaucratization in France, though, had little to do with centralization. Former local officers remained powerful. New central bureaucrats, such as the intendants, met with strong local networks which could not be subordinated to the central level. Most bureaucrats, after all, owned their office, and their loyalty to the state was overshadowed by concern to make a fortune as rapidly as possible.[9] France was certainly less centralized than is generally assumed. In the eighteenth century, the Minister of Finance, Calonne, complained:

> The disparity, the discord, the incoherence of the different parts of the body of the monarchy is the principal of the constitutional vices which enervate its strength and hamper all its organization; [. . .] one cannot destroy any one of them without attacking them all in the principle which has produced them and which perpetuates them; [. . .] a Kingdom whose provinces are foreign to one another, where multifarious internal barriers separate and divide the subjects of the same sovereign, where certain areas are totally freed from burdens of which others bear the full weight, [. . .] where it is impossible to have either a constant rule or a common will, is necessarily a very imperfect kingdom [. . .].[10]

Although similar complaints could have been applied to the Dutch Republic, this was absolutist France!

As for Spain, the view that the late sixteenth and early seventeenth centuries were years of increasing bureaucratic centralism should be adjusted too. By 1632 the situation had been totally reversed as compared with 1560. It was a shift from central to centrifugal government and from public to private administration. This process typically served to circumvent parliamentary representation:

> [. . .] the contractor, for all his faults, could be seen as offering the prince the chance to free himself from the financial and administrative control of the entrenched power of his own domestic opponents. Where constitutional supremacy remained incompletely resolved and the activities of the royal administration or the power to raise revenue restricted by political inhibitions or the unco-operativeness of subjects and estates, the crown turned to the contractor and the tax farmer. It is for this reason that the farmer, the contractor and the monopolist were so much hated by the parliamentary and constitutionalist oppositions.[11]

At the same time, this process was accompanied by a revival of the aristocratic element in the state.

England has generally been treated as deviant from the continent. However, that 'low British level of bureaucratization' appears a misconception. A bureaucracy did develop, in some cases a quite rigid one, for example in the excises. At the end of the eighteenth century the civil service consisted of almost 16,000 officials, most of them to be found in the revenue raising machine.[12] Yet England was successful in that it combined centralization with the incorporation of traditional local government. At that point France failed, and as a result the latter needed a constant extension of its bureaucracy. Bureaucratization in France developed by imposing and adding central bureaucrats upon local systems of former central bureaucrats, not by replacing them. As a result, the regional parliaments and provincial Estates remained barriers to any increased bureaucratic control from the centre.[13]

In addition, virtually all seventeenth-century states were hampered in their public functions by privatization, be it in the form of mercenary soldiers, tax farmers, state financiers, or the sale of offices. As a matter of course, local elites tried to obtain their share in state building. Offices constituted a major stepping stone of social advancement in France and Spain. Gifts, bonuses, and gratuities were a normal and substantial part of an official's income. Even the salaries of the lowest clerks were a kind of *grâce*, a personal arrangement.[14] City-state Venice had no clear-cut separation of private and public affairs either. There, too, local magistrates were essentially collaborators with the central power, but they were also obstacles to increased centralization and to schemes of direct taxation.[15]

Training of personnel might be a way to serve the causes of centralization and bureaucratization. Carl Friedrich, who analysed the introduction of cameralism in Prussia, concluded that it was used by the state to increase its influence upon the civil service and society and to combat feudal and local privileges. However, in England and Holland the rule of law as right reason was embraced. That in itself entailed a significant reactionary tendency, as vested privileges were defended and administration came to be based upon precedent.[16]

Yet warfare did necessitate immense administrations. Sweden and Prussia are the outstanding examples of highly militarized states. In Sweden army officers even came to be represented separately in the Estates. A quite coherent bureaucracy was developed. The *Postulata nobilium* of 1594 regulated a fixed salary system and differentiated positions with clearly defined areas of competence, and in the 1620s the chancellor Axel Oxenstierna created a highly effective central administration. In Prussia the highest civil servants subjected public matters to military affairs, resulting in a militarization of the state. Both Sweden and Prussia became models of bureaucratic rule.[17]

Those centralized governments were costly. Historical bureaucracies with conspicuous courts had the disadvantage that means were diverted from actual warfare. Any monarchy tended to be quite expensive, if only because of its extended pension system and patronage. In France, Richelieu estimated the war burden to have been 36 million livres in 1642, whereas salaries for civic personnel amounted to 34 million livres in 1639. And even Denmark spent 25.1 per cent of its budget on the court and civil service.[18]

Generally, the governments of city-states were much more public and much cheaper than their monarchical counterparts. The Dutch state was significantly influenced by such city government traditions. No history of feudal centralization was conveyed, no bulky bureaucracy was inherited. Its central means were extremely limited, forcing the body politic into constant bargaining and coalition-making, which hampered the growth of autonomy within the state. Nevertheless, the war burden was extremely onerous. The previous chapters have showed how the necessary funds were raised in the three consecutive steps of the burden-shifting process. This chapter deals with the competition among the governing colleges, the number of civil servants and several bureaucratic features of administration. In all, the patterns of local bureaucratization clearly outstripped the developments of the centre during the last decades of the Eighty Years' War.

Failed monopolization of violence and taxation

The military organization of the Dutch Republic was loosely structured under the central command of the Prince of Orange. It did not exclude semi-private fleets, nor local regiments like *waardgelders* serving city magistrates rather than central commanders. Paymaster provinces claimed a say in the management of the armed forces. Repeatedly, the authority of the centre – in particular that of the Council of State – was questioned as to the appointment rights of officers and marching orders. An attempt to establish a centralized navy board at Hellevoetsluis in the 1630s was short-lived. It was simply wrecked on the rock of oligarchical prejudices.

The monopoly of violence as such was only weakly advanced. Nevertheless, some bureaucratization occurred in the army, as the number of officers grew in relation to the number of troops (cf. Chapter Two). But the military did not impose themselves upon the domain of public domination, as army leaders only rarely proceeded to a position in the governing colleges of the Republic. Despite the enormous size of the Dutch military forces, no 'militarization' occurred within the central state agencies. Partly, this was due to the absence of a powerful nobility. Military commanders did not tend to make a career in the governing corps of the Republic, perhaps because so many were of foreign origin. On the whole, the Dutch army and navy remained subordinate to civil society.

Another circumstance that halted bureaucratization was the infrequent sale of offices, although in the army of the Dutch Republic the sale of offices was not unknown. Particularly in the French regiments of the army, the *vénalité* was common practice. Also, in some of the peripheral provinces the sale of a bureaucratic post constituted an option for the provincial rulers. The Estates General and the Council of State opposed the custom, but only after 1650 was an official interdiction proclaimed.[19] Another factor checking bureaucratization was the fact that the Dutch state did not grant or sell new noble titles. On the whole, the Dutch bourgeoisie did not seek advancement in status through state office as in France. A shorter cut was to buy a manor with the title of *heerlijkheid* attached to it.

Neither did the central state monopolize the means of taxation. The financial independence of provinces, cities and rural quarters hampered the development of any such process. Control was diffuse, and the position of the centre was weak (see Figure 7.1).

In this system, only a fraction of resources was transferred through what should have been the central organ of the body: the office of the

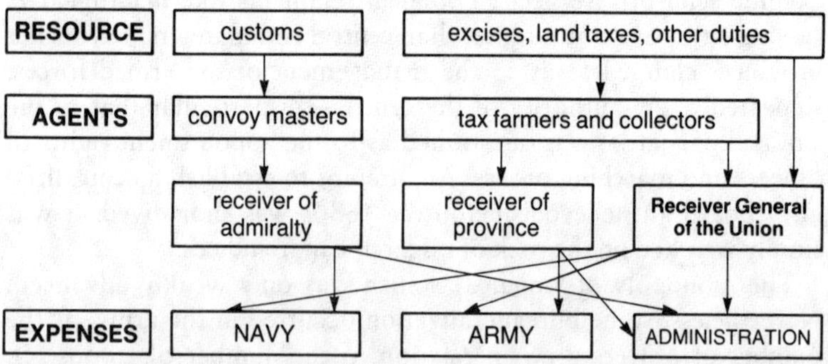

Figure 7.1 Financial system of the Dutch Republic, 1620–1650

Receiver General of the Union. Many funds were spent by the local or regional receivers directly. No state autonomy could be derived from the command of independent resources. Moreover, any concentration of resources was highly contested. The ill-fated tax farm of the customs, the repeated proposals for equalization of five taxes, and the reduction of the generality salt tax are three examples among many.

Also, within the revenue-raising machinery of the Dutch, semi-private contracts predominated. Whereas direct taxes were levied through local appointed officers, the bulk of the revenue came from excises and semi-direct taxes, and these imposts were typically farmed out to private entrepreneurs. Tax farming entailed selling the right of collection for a given period in exchange for payment of a capital sum stipulated in a contract. The farm was auctioned in public to the highest bidder. Contracts lasted in general one year, sometimes six or three months, or two years. Also, districts were small. Especially in the rural districts, excises were unlikely to be profitable at all. Remote villages with a high degree of self-sufficiency would not readily yield much profit. Some tax farms were as low as 100 guilders. Other difficulties for the tax farmers included extensive smuggling near provincial and republican frontiers or a decline in trade as a result of war.[20] Most tax farmers were men or women of moderate means.

Although the Dutch tax farmers never acquired the power of a French *fermier*, they were not particularly popular among the population. In the 1740s a series of riots resulted in the abolition of the farming of a couple of excises in some provinces. But in all probability, the profits of tax farmers were restricted: it was found in 1749 that about 10 per cent of the revenue might have proceeded to the tax farmer, who had to pay his staff from these funds as well. A state bureaucracy could hardly have been cheaper. Another advantage of tax farming was that local magistrates had less control over tax farming as compared with tax collection. Thus farming tended to reduce fraud. Proposals by the tax farmers to allow them three or five-year leases were generally declined by the Dutch authorities.[21]

In the system of public credit most receivers, who were responsible for the issue of the loans, mingled their private banking functions with those of the state. A famous example was the semi-official state banker, the office of Receiver General of the Union, which came to be connected with the family of Doubleth. Philips Doubleth, the descendant of a family of bureaucrats in Mechlin, was the first to obtain this post in 1586. When Philips Doubleth died in 1612, his son Johan Doubleth took over the office, until he was appointed Receiver General himself in 1618. Johan was succeeded in 1628 by his brother Philips, whereas in 1652 another relative, again with the name of Philips Doubleth, took care of the office until 1667. Thus, the Doubleths monopolized the office of Receiver General for almost eighty years. They also became one of the wealtiest families of the Hague.[22]

Their remuneration was considerable. The salary in itself was one of the highest of all civil servants in The Hague (2,000 guilders), but still insignificant compared with payments arising out of the contracting of obligations: for the semi-private loans of the Union 0.5 per cent commission (*makelaardijgeld*) upon the issue of the loans and, up to 1644, upon the interest payments too.[23]

A problem with semi-private arrangements was the possible loss of state funds due to personal bankruptcies. An example of a failed tax farmer was Claes Janszn Cruyk. He collected the generality salt duty in Hoorn, but his office of 1633/1634 landed him in difficulty. He died before his business affairs were settled. His widow Aeltjen Pieters Dirxdr took over his affairs, but she too died before the funds had been handed over to Receiver General Doubleth. A special committee was set up, and went to Hoorn, where it turned out that everything had been sold already. The committee reported that it had interviewed two of the daughters, who had wept and said that they could not possibly pay all the debts of their father. The eldest had four children and was pregnant, while she had to look after the three orphans of her sister as well. Moreover, there were other creditors: Cruyk had rented some of the Holland taxes, and they had the prior claims as their contracts had been established earlier. In the end, the committee managed to squeeze 800 guilders out of the heirs. This sum bore no relation, however, to Cruyk's debt to Doubleth, which was valued at 35,000 guilders.[24]

Yet the province of Groningen had found an answer to the possibility of mismanagement by tax farmers. After 1622 leases were sold in January and July, instead of April and October, which facilitated annual accounting. In 1631 the system of tax farming was reformed altogether. Thereafter, tax farmers did not employ their own personnel any more, but civil servants appointed by the province. Their salaries were paid by the tax farmers. As a result the arrears of the tax farmers declined. Fraud in the grain duties, so important for the Groningen budget, was further diminished by demolishing thirty-five of the province's 122 mills and by having controllers appointed at the remaining ones. These officers became known as *sarries*, after the official name of *cherchers*. Their effectiveness made them the most hated representatives of the state in the region and as such a direct target during food and tax riots.[25]

All told, the Groningen reforms proved a valuable reorganization of the provincial finances. Groningen had caught up with the 'west' by the early 1630s. However, despite the fact that other provinces learned about the Groningen methods, and Holland even acclaimed them, they were never copied.

The bureaucrats within the centre

As much was left to local and regional governments, the central administration costs remained low for the Dutch. No juridical high courts existed for the Republic, only Holland and Zeeland shared a High Court of Appeal. Most responsibilities of policing, justice, provision for the poor, and church matters were taken care of by local authorities. As a result, out of the reconstructed budget for around 1641 (see Chapter Three), only 4.6 per cent was spent on administration. Expenses for the central government declined even in the last decade of the war. The ordinary costs of the central bureaucracy amounted, according to the *Staat van Oorlog*, to 220,000 guilders in 1642, but to only 133,000 in 1649. These funds were used for the salaries and costs of the Estates General (with the office of the First Clerk), the Council of State (in particular for the *Kamer der Tresorie* and the secretary's office), the Chamber of Accounts (*Generaliteitsrekenkamer*), and the Councils for Brabant and Flanders. Additional administration charges, most of them concerning travel, attendance and embassies, comprised 145,000 and 136,000 guilders respectively.[26]

During the Eighty Years' War a slight overall increase in the number of personnel was noted in the office of the First Clerk of the Estates General. In 1618 the provinces claimed the right to have a clerk of their own in this office, which was conceded. These clerks, though, were paid by the provinces. The number of centrally paid civil servants remained small: the First Clerk, two secretaries, an agent keeping the charts, two clerks for each secretary, two ushers, three postmen and twenty-two messengers.[27]

The Council of State supervised the administration and finance of the army establishment and the generality lands. Yet the number of civil servants within the Council of State hardly increased, despite additions to the council's responsibilities. In all, the following received central salaries: the secretary, the treasurer, a clerk for the secretary, nine to ten clerks in the Chamber of Finance (*Kamer der Tresorie*), two ushers and a number of messengers. The Receiver General was officially under the Treasurer General of the Council. He employed two to four clerks, but they were in his private service.[28]

Some extensions were noted in the Chamber of Accounts. This institution was established in 1608 at the request of Friesland, with the aim of improving control over the accounts of the generality officers. Before that date, much of the auditing had been within the competence of the Chamber of Finance of the Council of State, which continued to run the financial administration. The civil service consisted of one secretary and three clerks, but soon another secretary was added and the number of clerks came to vary between three and six. Two ushers complemented the staff.[29]

The Mint Office of the Republic was composed of three General Masters of the Mint, one Assayer, and three clerks. The number of General Masters had been extended to five in the early seventeenth century, but reduced again to three in 1617. There was some centralization within this office, since the General Masters convened regularly in The Hague and an office was installed at the Binnenhof in 1618.[30] A new establishment was the office of the *klein zegel* for the generality in 1635, the stamp duty. It was composed of a commissioner, a controller, a designer and three clerks. The commissioner, however, had bought the office in a farm.[31]

As for the bureaucracy in the generality lands, which was commanded by the Council of State, little room was left for manoeuvre, as most former magistrates remained in their posts. For the judicial appeal court, two councils were installed: one for Brabant and Overmaze, which was situated in The Hague, and one for Flanders, with a seat in Middelburg. For generality taxation some new offices were needed. Four offices were created for the contributions. In the main cities a receiver of taxes was appointed, and one receiver of the *beden* was installed (see Chapter Four). In all, this bureaucracy numbered by 1650 only about fifty civil servants.[32]

These limited numbers constituted the central apparatus of the whole Union. The increase in numbers of the central bureaucracy was very small indeed. Including some temporary or semi-private clerks, peat-carriers, and other minor places, estimates would range between 100 and 200 for the beginning of the seventeenth century, and perhaps about 300 in 1800.[33]

Yet bureaucratization not only entailed growth. Regimentation of areas of competence and growing internal formalization were aspects that should be considered as well. However, there were few signs of either.[34] Several officers worked without any instruction at all. Areas of competence were not strictly separated. The Chamber of Accounts was an institution which might have been an efficient guard against irregularities, yet the actual scope was limited as sanctions were lacking. One of the most important civil servants of the generality, the Receiver General of the Union, began to undergo formal instruction only in 1628 whereas the office had existed since 1586. Receivers of the 'half-licence' (customs) duty in Zeeland operated without instruction for more than thirty years.[35]

Between the colleges, hierarchy relations remained unclear, making it hard to speak of a single system. In addition, higher officers employed their own clerks, who performed state duties but were responsible only to them.[36] Furthermore, the administration costs of the generality's offices were hard to control. Increases in salary were only partly decided upon by the 'centre'. Provincial decisions often preceded central ones. Zeeland increased the salary of the checkers of the admiralty from twenty-five to fifty guilders in 1631. The Estates General, that had refused similar increases for the admiralty of Rotterdam, approved them in 1632 and then increased the salaries of the other checkers as well. Salaries of the generality messengers were generally lower as those of Holland. And a muster commissioner for the army in the service of the Estates General received a lower wage as compared with those working for the province too.[37] Provinces, repeatedly, paid better than the central government: not much incentive for centralizing tendencies there either!

In appointments, patronage was strong, and was enhanced by the system of voluntary resignation. As, in principle, a civil servant was never fired, the officer could appoint his successor, whereby the resigning officer would come to an agreement with his successor about an annual payment out of the salary for his own keep. The practice was never officially endorsed, but it was condoned. It was quite usual for a son or a son-in-law to succeed his father. For example, in the Chamber of Accounts the secretary Gijsbert Ruysch asked to have his son Cornelis Ruysch appointed after his own resignation in 1624. Cornelis's son Floris, in turn, became a clerk in the office. In 1641 Cornelis Ruysch was eager to arrange his succession, and with the agreement of the Estates General it was decided that Floris Ruysch would be the new secretary when his father died. Floris obtained some promotion too: he became *commies*, a special clerk, separating him from the other clerks in salary and prestige.[38] In the case of a financial office, such succession had the advantage that it could save the state from the burden of settling all the remaining payments and debts of the officer: in the end, it would only be deducted from an inheritance.[39] These arrangements, though, decreased central authority and increased the impact of local networks.

Appointments, then, were irregular. They could even involve considerable costs. Payments to obtain positions were formally not allowed, as the sale of offices was prohibited, but the resignation system could be very costly. When the Chamber of Accounts learned that Arent van der Haer, who was nominated successor by the usher Cornelis Verschuyr, had to pay considerable sums (how much is not known), the Chamber decided that Van der Haer need not pay more than 1,000 guilders. More would have been a contradiction of the 'rules of the country'.[40]

Technical training was unimportant for appointments. As for the clerks, they needed to be able to read and write, which was not a stiff condition in a country with such high literacy rates. Yet many higher officers were appointed because they had been clerk, *commies* or deputy in a certain office. Experience seems to have been a major asset. Training in law became more common for the higher officers too, though it never became an official requirement. Financial officers, generally, were selected on account of their wealth. A surety was always obligatory, either by the office holder himself or by his family and friends, which again increased the power of patronage.[41]

For many a civil servant, the salary was not a fixed payment. Most ordinary salaries were supplemented by compensation or rewards. The ushers of the Chamber of Accounts received an annual extraordinary payment to be used for the pension of the widow of a deceased colleague. An usher could also be rewarded for finding a long-lost document in the piles on the shelves. In addition, ushers living in the office received special emoluments because of all the minor extra duties of cleaning, receiving guests and keeping the fire going.[42] Many writing clerks of the central government colleges in The Hague did not receive a conventional salary at all. Instead, all their earnings were based on the output of duties and orders: for each page written there was a fixed payment. Some improvement came about when it was decided in 1631 to fix the payment of some regular recurrent tasks, such as the writing of certain accounts, instructions and regulations. However, when the work ran out, no pay was received. Only in 1653 was it stipulated that clerks were to receive a fixed salary.[43]

The separation between private and public was poor. Some offices were run from the houses of the officers themselves, with the result that official papers could be confused easily with private documents. Even worse, official funds were frequently mixed with private capital. Tax receivers performed banking functions for others, above all the Receivers General of the Union, who held their office at their house on the Lange Voorhout. A large part of the tax collection remained a totally private matter because of the system of tax farming. As noted in Chapter Six, receivers issued their semi-private obligations, and in Chapter Two it was seen that semi-private fleets were fitted out, while *solliciteurs-militair* advanced private funds to captains in the army.

The private service of clerks generated particular problems. For example, Van Volbergen had been a clerk to Receiver General Johan Doubleth, but he was later Treasurer to the Stadhouder. During a lawsuit, he refused to cooperate in finding evidence of a 'lost' sum of 120,000 guilders belonging to the former Receiver General. After all, he declared, he was not bound by oath to the generality.[44]

Moreover, not even all the writing of the government colleges was performed by 'official' clerks. Translations were provided by certain persons outside the regular pay of the government. The clerk of the Chamber of Accounts, Jan van Loo, asked, for example, to be allowed to employ his nephew to do the writing, using the argument that his wife was ill and could not do the job. In the case of Jan van Loo himself, his position as a deacon of the church took up so much of his time that the Chamber complained that his office work suffered. And his colleague Leonart Casembroot was a clerk for several companies in the army.[45]

Other officers in the service of the state, such as receivers, often asked clerks in The Hague to write their accounts. Time and again the clerks were forbidden to write for others, but as this warning was heard often, it probably did not have a significant effect. In addition, it took years before rules were implemented. For example, Zeeland's admiralty used another unit of calculation, the Flemish pound, which was about six times the value of the pound of forty groats used by the other provinces. Also, the Zeeland accounts started in October of each year instead of January.[46]

The whole fabric was controlled by the representatives of the provinces. Yet these gentlemen deputies in the Hague were often absent, as complaints about low attendance were frequent. The continuity of the governing institutions was also hampered by the fact that the representatives stayed only a couple of years.[47]

On the whole, the Dutch central government establishment was to a certain degree a 'bureaucracy' but there were few signs of growing rigidity, impersonality or formalization within the governing colleges. The bureaucracy as such did not extend its power beyond its initial purpose. On the contrary, there was even privatization. As a result, there was neither a development of a certain *esprit de corps* nor any emphasis by the bureaucrats upon the extension of their power. The regents and provincial deputies were not replaced by bureaucrats as state makers.

The Hague and its competing colleges

In the 1570s, The Hague was chosen as the seat of the central government, as well as of the Estates of Holland, but only after protracted debate. The impoverished condition of this unwalled place had rendered the choice acceptable: to avoid all rivalry, as the decision expressed it in 1578. Thereafter, the bureaucratic centre was restrained from all sides. Although The Hague had been no threat to the other cities, it expanded and its population increased rapidly. The inhabitants even became on average the wealthiest of the Republic, as the highest Republican officers lived there. Sir William Brereton, visiting the place in 1634–1635, wrote: 'It is but a *Dorpe*, but the finest in all the land.'[48]

But the other cities would not have The Hague assert more power as a city. No local receiver of taxes was appointed, and no voting rights in the Estates were granted. The government of The Hague was financially and juridically subordinated to the *Societeit*, a peculiar organization in which the Court of Holland, the High Council, and the Chamber of Accounts of the province of Holland were represented alongside the two local burgomasters.[49]

Attempts by the local magistrates of The Hague to act outside the *Societeit* were put down. Delft, keen on becoming the bureaucratic centre itself and fearing its neighbour The Hague, played a leading role in keeping the town curtailed, and opposed the building of a wall around the city. In 1575 Delft had even proposed to burn the place down, alleging that it was a potential base for the enemy. The proposal was not accepted by the Prince of Orange, but throughout the seventeenth and eighteenth centuries the rivalry with Delft was very strong and no other city in Holland would support The Hague's claims.[50]

As a result, although The Hague would become one of the major urban centres, it did not act as a centralizing power. Not even the fact that the Stadhouder had his court there seemed to make much difference, although it did attract nobles and foreign envoys, all of whom added a certain stature to The Hague. His court had its own councillors, bureaucrats, treasury, and a special guard. Foreign princes had their exile courts in The Hague: Brandenburg, and the relatives of Charles I. But the Prince-Stadhouder did not control the highest civil servants of the state. That was left, in theory, to the Estates General and Council of State. Nor did he exert direct control over public revenues, which limited the power and patronage of his own court.[51]

Yet the centre itself was divided as well. Financial control invoked frequent competence struggles between the Estates General and the Council of State. Between many of the rifts stood the Chamber of Accounts. It was set up in 1608 with the aim of checking the accounts of the financial officers of the generality and of the sums approved by the provinces, taking over a task assigned previously to the Council of State. Central control through the Chamber of Accounts was thought to remove the distrust of the provinces in each other and to strenghten the 'sinews of war'. At first, only the accounts of the admiralties, the Receiver General of the Union, and the receivers of the provinces in respect of the quotas were to be audited. But the Chamber of Accounts claimed control over the directors of semi-private fleets too. This demand was met in 1642. After 1651 the control of the officers of the generality lands and the army clerks were added to its remit as well.[52]

Significant, though, were refusals by the Council of State to support the Chamber of Accounts in its attempt to audit the accounts of the Receiver General of the Union, who came under their Treasurer General. The council withheld documents or was prepared to furnish only one at a time. Also, the Council of State refused in 1626 to hand over the accounts of the receivers in the generality lands.[53]

A prolonged tug-of-war emerged about the provincial quota accounts. In 1622 it was confirmed in the Estates General that they should be brought to the Chamber of Accounts. Zeeland agreed to have its accounts checked, on condition that they were returned to the province and not kept in The Hague. Everything seemed settled, but then the Council of State would not have it so. In 1623 the Gelderland Quarters of Zutphen and Veluwe handed over their accounts to the Council of State. It was also the time of frequent debates over the quotas of Gelderland and Overijssel, which had been lowered temporarily. Gelderland even declared openly that it would bring its books to the council henceforth. The situation worsened. In 1627 not only Gelderland, but Overijssel and Drenthe too ignored the Chamber of Accounts. The council actively pursued the policy of obtaining the accounts for its own Treasury Chamber, emphasizing the council's rights. In turn, delegates of the Chamber of Accounts went to Overijssel to ask for the accounts in person, followed by a letter declaring that uniformity (*eenpaericheyt*) in the business of the chamber should be observed.[54]

The Estates General, formally the highest authority, decreed on 10 November 1628 that all accounts should be brought to the chamber, except the payments on orders by the Council of State. The chamber protested, as this was by no means a final solution: in fact, all payments, even the ordinary ones, could be interpreted as having been received by order of the Council of State. Finally, in January 1629, the Estates General issued a resolution containing the requirement that the chamber should receive all accounts, which seem to have been observed after 1630.[55]

Nevertheless, even after the provinces had agreed to bring the accounts to the chamber, it proved to be another matter to get hold of those accounts in The Hague at all. The province of Utrecht persisted in a resolution that no province was obliged to hand over its accounts unless all others had done so, with the result that no account of Utrecht was received after 1622. Other provinces were less outspoken, but their arrears accumulated too. An analysis of the dates when accounts were received shows that, after Utrecht, the provinces of Zeeland and Overijssel were most behind. By 1651 their latest accounts dated respectively from 1629 and 1632.[56] Thereafter, few improvements were noticed as to auditing. The number of years the accounts were behind increased. The province of Utrecht was most in arrears with accounting, followed by Zeeland and Overijssel.

The weakly defined competences caused rifts in policy-making too. In 1628, for example, the year of rapid reinforcement of Dutch troops, the Council of State was incensed about the fact that the Estates General held back important information concerning the country's policies. It drafted a letter, complaining about the abuses in finance and military discipline with the intention of sending it to the provinces. Among the matters raised were the arrears of the provinces, the fact that a petition of 36,000 guilders had not been approved, the fact that the Council of State did not know the arrears for the fleet of Admiral L'Hermite, and the fact that the Council of State did not know the revenue of the admiralties, which was a matter for the Estates General. The country seemed to be losing its credit through repeated loans, soldiers were short of cash, and a deputy of the council had been treated unworthily in the fortress of Steenbergen. The Stadhouder Frederick Henry disagreed strongly to the letter, fearing that the provinces, at that moment deliberating about petitions, would be unwilling to consent. The council sent the letter nevertheless. The Estates General were furious.[57]

Another recurring problem concerned appointment rights. Shortly after the peace settlement of 1648, the Estates General discussed the replacement of the sitting officers in the generality lands. They nominated twenty-five receivers of taxes, domains and church property, without seeking the advice of the Council of State. The latter protested, and obtained the support of the Prince of Orange and of the Estates of Holland. The Estates General, though, had their way.[58]

Such rivalry between the governing colleges was likely to become overt at official representations, such as funerals. When Maurice died in 1625, the Chamber of Accounts wanted to make sure its members came next in procession after the Council of State and not behind the Estates of Holland. The latter were regarded as lower in rank, since they were a provincial board and not a central one. And at another funeral, the Chamber even bluntly refused to send a delegation when it learned that Holland was to march first.[59]

Furthermore, this jostling for position reduced the power of control, for instance as over the office of the Receiver General. By the time of the Truce, his administration had grown quite complicated. Provinces were always years behind with their accounts. Some smaller funds were never accounted for, like those from the passports, as they were immediately used for smaller disbursements of the central government boards. Under Johan Doubleth, the accounting system was improved in chronological order according to cameralistic principles.[60]

Yet chronology worked only when all former accounts were properly checked and approved. Problematic items accumulated as they were shifted to the following years. Disputes between the Chamber of Accounts and Johan Doubleth, supported by the Council of State, accumulated too. At regular intervals, exhortations were used, the chamber demanding that Doubleth deliver his books within two months, but his accounts continued to come in slowly. The situation came to a head in 1627. It was a year of extreme financial pressure upon the Republic. Dunkirk pirates raided Dutch fleets. Military prospects were gloomy. Breda had recently been lost to the Spanish, a major loss of face for the Dutch. The anti-Catholic league in central Europe did not gain successes, either, against the military commanders Wallenstein and Tilly. In The Hague, the failure of the most important semi-public banker was feared. In France, meanwhile, the major state banker Beaune de Semblançay was accused in 1627 of 'malfeasance' and he was hanged.[61]

The Dutch managed to find a less dramatic solution. The next year, 1628, Johan resigned his office, and requested that his younger brother Philips Doubleth should be appointed, who had been 'raised in the office' like him. Under the circumstances it was the best possible solution. State credit remained connected to the same family. The investors continued to visit the Voorhout, former clerks (in private service) stayed on and the books were continued in similar fashion.[62]

Although Philips Doubleth seem to have been a better manager, the problems of former accounts had not been solved. Johan Doubleth remained responsible for handling them. Irritations between the Chamber of Accounts and the former Receiver General likewise continued. The Council of State repeatedly refused to furnish documents. On top of that, one of the Receiver's former *commiezen*, Johan Schas, was twice accused of embezzling funds to the amounts of respectively 22,800 and 24,000 guilders.[63] At the beginning of 1635 the situation reached a dangerous climax. In the Estates General the provinces demanded the settling of the accounts of Johan Doubleth before they would consent to any quota. In Friesland a tax revolt broke out. The Union was put under threat, as Frisian troops were not paid. In August 1635, following help from his brother Philips Doubleth, the overdue accounts for 1628 were finally received by the chamber. A crisis had barely been averted.[64]

The growth of regional and local bureaucracies

In all, the bureaucracy in The Hague failed to constitute a centralizing power. Also, it increased only slightly in number and expense. Whatever parts of the Dutch bureaucratic apparatus may have grown, they were not situated in The Hague, but in the local branches of the central state: in the admiralties, some in the army, maybe some in the generality lands.

With its five boards, the navy had quite a costly establishment. Rotterdam, being the first board in rank, whose deputies had to travel a good deal to The Hague, carried a lot of additional costs. It took care of most transport for the army, maintained the river vessels, and provided the Stadhouder's vessel. Rotterdam also had most of the custom offices, as a major part of the generality lands (the 'conquered' regions) came under its governance. Overall, the number of custom offices gradually expanded too.[65] According to the budgets of 1628–1633, the admiralties were allowed to spend the sums presented in Table 7.1. Amsterdam spent most on salaries, despite the fact that Rotterdam and Zeeland boasted more officers. Rotterdam's salary costs were lower on average, but travel and

Table 7.1 *Number of officers, average annual budgeted sums for salaries and administration, 1628–1633, five admiralties*

navy board	*no. officers*	*salaries*	*administration*
Rotterdam	104	48,283	21,817
Amsterdam	91	70,002	7,998
Zeeland	101	47,678	422
Northern Quarter	72	33,408	6,684
Friesland	?	24,840	7,150

Source: RAZH SH 8052; ARA Adm 3399; RAZH Jacob Cats 41.

attendance costs figured high for this central board. Expenses for the Northern Quarter were actually quite modest, taking into account that the admiralty moved every three months between Hoorn and Enkhuizen. Zeeland's costs were reduced, because the Provincial Estates shared its administration with the admiralty. Friesland's administration spent relatively high sums for what must have been a small establishment.[66]

In the meantime, the admiralties had become entangled with local political networks. Positions as councillors and higher officers were much sought after by regents and magistrates. Rotterdam, for example, exerted pressure in the succession of its Receiver Vroesen: it could not accept a 'foreigner' (*niemand vreemd soude kunnen lijden*), and it managed to get a *Rotterdammer* named again. Johan van IJck became the new receiver. His power was strengthened by the fact that he moved his office from the main buildings to his own house. After his death, his mother-in-law was accused of having supplied the admiralty with butter, cheese and dried fish at extraordinarily high prices. His widow (a sister of the powerful Cornelis Musch, the First Clerk of the Estates General) had to face charges of illegal trade in generality payment orders. The latter had been sold at discounts of 30, 40 and even 50 per cent.[67]

In the Northern Quarter admiralty, it was found that cables, ropes and sails were being bought from the ropeworks of Cornelis van Neck, who was a brother of the Secretary of the Northern Quarter, Johan van Neck. Some councillors, the Advocaat Fiscaal and the Secretary also participated in the supply. They received an official warning from the chamber. In 1641, it was found that bullets were being bought from the same family at lower prices than they were accounted for in the books.[68]

These local bureaucrats commanded significant resources. This was proved, among others, in the case of the abolition of the commission on loans issued by receivers. The latter were to lose a significant portion of their income. The receiver of the Northern Quarter, Compostel, who had a salary of 900 guilders, claimed he would lose about 2,200 guilders per year if the brokerage were abolished. For Spiegel, the Receiver of the Admiralty of Amsterdam, who had an annual salary of 1,600 and 800 guilders (he combined the offices of receiver for the admiralty and convoy master in Amsterdam), the revenue from the commission alone amounted to 5,054 guilders per year in the early 1640s. His request to be allowed to keep the commission or to have his salary increased by 5,000 guilders was backed up by the burgomasters of Amsterdam.[69]

In contrast to the central state budget, the administration of Holland gradually assumed a larger share of the province's expenses. In the budgets which have survived for the period 1600–1640, sums spent on non-war items (that is, mostly administration) increased from 900,000 guilders to over 6 million. They were, at the same time, growing more rapidly than the expenses of war, as Table 7.2 shows. The province of Holland itself employed more personnel than the central state. In addition, the amounts spent on provincial administration were larger in absolute terms compared with those of the central government. In the 1670s, of the income tax upon salaries, 12 per cent was derived from the central bureaucracy of The Hague, whereas the provincial administration in the same town yielded 15 per cent of the total revenue.[70]

Table 7.2 *Sums spent on non-war expenses and percentage of all Holland's expenses, 1600–1640*

year	*amount*	*percentage of total*
1600	900,000	16
1620	1,997,645	27
1621	2,041,395	25
1628	2,800,000	n.a.
1630	4,200,000	31
1634	4,895,114	30
1635	5,105,781	29
1640	6,286,556	38

Source: RAZH Jacob Cats 22 (1634, 1635) and 23 and 84 (1630, 1640); FH 806; GAA 5030/153; Engels, *Belastingen*, 24.

Yet below the provincial administration there was another extensive layer of bureaucracies: those of the cities. The most important positions in Holland were, after all, the yearly rotating offices of the burgomasters. It became the rule that influential families divided the tenure of these positions among themselves. Manifold minor municipal offices were in the patronage of the mayors. In the distribution of the tax upon salaries mantioned above (concerning the 1670s), Amsterdam alone yielded 37 per cent against The Hague at 29 per cent – the latter including the central, provincial, and local government. In the early eighteenth century, Amsterdam burgomasters disposed of 3,262 offices. Even allowing the fact that many offices were positions as lowly as peat carrier or church chair guard, these magistrates were in a position to mobilize more support as compared to several higher civil servants in The Hague.[71]

Apparently, local bureaucrats were even better paid as compared to The Hague. From a career perspective, a city position was to be preferred to a central one, at least in the case of the larger urban centres. Such a fact reduced centralization, as the most talented did not readily join the central government. However, salaries, even for local bureaucrats, were never a sign of the most lucrative positions: that was reserved for the deputies in the admiralties and in the East India Company.[72]

The centre subordinated to oligarchies

Because of the high degree of urbanization and the spread of resources within the core area, several political elites watched each other jealously. These competing segments of the Dutch Republic blocked the formation of a centralized national state. No ideological or cultural centre developed. The oldest universities were in Leiden and Franeker, but they were not backed up by regional power formation. Nor did the dominant religion, Calvinism, provide a model for centralized organization. The basis was the local *gemeente*, regionally coordinated in *classes*, and one step higher was the provincial synod. A national synod could be convened, but this was not a rule. Thus, in religion, neither a hierarchy nor a centralistic domination was imposed from above either.[73]

The court of the Stadhouder was left out of many public functions. Nor could an economic centre take the lead. Amsterdam started to dominate only in the course of the seventeenth century, while a city like Dordrecht claimed superiority from of old. In the east, the more traditional centres claimed allegiance to the Holy Roman Empire. Groningen, Middelburg and Utrecht had all built up a powerful historical position with regard to their hinterlands, but in Holland the domination over the countryside was fragmented as a result of inter-city rivalries. In the bureaucratic centre of The Hague itself, the relation between the Estates General and the Council of State was characterized by innumerable disputes over competence. Instructions were vague and subject to more than one interpretation. The Estates General themselves operated without written rules. At the same time, the provincial government of Holland, also convening at the Binnenhof in The Hague, had a strong influence upon national policy-making.[74]

The rulers in The Hague commanded no more than a couple of hundred civil servants. Not much capacity, then, for pursuing an autonomous policy of the state. Although incidentally state makers like a Stadhouder, a Grand Pensionary, or a First Clerk exerted considerable influence within the Dutch Republic, their power was always curtailed, as a strong state apparatus did not exist and the centrifugal tendency of provinces and cities meant that they retained sovereign rights within the representative machinery.

The number of central officers remained small. Personal arrangements predominated over bureaucratic structures. Some officers in the state were assigned unusually large administrations, such as the Receiver General of the Union. But their position was not translated into political power. The influence of senior civil servants was not institutionalized, nor translated into a powerful official position. Bureaucrats did not replace the regents or delegates of the provinces in political decision-making. The secretariat of the Council of State, also, remained small, despite the increased burden of administration as a result of warfare. In all, the growth of public domination, state making as such, was a concealed process, occurring at regional and local level rather than in the central colleges.

Privatization figured large in the Dutch Republic. Yet that did not explain the absence of bureaucratization as such, since privatization proceeded apace in many another European state. Nor was the emphasis on the meso-level unique in Europe – France and Spain, for example, were less centralized then has generally been assumed. Could the low degree of centralization be ascribed to the absence of a powerful existing (feudal) centre? After all, Paris had few domestic contenders for central power; so had London, or Stockholm. However, looking at Prussia's development, such an argument may not stand up, as Berlin was, after all, by no means a strong centre. It was made so by the state makers, and Moscow may have been another example.[75]

In this respect the restrictions that encompassed The Hague are of particular importance. As a centre, it might well have extended its powers beyond their initial purposes. And The Hague did grow, it became in fact the third largest city of the Netherlands, while it was still a *dorp*. Its growth was due to bureaucrats and colleges, to the court and fiscal administration. The Doubleths, who had monopolized the office of Receiver General for nearly eighty years, had grown incredibly rich and both branches of the family had gained the title of *heer* (owner of a *heerlijkheid*). Their influence was similar to that of other bureaucratic dynasties such as Huygenses or Van Kinschots. But the number of such families was small in The Hague.[76] And the great personal influence of the Doubleth family was not translated into political terms. The receivers remained subordinate to the central institutions and they never achieved a political status like the Treasurer General of the Council of State or the First Clerk of the Estates General.

In this context, imagine a situation in which the capital would have constituted a combination of economic, financial and bureaucratic centre – in addition to an already quite extensive city bureaucracy. Probably, such a centre would have moved Holland towards a more centralized unity, and in turn, Holland would have stimulated a more rigid centralization of the Dutch state. The result would have been a higher degree of bureaucratization at the centre and a much greater symbolic power for the Dutch state. Yet as the political economy was dominated by urbanization, and thus ruled by different and competing socio-economic elites, any such possibilities of a strong and autonomous state lay elsewhere than in the Low Countries.

Notes

1 Charles Tilly, 'Sinews of war', *Mobilization, center–periphery, structures and nation-building*, ed. P. Torsvik, Bergen, 1981, 112; cf. Roberts, *Military revolution*, 21; Samuel E. Finer, 'State- and nation-building in Europe: the role of the military', *The formation of national states in Western Europe*, ed. C. Tilly, Princeton, 1975, 84–163.

2 Gerald E. Aylmer, 'Bureaucracy', *The New Cambridge Modern History* XIII, Cambridge, 1979; D.J. Roorda and A.H. Huussen, 'Das Heft in der Hand und das Geld im Kasten. Historische beschouwingen over vroegmoderne overheidsbureaucratie in Europa', *Tijdschrift voor Geschiedenis* 90, 1977, 303–27.

3 S.N. Eisenstadt, 'Bureaucracy and bureaucratization: a trend report and bibliography', *Current Sociology* 7, 1958, 103; Reinhard Bendix, *Nation-building and citizenship. Studies of our changing social order*, New York, 1964, 132; Michel Crozier, *The bureaucratic phenomenon*, Chicago, 1964, 187–98; Tom Burns, 'Sovereignty, interests and bureaucracy in the modern state', *British Journal of Sociology* 31, 1980, 495.

4 Guy Benveniste, *Bureaucracy*, San Francisco, 1977, 159–60; Rokkan, *Citizens, elections, parties*, 60 ff.

5 Pierre Birnbaum, *States and collective action. The European experience*, Cambridge, 1988, 8.
6 Elliott, *Richelieu and Olivares*, 53.
7 Quoted by Dessert, *Argent, pouvoir*, 67.
8 Financiers: officers who provided loans in exchange for a position in the bureaucracy. Bosher, *From business to bureaucracy*, 6; Dent, *Crisis in finance*, 20, 60.
9 Any officer escaped direct supervision and inspection, as long as he remained solvent. Dent, *Crisis in finance*, 233; Bosher, *From business to bureaucracy*, 11. The salt tax in France (*gabelle*) showed that, while its revenue rose from 3.3 million livres in 1598 to 23.7 million in 1687 and 59.6 million in 1788, it had served a refeudalization of society by enriching a peculiar kind of new seigneur rather than bureaucratization in a modern sense. Jean-Claude Hocquet, 'Qui la gabelle du sel de roi de France a-t-elle enrichi?', *Genèse de l'état moderne. Prélèvement et redistribution*, Paris, 1987, 209–20.
10 Quoted by William Doyle, *Origins of the French revolution*, New York, 1980, 52.
11 Thompson, *War and government*, 285.
12 See for the development of the British state the excellent study of John Brewer, *The sinews of power*; and more specifically: Emmeline W. Cohen, *The growth of the British civil service, 1780–1939*, London, 1941, 34; C.D. Chandaman, *The English public revenue 1660–1688*, Oxford, 1975, 39, 87.
13 Alfred Cobban, *Aspects of the French revolution*, London, 1968, 73–4.
14 Elliott, *Richelieu and Olivares*, 81; Bosher, *From business to bureaucracy*, 279.
15 Knapton, 'City wealth', 202.
16 Carl J. Friedrich, 'The continental tradition of training administrators in law and jurisprudence', *Journal of Modern History* 11, 1939, 130–2; see also Wolfram Fisher and Peter Lundgreen, 'The recruitment and training of administrative and technical personnel', *The formation of national states in Western Europe*, ed. C. Tilly, Princeton, 1975, 456–561.
17 Rosenberg, *Bureaucracy, aristocracy and autocracy*; Roberts, *Swedish imperial experience*, 56, 60.
18 Dent, *Crisis in finance*, 42, 58; Ladewig Pedersen, 'War, finance and the growth of absolutism', 48.
19 K.W. Swart, *Sale of offices in the seventeenth century*, The Hague, 1949, 72, 117; Van der Capellen, *Gedenkschriften* I, 47; Aitzema, *Historie of verhael* III, 102; *Groot Placaet Boeck* II, 455.
20 Kappelhof, *Belastingheffing Meierij*, 176, 220; A.C.J. de Vrankrijker, *Geschiedenis van de belastingen*, Bussum, 1969, 48.
21 For example, *Resolutiën* SG 22 March 1621, 16 March 1622; Kersberger, 'Adriana van Oringen', 87, 90.
22 Van Gelder, 'Haagsche Cohieren', 114; J.G. Frederiks, 'Het geslacht Doubleth', *Heraldische Bibliotheek*, 1880, 256–8; Fölting, *Vroedschap*, 80 and 110, mixes two Doubleths into one.

23 ARA CoA 90 Instruction Receiver General artt. 35 and 37.

24 Cruyk is sometimes writen as Cruyl. ARA CoA 17 September 1638, 26 May and 4, 16, 21 November and 14 December 1639.

25 RAG Res GS 17 September 1622; Matthey, 'Fiskaal compas'.

26 RAZH Jacob Cats 43; Van Slingelandt 247.

27 ARA CoS 2101 Ia: list of officers. Also, in 1637 a new clerk was added to assist the First Clerk. Th. van Riemsdijk, *De griffie van Hare Hoog Mogenden. Bijdrage tot de kennis van het archief van de Staten-Generaal der Vereenigde Nederlanden*, The Hague, 1885, 10–11, 56; for the eighteenth century: W.R. Hugenholtz and H. Boels, 'De griffie van de Staten-Generaal en van de Nationale Vergadering, 1780–1789', *Tijdschrift voor Geschiedenis* 90, 1977, 391–422.

28 ARA CoS 2101 Ia: list of officers; Van Deursen, 'Raad van State onder Republiek', 61; Smit, 'Ambtenaren', 381. See also Instruction for Receiver General in ARA CoA 94: he is allowed to have clerks to his own 'pericul en risico'.

29 ARA CoS 2101 Ia: list of officers; R. Bijlsma, 'De generaliteitscolleges en de regeling van de auditie der comptabelen van de Generaliteit 1588–1651', *Nederlands Archieven Blad* 45, 1937, 108; Capadose, *Algemeene Rekenkamer*, 34.

30 ARA CoA 04: 12 October 1617, 5 September 1635.

31 Van Riemsdijk, *Griffie*, 87; on his salary: ARA CoA 9: 17 June 1642.

32 Of whom twenty-eight receivers and twenty-two *commiezen*. List in RAZH Jacob Cats 77; ARA CoS 2108 II; CoS 2101 Ia; CoA 94: 16 November 1648. In 1648 they cost 17,200 guilders in salaries.

33 For figures and lists, see RAZH Jacob Cats 77; Van Slingelandt 247; ARA CoS 2102 Ia: list officers.

34 A bureaucracy may be identified along the lines of the following seven characteristics: (*a*) a set of defined rights and duties, prescribed in written regulations; (*b*) authority relations between positions, ordered systematically; (*c*) appointment and promotion regulated and based upon contractual agreement; (*d*) technical training (or experience) as a formal condition of employment; (*e*) fixed monetary salaries; (*f*) strict separation of office and incumbent in the sense that the employee does not own the means of administration and cannot appropriate the position; (*g*) administrative work as a full-time occupation. Following Weber and Bendix; see Bendix, *Nation-building and citizenship*, 132.

35 Instruction: ARA CoA 90 147 v.

36 For an example: see ARA CoA 8: 31 March 1633 (Pietersen), or 9: 9 February 1652 (Van Arckel).

37 ARA CoA 94: 11 November 1630; 22 November 1631; 7 June 1632; 7 January, 30 November, 15 December 1641. On the muster commissioners: CoA 91: 6 May 1625.

38 However, when Cornelis Ruysch died in 1656, the decision was not as expected: instead of Floris, a certain Frans van der Poll, an educated lawyer and a delegated member of the Chamber for ten years, obtained the position. ARA CoA 7: 24 April 1624; 9: 20 December 1641; 10: 15 September 1656. As for the other secretary of the Chamber of Accounts,

Thijman van Volbergen got his son Jacob van Volbergen appointed as a clerk in the office and in due course Jacob succeeded his father as secretary. ARA CoA 8: 9 January 1632.

39 Auke van der Goot, 'Rond resignatie en ontslagneming. Kanttekeningen bij enkele vormen van ambtsbeëindiging ten tijde van de Republiek', *Holland. Regionaal-Historisch Tijdschrift* 19, 1987, 89; Smit, 'Ambtenaren', 183. For example, the receiver of the Friesland admiralty Jan Hendriksz Jarichs van der Ley was succeeded by the son of his sister Jacob Jacobsz in 1621, because the latter was prepared to accept Van der Ley's debt (*Resolutiën* SG 29 and 31 December 1621).

40 ARA CoA 8: 9 December 1630, 8 February 1631. For an interesting case in which the remaining clerks collectively paid the sum for the resignation of one of their colleagues, ARA CoA 8: 10 January 1637, 9: 10 and 14 March, 10 May 1640.

41 Hart, *Geschrift en getal*, 178. For appointments, see ARA CoA 91–4.

42 ARA CoA 7: 31 August 1621, 8: 5 October 1637, 24 February 1637, 8: 18 August, 19 September 1639, 9: 5 January 1645, 7 March 1647.

43 Smit, 'Ambtenaren', 382. ARA CoA 7: 26 June 1622; 8: 11 February 1631; 10: 13 October 1653.

44 ARA CoA 94: 9 February 1640, 31 January 1641, 31 October 1642, 9: 13–17 April 1643. On problems with Johan Schas, another former *commies*: ARA CoA January–February 1640.

45 ARA CoA 7: 6 February 1626 and 8: 15 December 1628.

46 ARA CoA 9: 16 April 1646 and 13 February 1649; see also 14 January 1650. On Zeeland ARA CoA 7: 6 July 1621, 11 November 1622, 8 July and 17 September 1624, 28 July 1625.

47 On the penalty for absence, ARA CoA 7: 11 October 1621; on the *leggeld*, CoA 7: 18 January 1624 and 8: 27 January 1629, 7 May 1632; on the writing to the deputies, CoA 9: 2 September 1641; 29 November 1644; 5 March 1652.

48 William Brereton, 'Travels in Holland, the United Provinces, England, Scotland and Ireland [1634]', *Remains of the Chatham Society* I, 1844, 28: *Dorp*: a village. On 1578: Van Gelder, *'s-Gravenhage in zeven eeuwen*, 110, quoting Bor; J. Smit, *Den Haag in geuzentijd*, The Hague, 1922, 286.

49 Major parts of the city were assigned to the control of the Court of Holland and the provincial Chamber of Accounts. See Gemeente Archief Den Haag (GADH) 845: Stukken betreffende financiële bemoeiingen Sociëteit 1624–1653.

50 Smit, *Den Haag in geuzentijd*, 286.

51 Van Gelder, *'s-Gravenhage in zeven eeuwen*, 113, 118. That nobles tended to have a costlier establishment as compared with bourgeois state makers was shown by a general complaint in 1644 about the administration of the governor of Maastricht, the Count of Solms, who was a brother-in-law of the Prince. Much revenue from the countryside was diverted into his court. No one tried to stop him because of his close relation to the Stadhouder. Cf. complaint by Van der Capellen, *Gedenkschriften* I, 89.

52 ARA CoA 90: Punten van consideratiën . . ., 25 June 1621. On the

settlement of 1651: Capadose, *Algemeene Rekenkamer*, 46 ff.

53 ARA CoA 7: 5 February 1626; 8: 19 January 1637; 9: 9 July, 14 September, 24 November, 11 December 1640, 9 March, 12 June 1641, 27 November 1642; ARA CoA 94: 24 December 1631, 2 January 1632, 17 July 1634; ARA SG 12548.265 16, 29 June, 24 November, 4 December 1640; 28 January, 24 April, 14 June, 5 August 1641; 12, 15 March, 12 May, 3 June, 3, 13, 22, 24 September, 1, 2 October 1642. Bijlsma, 'Generaliteitscolleges', 112.

54 ARA CoA 7: 11 March, 3, 4 August, 18 October 1623, 16, 18 September 1624; 94: 4 August 1623. ARA CoA 94: 8 November, 13 December 1627, 24, 19 June 1628; CoA 7: 10 November, 15, 16 December 1627; 8: 25 February, 15, 21 March 1628. See also Capadose, *Algemeene Rekenkamer*, 44.

55 ARA CoA 8: 25 and 18 June, 24 November, 8 December 1628. CoA 94: 10 November 1628, 8: 31 January 1629.

56 As for 1651, CoA 9: 22 November 1651. That this actually did not improve is shown by a list made up in 1766 which recorded all accounts available in the Chamber of Accounts: ARA CoA 98. Utrecht, still, had not given its account since 1622. Capadose, *Algemeene Rekenkamer*, 41, mentions Zeeland as the worst furnisher of accounts, yet he overlooks Utrecht. The accounts were in *kameraalstijl*: the year of service was the guiding line, all non-payments were simply transferred to the next year. The accounts therefore could only be understood with previous years.

57 Van der Capellen, *Gedenkschriften* I, 461–3.

58 Kappelhof, *Belastingheffing Meierij*, 227; see also CoS 2102 I: list of officers to be appointed by the Estates General.

59 ARA CoA 7: 6 September 1625, 8: 22 October 1634 (funeral of Heer van Bronckhorst).

60 There were additional problems: he had to accept 30,000 guilders in double stuyvers, and another time he was paid in bad money. ARA CoA 7: 4 May 1627 (controller); CoA 9: 14 January 1640 (passports); Capadose, *Algemeene Rekenkamer*, 31; *Resolutiën* SG 13 February 1620 and 4 May 1621 (bad money).

61 ARA CoA 7: 26 November 1627. On France: Webber, *History of taxation*, 253.

62 For a reconstruction of the Doubleth case: 't Hart, 'Staatsfinanciën als familiezaak', *passim*; Bijlsma, 'Generaliteitscolleges', 110.

63 For which he was at least initially held responsible, as Schas had been in his private service. ARA CoA 94: 29 April 1637, 29 February 1640, 11 January 1641, 8: 10 February, 7, 15, 28 April, 18 May, 17 June 1637; 9: 5, 6, 9, 10, 12, 24 January, 9, 12 February, 12 December 1640.

64 ARA CoA 8: 27 February, 17 July 1634; 13, 15, 27 February 1635.

65 In 1650, Amsterdam maintained thirty-one customs officers outside the city itself, Rotterdam had ninety-four customs officers (and thirty-one civil servants in the central office), the Northern Quarter counted thirty-two civil servants and thirty-one customs officers. Becht, *Statistische gegevens*, 186.

66 On Rotterdam: ARA CoA 94: 9 December 1642. In the budget of

1631, Friesland was the admiralty spending 18.2 per cent as compared with 6.2 per cent for the whole navy on administration.

67 ARA SG 12561.112; ARA CoA 9: 5 July and 22 September 1645, 3 January and 16 June 1646. Hazewinkel, *Geschiedenis van Rotterdam* II, 15–16.

68 Their father Willem van Neck had been secretary before him. ARA CoA 8: 27 September and 21 October 1639, 9: 9 March 1640. On the bullets: ARA CoA 9: 5 March 1642.

69 *Resolutiën* SG 21 January 1622; ARA SG 12548.252 Spiegel request 14 December 1640; other receivers' complaints: Doubleth and Receiver of Northern Quarter 12 December 1640: ARA SG 12548.252 Stukken betreffende makelaardijgeld; 12561.108 'makelaarsgelden'; ARA CoA 94: 19 December 1642.

70 GAA 5028.669. The provincial administration consisted of the College of Nobles, Estates of Holland, stamp duty office, Chamber of Finance, Receiver of Holland, Chamber of Accounts, Chamber of Vassalage of the County, College of Forests, Chamber of Domains, High Court, and the Court of Holland and Zeeland. Clerks, secretaries and ushers added up to 116, but with extraordinary clerks, messengers, housekeepers, an estimate of 200 to 300 civil servants would be reasonable. *Tegenwoordige Staat der Vereenigde Nederlanden* XIV, Amsterdam, 1739; Smit, *Inventaris*, xxviii; RAZH Hoornbeek 66 for a list in 1650.

71 GAA 5028.669; J.A.F. de Jongste, 'Hollandse stadspensionarissen tijdens de Republiek. Notities bij een onderzoek', *Bestuurders en Geleerden*, Amsterdam, 1985, 92.

72 Swart, *Sale of offices*, 71, 75–7; De Jongste, *Onrust aan het Spaarne*, 55, 87.

73 J.J. Woltjer, *Een niew ende onghesien dingh. Verkenningen naar de positie van de kerkeraad in twee Hollandse steden in de zestiende eeuw*, Leiden, 1985, 4. Cf. Joseph R. Strayer, *On the medieval origins of the modern state*, Princeton, 1970, 9, in which the religious model is regarded as crucial in bringing about a centralized state.

74 Van Deursen, 'Raad van State onder Republiek', 67; Zwitzer, 'Gezag van het leger', 6.

75 Cf. W.D. Voorthuysen, *De Republiek der Verenigde Nederlanden en het mercantilisme*, The Hague, 1965, 39–40: non-centralization does not result from a weak centre but from strong local traditions.

76 Smit, 'Ambtenaren', 379, 390; O. Vries, 'Geschapen tot ieders nut. Een verkennend onderzoek naar de Noordnederlandse ambtenaar in de tijd van het Ancien Regime', *Tijdschrift voor Geschiedenis* 90, 1977, 328–49.

8

State finances and patterns of state formation

Frequent wars and high taxation have for long been the major factors in explaining the rise of absolutist states. Yet the example of the Dutch Republic wipes out this causal regularity. Whereas warfare, taxation and finance often did serve as levers of state centralization and bureaucratization in other cases, in the Dutch Republic they linked the interests of local elites with those of the state, especially through bourgeois investment in the public debt. Much of the misapprehension in explaining state making has been due to so-called mechanisms of 'centralization' and 'bureaucratization'. Both processes were thought to have been preferred by state makers for their ease of supervision and manageability, their policies hinging upon the establishment of flexible financial institutions. Yet as Tilly has pointed out, states followed different patterns in the formation of power and prestige. Structures that set limits on the options of state makers in the process of shifting the burden of war onto society were determined by geographical, economic, social and political circumstances. And these conditions provided a significant part of the explanation.[1]

Some states, clearly, were more advantaged than others in shifting the burden of war on to society. First of all, economic growth was a great benefit for a belligerent state as it enabled the state to tap wealth from society for its own purposes. The most ready resources for war stemmed from commerce.[2] Second, the advantage of a developed and differentiated economy provided state makers with a wide choice of resources and a broad tax base. Differentiation was linked with the third advantage: urbanization. Figures on urban population for around 1650 have been provided by Jan de Vries: Scandinavia 2.4 per cent, Austria 2.4, Germany 4.4, France 7.2,

England and Wales 8.8, Spain 9.6, northern Italy 14.3, Portugal 16.6, and Belgium 20.8 per cent. The Netherlands stood out with 31.7 per cent.[3]

Urbanization, in turn, favoured political representation, which was the fourth advantageous condition. Municipal governments were almost always much more 'public' than their monarchical counterparts, and bargaining in regions with a high proportion of the populace living in larger cities was already an established tradition.[4] And although feudal structures could be profitable in supplying state rulers with independent central measures, they were likely to limit the future tax base. In France, for example, it was estimated that feudal and church duties took 30 to 40 per cent of production.[5]

Thus the 'Great Seventeenth Century Exception' of the Dutch Republic was partly set by relatively favorable conditions for warfare in comparative perspective. Yet some conditions were of a negative kind. The Dutch were dependent upon international trade, but those trading patterns were liable to be disrupted by war. In the 1620s the Hanseatic grain trade was given a boost at the expense of the Dutch in this field. Others took over the Iberian trade. The river blockades hurt Dordrecht especially, and fisheries declined because of the Dunkirk privateers. At least until 1627 the Spanish could argue with justification that they had harmed Dutch trade and commerce effectively. Yet the Dutch economy was sufficiently varied to absorb the shock. Home industry and the Far East colonial trade flourished during most of the period of the Golden Age.

Other negative conditions were a relatively small population, the lack of natural resources, and the absence of central state power. And indeed, these factors started to count as the British, French and Prussian states managed to strengthen their efficacy in competition overseas in the eighteenth century.

Yet during the early seventeenth century, the positive factors clearly outweighed the negative ones. For the answer to the question how the Dutch managed to carry on prolonged warfare without creating a large bureaucratic apparatus as compared to other major nation-states, the argument was structured in a triptych: first, the reconstruction of the extent and the nature of the burden of warfare; second, the scope for and means of shifting that burden on to society; and third, the consequences thereof for possible centralization and bureaucratization processes within the newborn state.

The long and costly war against Spain was sustained by erecting effective military institutions such as the standing army and the navy establishment. Facilitating conditions for the Dutch were a military revolution that modernized warfare methods under capable military leadership. Among others, the Stadhouders Maurice and Frederick Henry managed to safeguard the Republic's territories against foreign incursions, whereas Admiral Tromp halted the Spanish armada in the Downs in 1639. In the army, professionalization proceeded, as revealed in the growing numbers of specialized officers. Another advantage for the Dutch as against other states was the high proportion of sea warfare. Naval forces were always less expensive as compared to a standing army.

Yet in those military institutions centrifugal tendencies were strong. In the army, the paymasters were the provinces and they obtained far-reaching powers as to appointment rights and marching orders. For officers, no clear path led to the bureaucracy in The Hague for advancement in status, as provision for fortifications, garrisons, lodgings, vessels, and salaries was decided upon in provincial meetings rather than central ones. In the navy, major trading ports were in a position to dominate marine tactics. As a result of manifold inter-city and inter-provincial rivalries, five admiralties had been established instead of one central navy board. Their administrations were merged with local oligarchies who were subsequently in a position to promote their own trade interests. Privatization in military institutions was overtly present too, showing in the establishment of semi-private fleets and the short-term loans of military solicitors in the army. The captains of infantry companies and war vessels alike acted as entrepreneurs within the military establishment.

The war burden increased considerably during the Eighty Years' War. Almost 90 per cent of the Union's budget was devoted to warfare. The spreading of that burden was the second act of our reconstructed state formation process. A condition facilitating such a shift was the prior existence of representative institutions. The provinces had agreed upon a common effort in the Estates General in The Hague, and their representatives legitimized the transfer of the burden onto their territories, mainly through voting for a budget of expenses called the *Staat van Oorlog*.

Three major options were open to the state makers in The Hague. The first was a move towards central sources of revenue, the second was provincial taxation, and the third was the floatation of loans. The central options consisted of measures such as a generality salt tax and the generality stamp duty. Also, taxation in the generality lands belonged to this category, as the Council of State was in charge of these territories. The customs, collected by the admiralties, were centrally decided upon as well, although the navy boards proved a dead weight in the actual implementation and control of the duties.

As to the central options, the Dutch Republic was restricted by comparison with most other European states at the time. Revenues from domains, colonies, state enterprises and state monopolies were neglegible. Two major trading companies controlled colonial profits. Moreover, the only central tax (on salt) declined in revenue. It proved imperative to raise custom levels owing to the subordination of the admiralties to local merchant cliques. The taxes in generality lands could not be increased, either, because revolts were feared (the state having a low legitimacy there) and political losses through outmigration to the less heavily taxed Spanish-controlled territories. Thus each germ of centralization in Dutch revenues was constrained on all sides, by the provinces and not least by the rival central colleges themselves.

The second option was contingent upon the provincial consent to the quotas. It constituted more than four-fifths of the ordinary revenue. Here, a clear variation was revealed in burden-sharing policies. The province of Holland with the adjacent territories of Zeeland and Utrecht developed a taxation structure which was quite exceptional in European perspective. Theirs was a broad tax base, facilitated by urbanization and commercialization, relying upon the wide extraction possibilities of excises. The bureaucracy could be restricted (as indirect taxes needed fewer personnel and excises were often farmed out) and the urban revolts (by their very nature localized) were manageable for the city magistrates. Army involvement was low, as city militias managed to control most of the outbreaks.

Yet in the more peripheral provinces inland, and in the north, the extraction structure was problematic and looked much more 'European'. The more distant provinces had fewer inhabitants, whose numbers even stagnated or declined. With lower degrees of commercialization and urbanization the predominant choice in the shift of the burden had to be direct taxes on land. Excises tended to be semi-direct. The political ceiling of taxation was low, as The

Hague and the profitable admiralties were more distant, and access to state policies was difficult. In addition, urban–rural dichotomies hampered the representative institutions in fiscal decision-making. Large parts of Overijssel, Gelderland, Brabant and Overmaze had to bear the painful brunt of passing and besieging armies as well. Their economies showed clearly the limits of taxation. Revolts, subsequently, were more widespread as compared with the *redoubt* area of the Republic, and central state enforcement and even army involvement followed the introduction of new taxes.

The third major option for state makers was the contracting of loans. The Dutch Republic enjoyed excellent credit, which was in particular due to Holland's tradition in that respect. Credit was facilitated by ease of access to international capital flows, control over financial markets through institutions like the Bank of Amsterdam and the Bourse, the extraordinary accumulation of wealth from trade, and the development of a substantial rentier class. Creditors were domestic, numerous, and even found among the lower middle classes.

The lion's share of the public debt of the generality had been contracted because of default on payments to troops by the provinces. At the Union level, the funding of debt charges was difficult, as central taxation was virtually absent. Its management was secured, though, through the intermediation of the powerful credit of Holland. The latter was assigned the interest payments, and this province took on huge parts of the Union's loans at the end of the war. Thus in debt management too the meso-level was accentuated. And even where the provincial debt was concerned, centrifugal tendencies were noticeable: local receivers came to outstrip the central receivers in funds. In addition, much of the loan policy entailed another semi-private arrangement, since receivers acted as state bankers and gained significantly from remunerative commissions. Yet Dutch public credit, on the whole, was outstanding and differed from Europe generally, as most loans were domestic and voluntary.

In all, the choices in the burden-shifting process were heavily geared towards the meso-level at the expense of the central state. The loose federal system provided ample opportunity for delegates to promote the vital interests of their own citizens and subjects. They preferred to deal with controversies in a discreet manner, avoiding open conflict as much as possible, setting up committees with rotating presidencies.[6] Provincial and local bureaucracies extended themselves as new demands were made of on military and fiscal resources. Centralization of the state was hampered by the fact that local bureaucracies simply paid better. They could even outbid the centre in status and political influence, at least in the larger urban areas. Moreover, the state bureaucracy was often not superior to semi-private undertakings. Attempts to increase central control were of no avail, such as the customs farm, the Hellevoetsluis project, and the egalization of taxes called the *Vijf Speciën*.

As control over revenues was diffuse, monopolization of taxation did not occur. Had the Council of State controlled all finances, the division of power might have been quite different. But no centre supervised the lax implementation of rules, and the hierarchies were weakly defined. There was little standardization, no impersonalisation or increased rigidity in the civil service, and no extension of the bureaucracy beyond its initial purposes. As indirect taxes prevailed at the core, war taxation did not contribute to national feeling, a new kind of consciousness of being the subject of a state. Much of the collection was privatized through tax farmers, thus state interests were not clearly recognized there either.

Holland frequently failed to act as a centralizing power as it was divided by inter-city rivalries itself. The Hague never combined its status as a bureaucratic centre with that of the intellectual, economic, cultural or religious centres. Compared with other states, those whose capitals combined several of these functions were able to draw much more on symbolic power and were likely to attract the cream of bureaucrats and rulers. A further reason for the weakness of the bureaucratization process was the absence of a powerful nobility. Nobles did not dominate military institutions, or the civil service.

National feeling had been weak from the start. Holland may have been the dominant force, but it could not survive without the support of the inland provinces. Although the latter had few opportunities to initiate new policies, often times they could block a Holland-centric decision in the Estates General. War against Spain was sustained, not by a sense of nationalism, but by the legitimacy of maintaining local privileges and preserving the freedom of the Calvinist religion. The whole political fabric was dominated by bargaining between elites and the balance of power, although some constituent elements (for example, Amsterdam or the Stadhouder) were always stronger than others.

Thus the central bureaucracy that emerged was not strong, as it did not develop coherent boundaries, rules, or capacity. Its penetration into society was only slight. Provinces proved stronger in that regard: they established more or less rational fields of administration for resource mobilization and the coordination of collective efforts. However, there were limits to provincial 'rationality', as only Utrecht prepared its taxation effectively for war, and only Groningen solved decisively its problems with tax farmers. As for the centre, the colleges in The Hague were even forced to cut back their expenses after the conclusion of peace. Bureaucratization did not get a chance to develop because not even the administration's budget was extended in proportion to the growth of population and economy.

The central state became highly dependent upon one of its constituent parts, Holland, both for the immediate provision of money (loans) and for more regular revenue (taxation). The Dutch state, therefore, was characterized by a low degree of state autonomy. As almost all creditors lived in the core province of Holland, Stadhouders and the Councillors of State always had to consider that province's political preferences, because provincial funds from the periphery came in too slowly. On all counts, the Dutch path in state making was characterized by oligarchization of public domination in this essentially bourgeois state. The state makers remained hidden behind the scenes, on commissions and in colleges, on secret missions and in local faction struggles.

The process of shifting the war burden elucidated the separate Dutch development in state formation, and may contribute to the explanation of state formation in general. Although fiscal apparatuses are never representative of the state *tout court*, they reveal the origins of state funds, the extent to which the state depends on private capital, and the nature of fiscal trade-offs in bargaining processes; they also tell about the potential capacity of state makers to act more or less independently of major pressure groups, which is crucial for understanding the characteristic domination of any modern state. A strong state, after all, is likely to command autonomous powers. The latter is demonstrated if the state can formulate and pursue its goals independently of the wishes of specific powerful classes in society. As state autonomy may increase and decrease over time, it is not a static concept.[7]

In early modern Europe, as long as states were not destroyed in wars, their governments were confronted with an increased financial burden as armed forces grew in size and had to be maintained throughout periods of both war and peace. Yet some rulers had already exploited their resources to the hilt in former wars. Their taxes had a 'low political ceiling' as a result of overburdening the peasant population, careless mint manipulation, the widespread sale of offices or a precarious loan policy. The crisis was worse if state makers refused opportunities for bargaining. Their borrowing would be likely to carry a high rate of interest, and weighed heavily upon the state budget. Such states, often poorly monetized agrarian economies, were faced with an absolute crisis.

The failure of state makers to find a solution to the financial crisis left the state an easy prey to incursions by neighbouring states. Moreover, domestic revolts were likely. Either a state bankruptcy occurred, or the rulers had to initiate a programme of thorough reform within the financial system itself, such as taxation of formerly exempt groups. Both policies entailed great risks to domestic order. Powerful creditors saw their funds disappear and property rights came under attack. As a consequence, elites were faced with the choice of joining with the lower classes in their grievances against the state. If, in addition, the state had low legitimacy the result could be widespread revolts and civil disorder. A revolution could even occur. Such a state was likely to become dependent upon the army, necessary to suppress revolts, as well as upon a strong bureaucracy with wide-ranging powers, necessary to impose exactions upon an unwilling population. Therefore, a constant drive for centralization was indispensable. The state's autonomy was likely to be restricted by the victorious group among the contenders for power.[8]

In the case of a relative crisis, the state makers were in a position to find new means within the existing system. Relative crises were more likely in countries with monetized ecomonies, with some economic development and population growth, all resulting in a wider range of options for the extraction of resources. A stabilized public debt, made possible by a financial revolution, permitted the option of shifting the burden on to the future, which eased the immediate effect of war and rendered the crisis at hand merely relative.

Also, the relative crisis might be solved by taking autonomous measures. This was the option state rulers preferred. Examples are increases in the yields of their domestic enterprises and domains through reorganization and retrenchment. This necessitated bureaucratization in the management of their properties. Or they could look for 'external' solutions, such as foreign loans and subsidies. They might have at their disposal conquests or colonies. On the whole, in avoiding bargaining with domestic elites, the result was a coherent bureaucracy with a strong *esprit de corps* and few powers delegated to representative institutions.[9]

An example of the latter path may be seen in Russia at the beginning of the twentieth century. The imperial state makers financed industrialization mainly through foreign borrowing. Foreign capital (mainly French) provided the state with powerful levers in society – among others, they established extensive state enterprises. Half the Russian industrial work force was employed by the state. Yet that dependence upon the autonomous option of foreign capital showed the poignant effects should the latter fail, as happened during the First World War. France was involved in war itself and needed all her available capital, whereas Russia was confronted with a domestic population unwilling and unable to support the state with funds, rendering the state an easy prey to the revolutionaries in 1917.[10]

When state makers were not in a position to choose from autonomous options, they had to engage in bargaining. This was facilitated by representative structures. Bargaining was more successful when the state had strong legitimacy, because of a 'just war' or a 'strong nationalist feeling'. Bargaining could involve also sale of offices and domains, or the offer of positions in the financial bureaucracy and army, or the promise of high returns on state loans. In the more agrarian economies, these proceedings resulted in a coalition between the state and the landed elite. This path paved the way to heavy direct taxation, especially on land, as funds could be had only by impositions on the peasantry. Direct taxes required a more extended bureaucracy as compared with indirect ones, so the financial bureaucracy grew in size. Army involvement was relatively large, because the tax burden often led peasants to revolt. In the end, the state was likely to be characterized by bloated bureaucratization. Centralization was not always a consequence, as much power was delegated to local elites in the suppression of the revolts. An example of such a state would be France in the seventeenth and early eighteenth centuries.[11]

But no state always followed any one of these 'pure type' paths. State agents could choose among more or less autonomous options and more or less bargaining, the range of options being determined by the socio-economic structure and political traditions. The strategies of state makers mattered, yet each choice was likely to evoke a specific response from their populations, contributing to the character of public domination again. Above all, the degree of constraint on central options counted for a good deal in making states autonomous powers. Prussia was highly autonomous, but had to resort to bargaining with the landed elite at some stage too.[12] The English state tried to follow a more autonomous path in the late sixteenth century, but was forced to cooperate with the new Parliament in the Civil War.

Despite the weak integration of state finances, Dutch state makers were able to mobilize resources on an unprecedented scale in the course of the Eighty Years' War. The Dutch were driven into a decentralized solution, as a contribution was required of all constituent members, and no central machinery existed in 1579 to manage the extraction of funds from the multiple elites. War, moreover, constituted the binding force of the federation for two centuries or so.

Specific to the Dutch case was the advantage of the financial revolution, through which a close link was established between wartime state demands and interests of the monied classes. England shared this advantage with the Dutch in the eighteenth century, but other countries necessarily concentrated on fiscalist or mercantilist policies. In Spain, no domestic elite profited from the state loans, as the bonds were placed among foreign circles. In France, the capital invested in royal finances was largely derived from the illegal exploitation of lower levels of financial administration, such as taxation, and reinvested in higher levels, such as state loans. Financiers constituted in this context a largely parasitic growth, their burden upon the whole administrative apparatus being enormous, mixed with bureaucratization and the incorporation of the elite within the state.[13]

After 1795, the Dutch state followed a different path in state making as compared with the choices of the preceding centuries. Centralization of the political system during the period of French domination (up to 1813) facilitated the establishment of a centralized tax system and a centralized bureaucracy. The Dutch path of state building converged with that of other nation-states. Yet specific traits of the past remained. Polarization split the country along religious and political lines. Dutch politics in the twentieth century were still the result of frequent bargaining, power being balanced among a multifarious domestic elite.[14]

Questions of state finance usually seem obscure, tedious, and peripheral to political struggles for power. The experience of European states, however, shows that fiscal strategies influence profoundly the forms of states, the power of rulers, and the relative positions of different social classes. War drove the formation of all European states, but it did not drive them all in the same direction. Differing arrangements for meeting the expense of war accounted for a significant part of the variation from state to state. Those arrangements, in turn, depended on the degree of commercialization of the economy, the importance of capitalist oligarchies, and the relation between landlords and merchants. The Dutch Republic showed the effects of great commercialization, powerful municipal oligarchies, sharp inter-city rivalries, and relative subordination of landlords to capitalists. But within its small compass, the Republic also displayed the consequences of variation in all these respects. The core of the Republic was much better endowed with high political ceilings of taxation and public loans. In that regard, credit should be given to Rabelais's Panurge. After all, he did foresee that public debt gave lenders an interest in the well-being of the new power, forging an enduring alliance between the nascent bourgeois state and its whole and half-capitalists.[15]

Notes

1 Tilly, *Coercion, Capital and European States*, 187–91.

2 Gabriel Ardant, *Histoire de l'impôt. De l'antiquité au XVIIe siècle*, Paris, 1971, 14; Krygier, 'State and bureaucracy', 10; Richard Bean, 'War and the birth of the nation state', *Journal of Economic History* 33, 1973, 204.

3 Jan de Vries, *European urbanization, 1500–1800*, Cambridge, 1984, 39, 160–2; Stein Rokkan, 'Dimensions of state formation and nation building. A possible paradigm for research on variations within Europe', *The formation of national states in Western Europe*, ed. C. Tilly, Princeton, 1975, 583; E.A. Wrigley, *People, cities, and wealth. The transformation of traditional societies*, Oxford, 1987, 181; cf. also Raymond W. Goldsmith, *Premodern financial systems. A historical comparative study*, Cambridge, 1987, 231, on the impact of urbanization upon pre-modern financial systems.

4 W.P. Blockmans, 'A typology of representative institutions in late medieval Europe', *Journal of Medieval History* 4, 1978, 206; see also

Downing, 'Constitutionalism, warfare', 7.

5 Robert Mandrou, *La France aux XVIIe et XVIIIe siècles*, Paris, 1967, 65; yet the burden was never uniform throughout France.

6 Boogman, 'Union of Utrecht', 389–92; J.L. Price, *Culture and society in the Dutch Republic during the seventeenth century*, London, 1974, 52; G. de Bruin, *Geheimhouding en verraad. De geheimhouding van staatszaken ten tijde van de Republiek 1600–1750*, The Hague, 1911, 119, 133; Richard H. Leach, 'The provinces in the Dutch system of government', *South Atlantic Quarterly* 69, 1970, 328.

7 Skocpol, 'Bringing the state back in', 17. See also the debate on the relative autonomy of the state, based upon Karl Marx's 'The Eighteenth Brumaire of Louis Bonaparte', *Marx–Engels Reader*, ed. Robert C. Tucker, New York, 1978, 594–617. On states as independent actors: J.P. Nettl, 'The state as a conceptual variable', *World Politics* 20, 1968, 559–92; Bob Jessop, 'Accumulation strategies, state forms, and hegemonic projects', *Kapitalistate* 10, 1983, 917; Karl Polanyi, *The great transformation. The political and economic origins of our time*, Boston, 1957, 152–3; Siep Stuurman, *De labyrinthische staat. Over politiek, ideologie en moderniteit*, Amsterdam, 1985, 53; Dietrich Rueschemeyer and Peter B. Evans, 'The state and economic transformation: towards an analysis of the conditions underlying effective intervention', *Bringing the state back in*, ed. P.B. Evans *et al.*, Cambridge, 1985, 55.

8 Cf. Theda Skocpol, *States and social revolutions. A comparative analysis of France, Russia and China*, Cambridge, Mass., 1979, part 2; Barrington Moore Jr, *Social origins of dictatorship and democracy. Lord and peasant in the making of the modern world*, Harmondsworth, 1966, 109; Charles Gomel, *Les causes financières de la révolution française*, Paris, 1892, 6; Fritz Karl Mann, *Finanztheorie und Finanzsoziologie*, Göttingen, 1959, 142–62; see also Siegwart Lindenberg, 'Theories of revolution and empirical evidence', *Theoretical models and empirical analysis*, ed. W. Raub, Utrecht, 1982, 63–75; Marjolein 't Hart, 'Hoe de staat zijn *raison d'être* verloor. Staat en revolutie in Frankrijk, 1775–1789', *Mens en Maatschappij* 60, 1985, 5–25.

9 Pierre Birnbaum, 'State, centre and bureaucracy', *Government and Opposition* 16, 1981, 59.

10 E.H. Carr, *The Bolshevik revolution, 1917–1923*, Harmondsworth, 1950, 81.

11 Tilly, *The contentious French*, especially chapter 7.

12 Perry Anderson, *Lineages of the absolutist state*, London, 1974, 271.

13 Fiscalism: concentrating on 'inside' credit. On France, see for example Martin Wolfe, 'Fiscal and economic policy in Renaissance France', *Troisième Conférence Internationale d'Histoire Economique*, Paris, 1968, 689; Bonney, *King's debts*, 242; on England, Brewer, *Sinews of power*.

14 Leach, 'Provinces in Dutch system of government', 327; Daalder, 'Consociationalism', 238.

15 'Whole' and 'half' capitalists follow the terminology in the Holland property tax registers.

Archives and sources

ALGEMEEN RIJKSACHIEF (ARA), The Hague:
Staten Generaal (SG) 1.01.1–1.01.7
Raad van State (CoS) 1.01.19
Generaliteitsrekenkamer (CoA) 1.01.43
Admiraliteiten (Adm) 1.01.47

RIJKSARCHIEF IN ZUID-HOLLAND (RAZH), The Hague:
Staten van Holland (SH) 3.1.4
Financie van Holland (FH) 3.1.28
Jacob Cats 3.11.15
Van Slingelandt 3.2.52
Hoornbeek 3.1.20

RIJKSARCHIEF IN GRONINGEN (RAG), Groningen:
Provinciale Staten

GEMEENTEARCHIEF IN AMSTERDAM (GAA), Amsterdam:
Archief Burgemeesters

GEMEENTEARCHIEF IN ROTTERDAM (GAR), Rotterdam:
Oud-archief

GEMEENTEARCHIEF IN 'S-GRAVENHAGE (GATH), The Hague:
Oud-archief

KONINKLIJKE BIBLIOTHEEK, The Hague:
Collection of pamphlets
Resolutiën der Staten-Generaal (*Resolutiën* SG) 1579–1609, ed. N. Japikse, N.H.P. Rijperman/Nieuwe Reeks, 1610–1670, ed. A.Th. van Deursen, J. Roelevink, and J.G. Smit, The Hague, 1915–1991, Rijksgeschiedkundige Publicatiën Grote Serie.
Groot Placaat en Charterboek van Vriesland, ed. G.F. Baron thoe Schwartzenberg, Leeuwarden, 1768.
Groot Placaet Boeck vervattende de placaten, ordonnantiën ende edicten van de Staten-Generaal der Vereenigde Nederlanden, ed. C. Cau, The Hague, 1644.
Groot Utrechts Placaatboek, ed. Johan vande Water, Utrecht, 1729.

Index